Keycloak - Identity and Access Management for Modern Applications

Harness the power of Keycloak, OpenID Connect, and OAuth 2.0 protocols to secure applications

Stian Thorgersen

Pedro Igor Silva

Packt>

BIRMINGHAM—MUMBAI

Keycloak - Identity and Access Management for Modern Applications

Group Product Manager: Wilson D'souza

Publishing Product Manager: Yogesh Deokar

Senior Editor: Shazeen Iqbal

Content Development Editor: Romy Dias

Technical Editor: Sarvesh Jayant

Copy Editor: Safis Editing

Project Coordinator: Shagun Saini

Proofreader: Safis Editing

Indexer: Pratik Shirodkar

Production Designer: Aparna Bhagat

First published: May 2021

Production reference: 1120521

Published by Packt Publishing Ltd.
Livery Place
35 Livery Street
Birmingham
B3 2PB, UK.

ISBN 978-1-80056-249-3

www.packt.com

To those that are fighting against COVID-19. Specifically, to Jadiel Filho, whose memory will be forever with us.

– Pedro Igor Silva

Contributors

About the authors

Stian Thorgersen started his career at Arjuna Technologies building a cloud federation platform, years before most companies were even ready for a single-vendor public cloud. He later joined Red Hat, looking for ways to make developers' lives easier, which is where the idea of Keycloak started. In 2013, Stian co-founded the Keycloak project with another developer at Red Hat.

Today, Stian is the Keycloak project lead and is also the top contributor to the project. He is still employed by Red Hat as a senior principal software engineer focusing on identity and access management, both for Red Hat and for Red Hat's customers.

In his spare time, there is nothing Stian likes more than throwing his bike down the mountains of Norway.

Pedro Igor Silva is a proud dad of amazing girls. He started his career back in 2000 at an ISP, where he had his first experiences with open source projects such as FreeBSD and Linux, as well as a Java and J2EE software engineer. Since then, he has worked in different IT companies as a system engineer, system architect, and consultant.

Today, Pedro Igor is a principal software engineer at Red Hat and one of the core developers of Keycloak. His main area of interest and study is now IT security, specifically in the application security and identity and access management spaces.

In his non-working hours, he takes care of his planted aquariums.

> *I want to thank my wonderful family for giving me the space and support*
> *I've needed to write this book. The whole Packt editing team has helped this*
> *first-time author immensely, but I'd like to give a special thanks to Romy*
> *Dias, who edited most of my work.*

About the reviewers

Hynek Mlnarik has over 20 years of experience in IT. Theoretical aspects of computer science were so attractive to him that to his own surprise, he eventually found himself holding a PhD in computer science. Yet as he likes the synergy of theory and practice, he has simultaneously worked on the architecture, development, quality engineering, and management of various IT systems, ranging from wholesale support and banking to virtualization and security. In the last few years, his main interest has been in Keycloak, which he has contributed a few lines of code to here and there, and now he reviews the lines contributed by others.

Siddhartha De holds an MS degree in systems engineering from BITS Pilani and holds around 10 years of experience in IT industries, which includes technical support, consultation, and infrastructure design. He is currently employed at Red Hat Inc. (India).

Łukasz Budnik holds a PhD in information systems and is an inside-outside technologist with over 20 years of experience designing and implementing IT solutions. He has worked on projects such as real-estate portals, car/home insurance, voice and video solutions, mobile banking, and medical systems. For the past 9 years, he has worked as a cloud architect on platforms such as AWS, Azure, Heroku, and Rackspace. Łukasz is an expert in cloud-native applications. He has been responsible for implementing rigorous security, governance, and compliance programs in the cloud.

Łukasz is a happy husband and a father to three energetic boys.

He is a huge fan of the cloud and doesn't mind the rain (at all)!

Łukasz goes by the handle @lukaszbudnik on GitHub and Twitter.

Table of Contents

Section 2: Securing Applications with Keycloak

3
Brief Introduction to Standards

4
Authenticating Users with OpenID Connect

5
Authorizing Access with OAuth 2.0

6
Securing Different Application Types

7
Integrating Applications with Keycloak

8

Authorization Strategies

Section 3: Configuring and Managing Keycloak

9

Configuring Keycloak for Production

10

Managing Users

11

Authenticating Users

12

Managing Tokens and Sessions

13
Extending Keycloak

Section 4: Security Considerations

14
Securing Keycloak and Applications

Assessments

Other Books You May Enjoy

Index

Preface

Keycloak is an open source identity and access management tool with a focus on modern applications such as single-page applications, mobile applications, and REST APIs.

The project was started in 2014 with a strong focus on making it easier for developers to secure their applications. It has since grown into a well-established open source project with a strong community and user base. It is used in production for scenarios ranging from small websites with only a handful of users up to large enterprises with millions of users.

This book introduces you to Keycloak, covering how to install Keycloak as well as how to configure it ready for production use cases. Furthermore, this book covers how to secure your own applications, as well as providing a good foundation for understanding OAuth 2.0 and OpenID Connect.

Who this book is for

This book is for developers, system administrators, and security engineers, or anyone who wants to leverage Keycloak and its capabilities to secure applications.

If you are new to Keycloak, this book will provide you with a strong foundation to leverage Keycloak in your projects.

If you have been using Keycloak for a while, but have not mastered everything yet, you should still find a lot of useful information in this book.

What this book covers

Chapter 1, *Getting Started with Keycloak*, gives you a brief introduction to Keycloak and steps on how to get quickly up to speed by installing and running Keycloak yourself. It also provides an introduction to the Keycloak admin and account consoles.

Chapter 2, *Securing Your First Application*, explains how to secure your first application with Keycloak through a sample application consisting of a single-page application and a REST API.

Chapter 3, Brief Introduction to Standards, provides a brief introduction and comparison of the standards Keycloak supports to enable you to integrate your applications securely and easily with Keycloak.

Chapter 4, Authenticating Users with OpenID Connect, teaches how to authenticate users by leveraging the OpenID Connect standard. This chapter leverages a sample application that allows you to see and understand how an application authenticates to Keycloak through Open ID Connect.

Chapter 5, Authorizing Access with OAuth 2.0, teaches how to authorize access to REST APIs and other services by leveraging the OAuth 2.0 standard. Through a sample application, you will see firsthand how an application obtains an access token through OAuth 2.0, which the application uses to invoke a protected REST API.

Chapter 6, Securing Different Application Types, covers best practices on how to secure different types of applications, including web, mobile, and native applications, as well as REST APIs and other backend services.

Chapter 7, Integrating Applications with Keycloak, provides steps on how to integrate your applications with Keycloak, covering a range of different programming languages, including Go, Java, client-side JavaScript, Node.js, and Python. It also covers how you can utilize a reverse proxy to secure an application implemented in any programming language or framework.

Chapter 8, Authorization Strategies, covers how your application can use information about the user from Keycloak for access management, covering roles and groups, as well as custom information about users.

Chapter 9, Configuring Keycloak for Production, teaches how to configure Keycloak for production, including how to enable TLS, configuring a relational database, and enabling clustering for additional scale and availability.

Chapter 10, Managing Users, takes a closer look at the capabilities provided by Keycloak related to user management. It also explains how to federate users from external sources such as LDAP, social networks, and external identity providers.

Chapter 11, Authenticating Users, covers the various authentication capabilities provided by Keycloak, including how to enable second-factor authentication, as well as security keys.

Chapter 12, Managing Tokens and Sessions, helps understand how Keycloak leverages server-side sessions to keep track of authenticated users, as well as best practices on managing tokens issued to your applications.

Chapter 13, Extending Keycloak, explains how you can extend Keycloak, covering how you can modify the look and feel of user-facing pages such as the login pages and account console. It also provides a brief introduction to one of the more powerful capabilities of Keycloak that allows you to provide custom extensions for a large number of extension points.

Chapter 14, Securing Keycloak and Applications, provides best practices on how to secure Keycloak for production. It also provides a brief introduction to some best practices to follow when securing your own applications.

To get the most out of this book

To be able to run the examples provided in this book, you need to have OpenJDK and Node.js installed on your computer. All code examples have been tested using OpenJDK 11 and Node.js 14 on Linux (Fedora). However, the examples should also work on newer versions of OpenJDK and Node.js, as well as with Windows and mac OS.

Software/hardware covered in the book	OS requirements
Keycloak 12	Linux (any), macOS, or Windows
OpenJDK 8+	Linux (any), macOS, or Windows
Node.js 14+	Linux (any), macOS, or Windows

If you are using the digital version of this book, we advise you to type the code yourself or access the code via the GitHub repository (link available in the next section). Doing so will help you avoid any potential errors related to the copying and pasting of code.

Download the example code files

You can download the example code files for this book from GitHub at `https://github.com/PacktPublishing/Keycloak-Identity-and-Access-Management-for-Modern-Applications`. In case there's an update to the code, it will be updated on the existing GitHub repository.

We also have other code bundles from our rich catalog of books and videos available at `https://github.com/PacktPublishing/`. Check them out!

Code in Action

Code in Action videos for this book can be viewed at `https://bit.ly/3h6kdDm`.

Download the color images

We also provide a PDF file that has color images of the screenshots/diagrams used in this book. You can download it here: `http://www.packtpub.com/sites/default/files/downloads/9781800562493_ColorImages.pdf`.

Conventions used

There are a number of text conventions used throughout this book.

`Code in text`: Indicates code words in text, database table names, folder names, filenames, file extensions, pathnames, dummy URLs, user input, and Twitter handles. Here is an example: "Keycloak supports the `authorization_code` grant type and the `code` and `token` response types."

A block of code is set as follows:

```
<Header>.<Payload>.<Signature>
```

When we wish to draw your attention to a particular part of a code block, the relevant lines or items are set in bold:

```
{
  "access_token": "eyJhbGciOiJSUzI1NiIsI…",
  "expires_in": 299,
  "token_type": "bearer",
  "scope": "profile email",
  …
}
```

Any command-line input or output is written as follows:

```
$ npm install
$ npm start
```

Bold: Indicates a new term, an important word, or words that you see onscreen. For example, words in menus or dialog boxes appear in the text like this. Here is an example: "Now click on **Load OpenID Provider Configuration**."

> **Tips or important notes**
> Appear like this.

Get in touch

Feedback from our readers is always welcome.

General feedback: If you have questions about any aspect of this book, mention the book title in the subject of your message and email us at customercare@packtpub.com.

Errata: Although we have taken every care to ensure the accuracy of our content, mistakes do happen. If you have found a mistake in this book, we would be grateful if you would report this to us. Please visit www.packtpub.com/support/errata, selecting your book, clicking on the Errata Submission Form link, and entering the details.

Piracy: If you come across any illegal copies of our works in any form on the Internet, we would be grateful if you would provide us with the location address or website name. Please contact us at copyright@packt.com with a link to the material.

If you are interested in becoming an author: If there is a topic that you have expertise in and you are interested in either writing or contributing to a book, please visit authors. packtpub.com.

Reviews

Please leave a review. Once you have read and used this book, why not leave a review on the site that you purchased it from? Potential readers can then see and use your unbiased opinion to make purchase decisions, we at Packt can understand what you think about our products, and our authors can see your feedback on their book. Thank you!

For more information about Packt, please visit packt.com.

Section 1: Getting Started with Keycloak

In this section, you will get up and running with Keycloak, including securing your first application in little to no time.

This section comprises the following chapters:

- *Chapter 1, Getting Started with Keycloak*
- *Chapter 2, Securing Your First Application*

1
Getting Started with Keycloak

If you are new to **Keycloak**, this chapter will quickly get you up to speed. We'll start with a brief introduction to Keycloak. Then, you will find out how easy it is to install Keycloak and get it up and running. After we have started Keycloak, you will learn about the **Keycloak admin console**, which provides a great interface for managing and configuring Keycloak. Finally, we'll take a quick look at the Keycloak account console as well, which lets users of your applications manage their own accounts.

By the end of this chapter, you will know how to get started with the Keycloak server, and understand how you can use the Keycloak admin console to manage Keycloak. You will learn how to prepare Keycloak with an example user in order to get started securing your first application in the next chapter.

In this chapter, we're going to cover the following main topics:

- Introducing Keycloak
- Installing and running Keycloak
- Discovering the Keycloak admin and account consoles

Technical requirements

For this chapter, in order to run Keycloak, you will need to have Docker (`https://www.docker.com/`) or JDK 8+ (`https://openjdk.java.net/`) installed on your workstation.

Check out the following link to see the Code in Action video:

`https://bit.ly/3nRLgng`

Introducing Keycloak

Keycloak is an open source **Identity and Access Management** tool with a focus on modern applications such as single-page applications, mobile applications, and REST APIs.

The project was started in 2014 with a strong focus on making it easier for developers to secure their applications. It has since grown into a well-established open source project with a strong community and user base. It is used in production for scenarios ranging from small websites with only a handful of users up to large enterprises with millions of users.

Keycloak provides fully customizable login pages, including strong authentication, as well as various flows, such as the recovery of passwords, requiring users to regularly update the passwords, accepting terms and conditions, and a lot more. All of this without any need to add anything to your applications, or any coding at all. All pages visible to your users support custom themes, making it very easy to modify the look and feel of the pages to integrate with your corporate branding and existing applications.

By delegating authentication to Keycloak, your applications do not need to worry about different authentication mechanisms, or how to safely store passwords. This approach also provides a higher level of security as applications do not have direct access to user credentials; they are instead provided with security tokens that give them only access to what they need.

Keycloak provides single sign-on as well as session management capabilities, allowing users to access multiple applications, while only having to authenticate once. Both users themselves and administrators have full visibility to where users are authenticated, and can remotely terminate sessions when required.

Keycloak builds on industry standard protocols supporting OAuth 2.0, OpenID Connect, and SAML 2.0. Using industry standard protocols is important from both a security perspective and in terms of making it easier to integrate with existing and new applications.

Keycloak comes with its own user database, which makes it very easy to get started. You can also easily integrate with existing identity infrastructure. Through its identity brokering capabilities, you can plug in existing user bases from social networks, or other enterprise identity providers. It can also integrate with existing user directories, such as **Active Directory** and **LDAP servers**.

Keycloak is a lightweight and easy-to-install solution. It is highly scalable and provides high availability through clustering capabilities. For additional redundancy, Keycloak also supports clustering to multiple data centers.

A lot of effort has gone into making Keycloak usable out of the box, supporting common use cases, but, at the same time, it is highly customizable and extendable when needed. Keycloak has a large number of extension points where you can implement and deploy custom code to Keycloak to modify existing behavior or add completely new capabilities. Examples of extensions that can be written to Keycloak include custom authentication mechanisms, integrations with custom user stores, and the custom manipulation of tokens. You can even implement your own custom login protocols.

This section was a very brief introduction to the features and capabilities of Keycloak. As this book aims to give you a practical guide to Keycloak, we will come back to many of these features in later chapters, where you will learn firsthand how you can put these to use.

Installing and running Keycloak

In this section, you will quickly learn how to install and run Keycloak. Once you have Keycloak up and running, we will take a look at the Keycloak admin console and the Keycloak account console.

Keycloak provides a few options on how it can be installed, including the following:

- Running as a container on Docker
- Installing and running Keycloak locally (which will require a Java virtual machine, such as OpenJDK)
- Running Keycloak on Kubernetes
- Using the Keycloak Kubernetes operator

If you already have Docker installed on your workstation, this is the recommended approach as it is simpler to get up and running this way.

If you don't have Docker installed, it is easier to get started by installing and running it locally. The only dependency required is a Java virtual machine.

Keycloak can also be easily deployed to Kubernetes, where you have the option of using the Keycloak Kubernetes Operator, which makes installation, configuration, and management even simpler. We are not going to provide instructions for Kubernetes in this book, as we instead want to focus on Keycloak and its features. If you are interested in knowing how to run Keycloak on Kubernetes, then the Keycloak website provides great *Getting started* guides at `https://www.keycloak.org/getting-started`.

In the next section, we will look at how you can run Keycloak as a container on Docker. If you prefer to run it locally, you can skip to the section titled *Installing and running Keycloak with OpenJDK*.

Running Keycloak on Docker

With Docker, it is very easy to run Keycloak as you don't need to install a Java virtual machine yourself, nor do you have to download and extract the Keycloak distribution.

To run Keycloak on Docker, simply execute the following command:

```
$ docker run -e KEYCLOAK_USER=admin -e KEYCLOAK_PASSWORD=admin
-p 8080 quay.io/keycloak/keycloak
```

As Keycloak does not ship with a default admin account, passing the environment variables, KEYCLOAK_USER and KEYCLOAK_PASSWORD, makes it easy to create an initial admin account. We are also using -p 8080 to publish the port used by Keycloak to the host, so as to make it easy to access Keycloak.

After a few seconds, you will see a message along the lines of the following, meaning Keycloak has started successfully:

Figure 1.1 – Start up message

You can verify that Keycloak is running by opening `http://localhost:8080`.

Congratulations! You now have Keycloak running as a Docker container and can get started with trying Keycloak out by first discovering the Keycloak admin and account consoles.

Installing and running Keycloak with OpenJDK

As Keycloak is implemented in Java, it is easy to run Keycloak on any operating system without the need to install additional dependencies. The only thing that you need to have installed is a Java virtual machine, such as OpenJDK.

In the next section, we will install OpenJDK, which is required before running Keycloak. If you already have a Java virtual machine installed, you can skip the next section and go directly to the section entitled *Installing Keycloak*.

Installing OpenJDK

The best way of installing OpenJDK depends on the operating system you are using. Most Linux distributions, for example, include OpenJDK packages in the default repositories.

By way of an example, on Fedora, you can install OpenJDK by executing the following command:

```
$ sudo dnf install java-latest-openjdk
```

For instructions specific to your operating system, use one of the following URLs to find the relevant instructions:

- Windows: https://www.google.com/ search?q=install+openjdk+windows

- macOS:https://www.google.com/search?q=install+openjdk+macos

- Ubuntu: https://www.google.com/ search?q=install+openjdk+ubuntu

Another simple way to install OpenJDK is to download one of the ready builds at https://jdk.java.net/. Open this page in your browser and then click on the **JDK 15** link next to **Ready for use**. Download the build for your operating system, and then extract it to a suitable location. Once extracted, set the JAVA_HOME environment variable to point to the extracted directory.

The following screenshot shows an example of installing a ready build of OpenJDK on Linux:

```
$ mkdir ~/kc-book
$ cd ~/kc-book
$ tar xfvz ~/Downloads/openjdk-14.0.2_linux-x64_bin.tar.gz
$ export JAVA_HOME=~/kc-book/jdk-14.0.2
$ $JAVA_HOME/bin/java -version
```

The last command (`java -version`) verifies that Java is working properly.

Now that you have OpenJDK installed, we will move on to installing Keycloak.

Installing Keycloak

Once you have the Java virtual machine installed on your workstation, the next step is to download the distribution of Keycloak from the Keycloak website. Open `https://www.keycloak.org/downloads`, and then download either the **ZIP** or the **TAR.GZ** archive of the server (standalone server distribution). Once downloaded, simply extract this archive to a suitable location.

The following screenshot shows an example of installing Keycloak on Linux:

```
$ cd ~/kc-book
$ unzip ~/Downloads/keycloak-11.0.1.zip
$ cd keycloak-11.0.1
$ export KC_HOME=~/kc-book/keycloak-11.0.1
```

Before starting Keycloak, we will create an initial admin account.

Creating an admin account

Keycloak does not ship with a default admin account. This is to prevent anyone from running Keycloak with a default username and password in production.

This means that prior to using Keycloak, you need to create an initial admin account.

To create an admin account on Linux or macOS, execute the following command in a terminal:

```
$ cd $KC_HOME
$ bin/add-user-keycloak.sh -u admin -p admin
```

On Windows, execute the following command:

```
> cd %KC_HOME%
> bin\add-user-keycloak.bat -u admin -p admin
```

> **Important note**
>
> For production systems, you should obviously use a more secure password, including strongly considering using strong authentication, especially for the admin account. Later in the book, we will cover how you can easily enable two-factor authentication with Keycloak.

You are now ready to start Keycloak, which we will cover next.

Starting Keycloak

Once you have installed Keycloak and created the initial admin account, it's easy to start Keycloak.

On Linux or macOS, start Keycloak with the following command:

```
$ cd $KC_HOME
$ bin/standalone.sh
```

Or, on Windows, execute the following command:

```
> cd %KC_HOME%
> bin\standalone.bat
```

After a few seconds, you will see a message along the lines of the following, meaning Keycloak has started successfully:

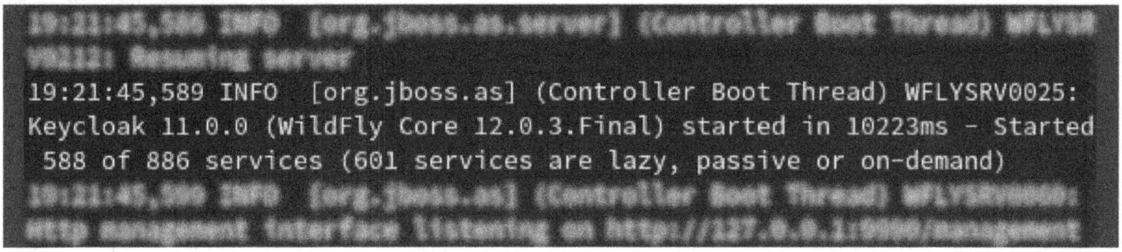

Figure 1.2 – Start up message

You can verify that Keycloak is running by opening `http://localhost:8080`.

Congratulations! You now have Keycloak running on your workstation and can get started with trying Keycloak out by first discovering the Keycloak admin and account consoles.

Discovering the Keycloak admin and account consoles

In this section, we will take a look at the Keycloak admin and account consoles. The admin console is an extensive console that allows you to configure and manage Keycloak. The account console, on the other hand, is there to allow your end users to manage their accounts.

Getting started with the Keycloak admin console

In this section, you will learn how to log in to the Keycloak admin console as well as learn how to set up the basic configuration needed to secure your first application.

The Keycloak admin console provides an extensive and friendly interface for administrators and developers to configure and manage Keycloak.

To access the admin console, open `http://localhost:8080/auth/admin/` in a browser. You will be redirected to the Keycloak login pages, where you can log in with the admin username and password you created in the previous section while installing Keycloak.

Once you have logged in, you will see the configuration for the master realm in Keycloak, as shown in the following screenshot:

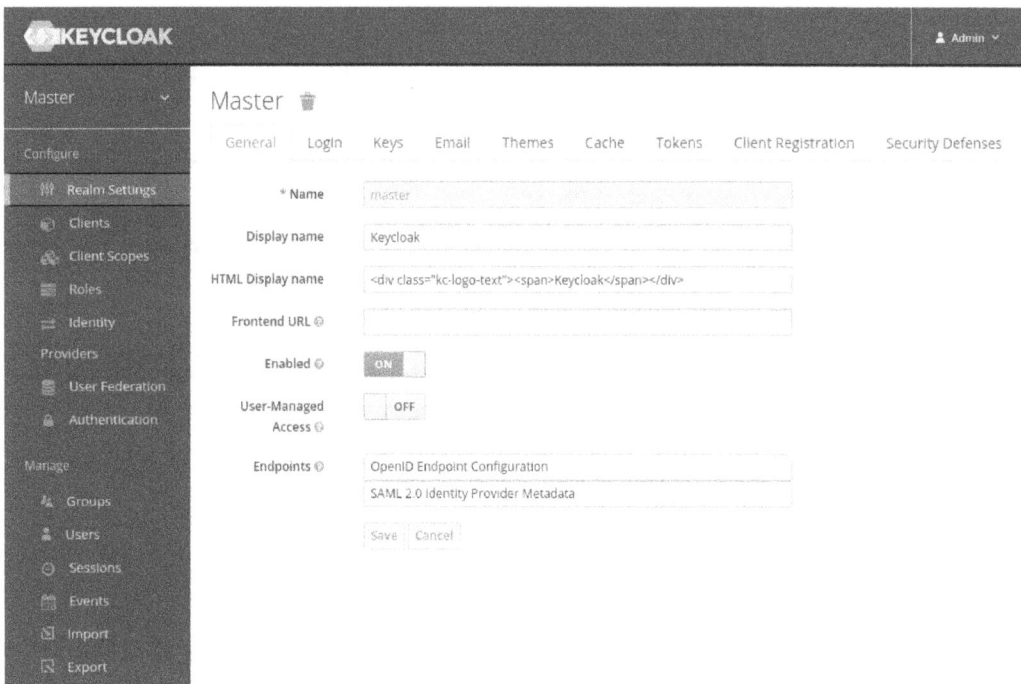

Figure 1.3 – The Keycloak admin console

You will learn a lot more about the admin console throughout the book, but let's go through a few steps to make your Keycloak application ready to start securing applications.

Creating and configuring a realm

The first thing you will want to do is create a realm for your applications and users. Think of a realm as a tenant. A realm is fully isolated from other realms, it has its own configuration, and its own set of applications and users. This allows a single installation of Keycloak to be used for multiple purposes. For example, you may want to have one realm for internal applications and employees, and another realm for external applications and customers.

To create a new realm, hover your mouse over the realm selector in the top-left corner (just below the Keycloak logo). When hovering your mouse over the realm selector, you will see a list of realms, including a button to create a new realm. Click on the **Add realm** button:

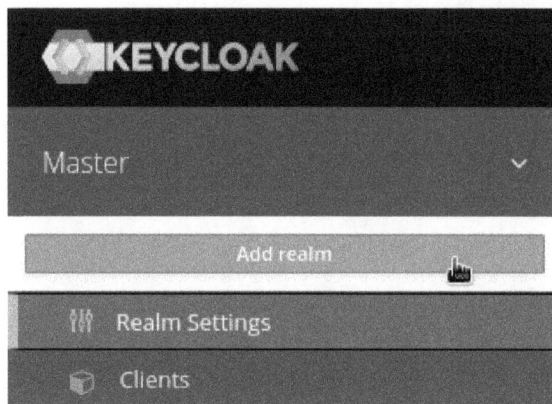

Figure 1.4 – Realm selector

On the next page, enter a name for the realm. As the name is used in URLs, the name should ideally not use special characters that need escaping in URLs (such as spaces). Once created, you can set a human friendly display name. For example, use `myrealm` for the name, and `My Realm` for the display name.

Creating a user

Once you have created the realm, let's create the first user in the realm:

1. From the left-hand menu, click on **Users**, and then click on **Add User**.

2. Enter a memorable username, and also enter a value of your choice for email, first name, and last name.

   The **Email Verified** option can be selected by an administrator if they know this is the valid email address for the user.

3. **Required User Actions** allows an administrator to require a user to perform some initial actions on the next login; for example, to require the user to review their profile, or to verify their email address.

4. Remember to click on **Save** after you have completed the form:

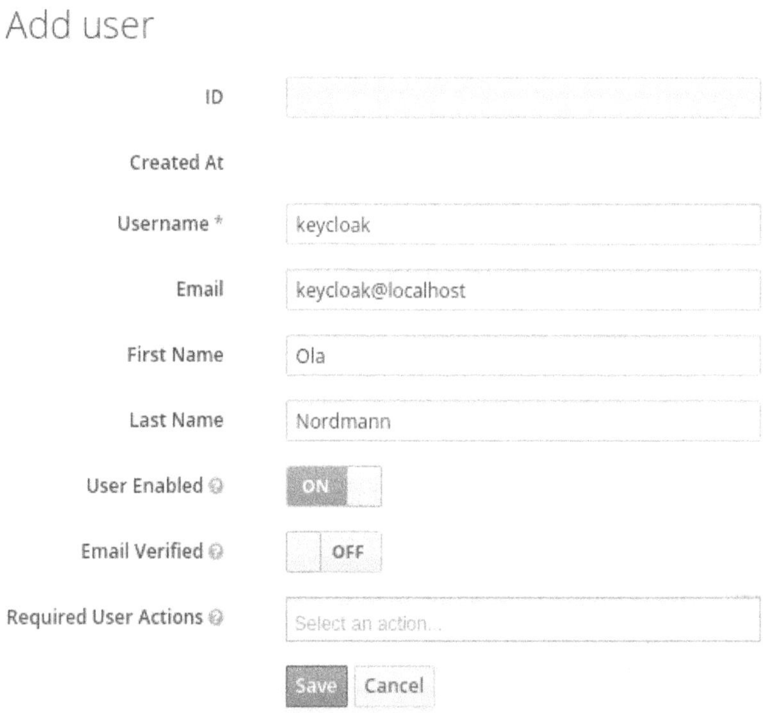

Figure 1.5 – The Add user form

A user has a few standard built-in attributes, such as first name, but it is also possible to add any custom attributes through the **Attributes** tab.

Before the user can log in, you have to create an initial temporary password. To do this, click on the **Credentials** tab. In the **Set Password** section, enter a password and click **Set Password**.

If the **Temporary** option is enabled, the user is required to change the password when logging in for the first time. In cases where an administrator creates the user, this makes a lot of sense.

Creating a group

Next, let's create a group and add the user we previously created to the group. From the menu on the left-hand side, click on **Groups**, and then click on **New**.

Enter a name for the group, for example, `mygroup`, and then click on **Save**.

Once you have created the group, you can add attributes to the group. A user inherits all attributes from a group it belongs to. This can be useful if, for example, you have a group for all employees in an office and want to add the office address to all employees in this group.

You can also grant roles to a group, which again is inherited by all members of the group.

To add the user to the group, go back to the **Users** page. Click **View all users** and select the user you created previously.

Next, click on the **Groups** tab. In the right-hand column, select the group you created previously and click on **Join** to add the user to the group.

Creating a global role

To create a global role, click on **Roles** in the menu on the left-hand side, and then click on **Add Role**. Enter a role name, for example, `myrole`. You can also add a description to the role, which can be especially useful if there are other administrators.

Any role in Keycloak can be turned into a composite role, allowing other roles to be added to the role. A user who is granted a composite role will dynamically be granted all roles within the composite role. Composite roles can even contain other composite roles. This feature can be very powerful, but, at the same time, should be used with some care. Composite roles can be a bit difficult to manage, and can also have a performance overhead if overused, especially if there are many layers of composite roles.

To add the user to the role, go back to the **Users** page. Click **View all users** and select the user you created previously.

Next, click on the **Role Mappings** tab. In the left-hand column, select the role you created previously and click on **Add selected** to add the user to the role.

You have now created all the required initial configuration to get started securing your first application, but first let's take a look at the Keycloak account console, which lets users manage their own accounts.

Getting started with the Keycloak account console

The Keycloak account console provides an interface where users can manage their own accounts, including the following:

- Updating their user profile
- Updating their password
- Enabling second factor authentication
- Viewing applications, including what applications they have authenticated to
- Viewing open sessions, including remotely signing out of other sessions

To access the account console, open `http://localhost:8080/auth/realms/myrealm/account/` in a browser (if you used a different realm name in the previous section, replace `myrealm` with the name of your realm). You will be redirected to the Keycloak login pages, where you can log in with the username and password you created in the previous section while creating your first user:

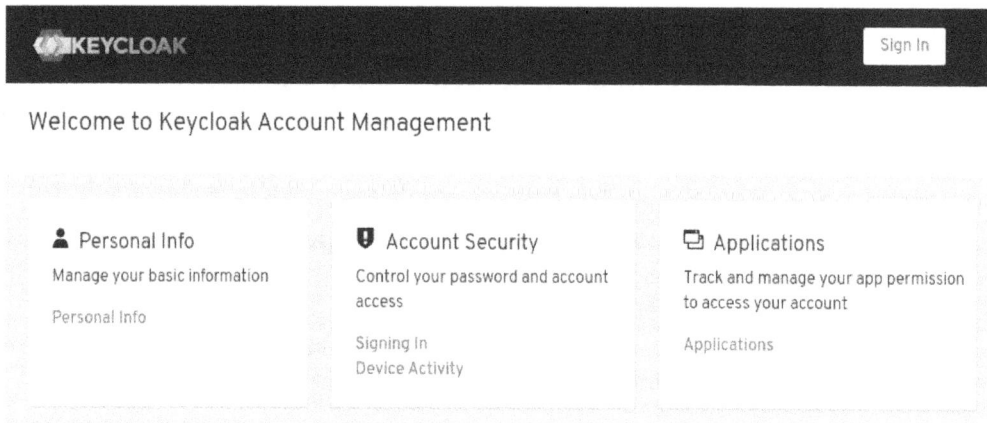

Figure 1.6 – The Keycloak Account Console

> **Tip**
> You can also find the URL of the account console through the Keycloak admin console. In the admin console, click on **Clients**, and then you will find the URL of the account console next to the account client.

You have now learned how Keycloak not only provides an extensive admin console, but also a self-management console for users of your applications to manage their own accounts.

Summary

In this chapter, you have learned how to install Keycloak and get it up and running. You also learned how to use the Keycloak admin console to create your first realm, including an example user with an associated role. This provides you with the foundation on which to continue building throughout the book.

In the next chapter, we will use what you have learned in this chapter in order to secure your first application with Keycloak.

Questions

1. Can you run Keycloak on Docker and Kubernetes?
2. What is the Keycloak admin Console?
3. What is the Keycloak account console?

2
Securing Your First Application

In this chapter, you will learn how to secure your first application with **Keycloak**. To make things a bit more interesting, the sample application you will be running consists of two parts, a **frontend web application** and a **backend REST API**. This will show you how a user can authenticate to the frontend, and also how the frontend is able to securely invoke the backend.

By the end of this chapter, you will have a basic understanding of how applications can be secured by Keycloak by leveraging **OpenID Connect**.

In this chapter, we're going to cover the following main topics:

- Understanding the sample application
- Running the application
- Understanding how to log in to the application
- Securely invoking the backend REST API

Technical requirements

To run the sample application included in this chapter, you need to have Node.js (`https://nodejs.org/`) installed on your workstation.

You also need to have a local copy of the GitHub repository associated with the book. If you have Git installed, you can clone the repository by running this command in a terminal:

```
$ git clone https://github.com/PacktPublishing/Keycloak-
  Identity-and-Access-Management-for-Modern-Applications.git
```

Alternatively, you can download a ZIP of the repository from

`https://github.com/PacktPublishing/Keycloak-Identity-and-Access-Management-for-Modern-Applications/archive/master.zip.`

Check out the following link to see the Code in Action video:

`https://bit.ly/3nQjU0W`

Understanding the sample application

The sample application consists of two parts – a frontend web application and a backend **REST API**.

The frontend web application is a **single-page application** written in **JavaScript**. As we want to focus on what Keycloak can offer, the application is very simple. Furthermore, to make it as simple as possible to run the application, it uses *Node.js*. The application provides the following features:

- Login with Keycloak.
- It displays the user's name.
- It displays the user's profile picture, if available.
- It shows the **ID token**.
- It shows the **Access token**.
- It refreshes the tokens.
- It invokes the secured endpoint provided by the backend.

The backend REST API is also very simple, and is implemented with Node.js. It provides a REST API with two endpoints:

- `/public`: A publicly available endpoint with no security
- `/secured`: A secured endpoint requiring an access token with the `myrealm` global role

Node.js is used for the example applications as we want to make the code as easy to understand and simple to run as possible, regardless of what programming language you are familiar with.

The following diagram shows the relationship between the frontend, the backend, and Keycloak. The frontend authenticates the users using Keycloak, and then invokes the backend, which uses Keycloak to verify that the request should be permitted:

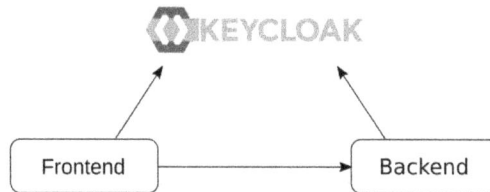

Figure 2.1 – Application overview

Now that you have a basic understanding of the sample application, let's look at some more details on how it all comes together.

When the user clicks on the login button in the frontend application, the browser is redirected to the **Keycloak login page**. The user then authenticates with Keycloak, before the browser is redirected back to the application with a special code called an **authorization code**. The application then invokes Keycloak to exchange the authorization code for the following tokens:

- An ID token: This provides the application information pertaining to the authenticated user.
- An access token: The application includes this token when making a request to a service, which allows the service to verify whether the request should be permitted.
- A refresh token: Both the ID and the access token have short expirations, by default, 5 minutes. The refresh token is used by the application to obtain new tokens from Keycloak.

The flow described is what is known as the **authorization code flow** in OpenID Connect. If you are not already familiar with **OAuth 2.0** or OpenID Connect, they can be a bit daunting at first, but once you become familiar with them, they are actually quite simple and easy to understand.

Luckily, the example application uses the Keycloak JavaScript and Node.js libraries, which means you don't actually have to understand these specifications to get started using Keycloak.

To help visualize the login process, a simplified sequence diagram is provided as follows:

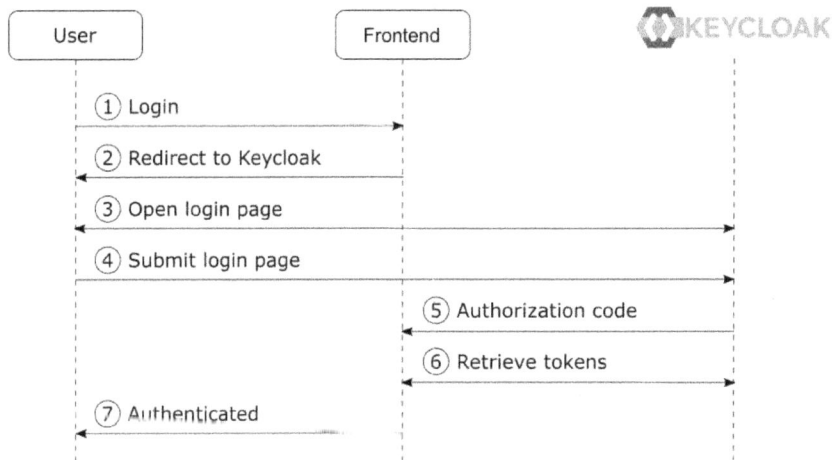

Figure 2.2 – Authorization code flow in OpenID Connect simplified

The steps in this diagram are as follows:

1. The user clicks on the login button.

2. The application redirects to the Keycloak login page.

3. The Keycloak login page is displayed to the user.

4. The user fills in the username and password and submits the results to Keycloak.

5. After verifying the username and password, Keycloak sends the authorization code to the application.

6. The application exchanges the authorization code for an ID token and an access token. The application can now verify the identity of the user by inspecting the ID token.

> **Tip**
> By delegating authentication of the user to Keycloak, the application does not have to know how to authenticate the user. This is especially relevant when the authentication mechanisms change. For example, two-factor authentication can be enabled without having to make changes to the application. This also means the application does not have access to the user's credentials.

The next step related to Keycloak is when the frontend invokes the backend. The backend REST API has a protected endpoint that can only be invoked by a user with the global role, `myrole`.

To be completely accurate, the frontend is granted permissions to invoke the backend on behalf of the user. This is part of the beauty of OAuth 2.0. An application does not have access to do everything that the user is able to do, only what it should be able to do.

When the frontend makes a request to the backend, it includes the access token within the request. By default, Keycloak uses **JSON Web Signature** (**JWS**) as the token format. These types of tokens are often referred to as **non-opaque tokens**, meaning the contents of the token are directly visible to the application.

The token also includes a digital signature, making it possible to verify that the token was indeed issued by Keycloak. In essence, this means that the backend can both verify the token and read the contents without a request to Keycloak, resulting in less demand on the Keycloak server and lower latency when processing requests to the backend.

To help visualize what happens when the frontend sends a request to the backend, take a look at the following diagram:

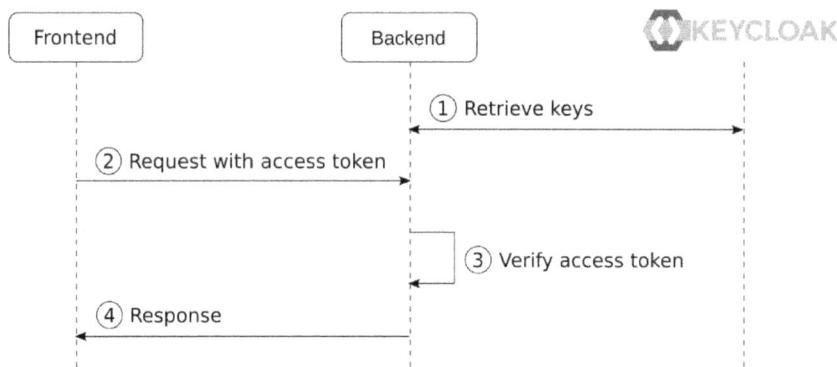

Figure 2.3 – Secured request from the frontend to the backend simplified

The steps in the diagram are as follows:

1.   The backend retrieves Keycloak's public keys. The backend does not need to do this for all requests to the backend, but can instead cache the keys in memory.

2.   The frontend sends a request to the backend, including the access token.

3.   The backend uses the public keys it retrieved earlier to verify that the access token was issued by a trusted Keycloak instance, and then verifies that the token is valid and that the token contains the role, `myrole`.

4.   The backend returns the results to the frontend.

You now have a basic understanding of how the sample applications is secured with Keycloak. In the next section, you will learn how to run the sample application.

Running the application

In this section, you will learn how to run the sample application.

If you don't already have Node.js installed on your workstation, go to `https://nodejs.org/` for instructions on how to install it.

To run the frontend on Node.js, open a terminal and run the following commands:

```
$ cd Keycloak Identity-and-Access-Management-for-Modern-
Applications/ch2/frontend/
$ npm install
$ npm start
```

Next, open a new terminal to run the backend using the following commands:

```
$ cd Keycloak-Identity-and-Access-Management-for-Modern-
Applications/ch2/backend/
$ npm install
$ npm start
```

Now that you have the sample application running with Node.js, you can register it with Keycloak, which we will cover in the next section.

Understanding how to log in to the application

In the previous chapter, covering how to get started with Keycloak, you learned how to run Keycloak, as well as how to create your first realm. Prior to continuing this section, you should have Keycloak running with the realm created as covered in the previous chapter. In summary, what you require before continuing is the following:

- Keycloak up and running
- A realm named `myrealm`
- A global role named `myrole`
- A user with the preceding role

Before an application can log in with Keycloak, it has to be registered as a client with Keycloak.

Before registering the frontend, let's see what happens if an unregistered application tries to authenticate with Keycloak. Open `http://localhost:8000` and then click on the **Login** button.

You will see an error page from Keycloak with the message **Client not found**. This error is telling you that the application is not registered with Keycloak.

To register the frontend with Keycloak, open the Keycloak admin console. At the top of the menu on the left-hand side, there is an option to select what realm you are working with. Make sure you have selected the realm named `myrealm`. In the menu on the left-hand side, click on **Clients**, and then click on **Create**.

Fill in the form with the following values:

- **Client ID**: `myclient`
- **Client Protocol**: `openid-connect`
- **Root URL**: `http://localhost:8000`

The following diagram shows the **Add Client** form with the values you need to fill in:

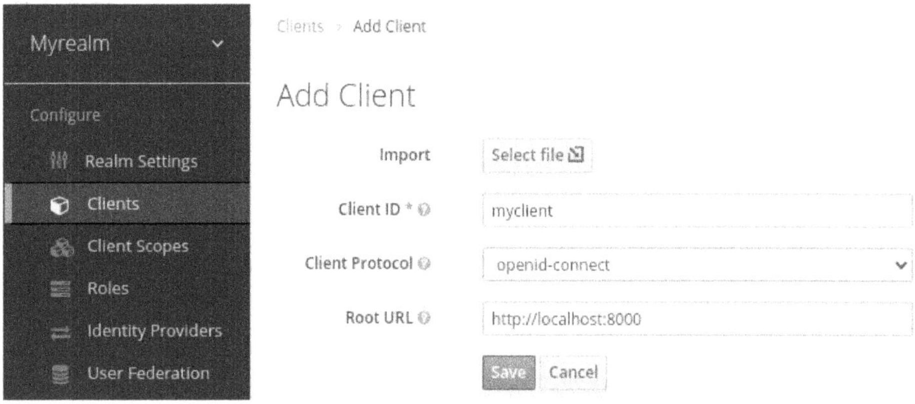

Figure 2.4 – Creating the client in the admin console

Once you have filled in the form, click on **Save**. After you click **Save**, you will see the full configuration for the client. There are two configuration options that are particularly interesting at this point:

- **Valid Redirect URIs**: This value is very important in an OpenID Connect authorization code flow when a client-side application is used. A client-side application is not able to have any credentials as these would be visible to end users of the application. To prevent any malicious applications from being able to masquerade as the real application, the valid redirect URIs instruct Keycloak to only redirect the user to a URL that matches a valid redirect URI. In this case, since the value is set to `http://localhost:8000/*`, an application hosted on `http://attacker.com` would not be able to authenticate.

- **Web Origins**: This option registers the valid web origins for the application for **Cross-Origin Resource Sharing** (**CORS**) requests. To obtain tokens from Keycloak, the frontend application has to send an AJAX request to Keycloak, and browsers do not permit an AJAX request from one web origin to another, unless **CORS** is used

Now you can go back to the frontend by opening `http://localhost:8000`. This time, when you click on the **Login** button, you will see the Keycloak login page. Log in with the username and password you created during the previous chapter.

Let's take a look at the ID token that Keycloak issued. Click on the **Show ID Token** button. The ID token that is displayed will look something like the following:

```
{
    "exp": 1603912252,
    "iat": 1603911952,
```

```
    "auth_time": 1603911952,
    "jti": "363b94b8-7e0c-4852-8287-d331c98153f2",
    "iss": "http://localhost:8080/auth/realms/myrealm",
    "aud": "myclient",
    "sub": "67855660-fd6e-4416-96d1-72c99db5e525",
    "typ": "ID",
    "azp": "myclient",
    "nonce": "b59c4dbf-d196-4af7-9451-8020b153caff",
    "session_state": "32e2501f-f5ca-4d73-9fad-067d4c52835a",
    "at_hash": "7p1VYLHv2T5qRAf2X9UzSw",
    "acr": "1",
    "email_verified": false,
    "realm_access": {
      "roles": [
        "offline_access",
        "uma_authorization",
        "myrole"
      ]
    },
    "name": "Stian Thorgersen",
    "preferred_username": "st",
    "locale": "en",
    "given_name": "Stian",
    "family_name": "Thorgersen",
    "email": "st@localhost"
}
```

Here is a list of some of the more interesting values within the ID token:

- exp: This is the date and time the token expires in seconds since 01/01/1970 00:00:00 UTC (often referred to as Unix or Epoch time).

- iss: This is the issuer of the token, which you may notice is the URL of the Keycloak realm.

- sub: This is the unique identifier of the authenticated user.

- name: This is the first name and last name of the authenticated user.

- `preferred_username`: This is the username of the authenticated user. You should avoid this as a key for the user as it may be changed, and even refer to a different user in the future. Instead, always use the sub field for the user key.

The ID token is used by the application to establish the identity of the authenticated user.

Next, let's take a look at the access token. Click on the **Show Access Token** button. Let's also take a look at some fields in this token:

- `allowed-origins`: This is a list of permitted web origins for the application. The backend service can use this field when deciding whether web origins should be permitted for CORS requests.

- `realm_access`: This contains a list of global roles. It is the intersection between the roles granted to the user, and the roles the client has access to.

- `resource_access`: This contains a list of client roles.

- `scope`: Scopes can be used both to decide what fields (or claims) to include in the token, as well as be used by backends to decide what APIs the token can access.

Currently, the information within the tokens are the default fields available in Keycloak. If you want to add additional information, Keycloak is very flexible in allowing you to customize the contents within the tokens.

Let's give this a go by adding a picture for the user. Leave the tab with the frontend open, and then open a new tab with the Keycloak admin console. In the menu on the left-hand side, click on **Users**, then click on **View all users**, and select the user you created previously. Now let's add a custom attribute to the user. Click on **Attributes**. In the table, there will be two empty input fields at the bottom. In the **Key** column. set the value to `picture`, and in the **Value** column, set the value to the URL to a profile picture (in the following screenshot, I've used my GitHub avatar). Then, click on **Add**:

Figure 2.5 – Adding a custom attribute to a user

Now, go back to the tab where you have the frontend open. To display the profile picture, you can click on the **Refresh** button. When you click on this button, the tokens will be refreshed, and the new ID token will now contain the picture attribute you just added, which allows the application to display a profile picture for the user.

Next, you will learn how to securely invoke the backend from the frontend.

Securely invoking the backend REST API

Now, open `http://localhost:3000/` and click on the **Public endpoint** link. You will see a message saying **Public message!**. The public endpoint is not secured by Keycloak, and can be invoked without an access token.

Next, let's try the secured endpoint that is protected by Keycloak. Open `http://localhost:3000/` again. This time, click on the **Secured endpoint** link. Now you will see a message saying **Access denied**. The Keycloak Node.js adapter is denying requests to this endpoint as it requires a valid access token to invoke the endpoint.

Let's now try to invoke the secured endpoint from the frontend. Open `http://localhost:8000/` and click on **Invoke Service**. You will now see a message displayed saying **Secret message!**. If instead you get the message **Access Denied**, this is most likely caused by the user not having the `myrole` role.

When you click **Invoke Service**, the frontend sends an AJAX request to the backend service, including the access token in the request, which allows the backend to verify that the invocation is done on behalf of a user who has the required role to access the endpoint.

Summary

In this chapter, you learned how to secure your first application, consisting of a frontend web application and a backend REST API with Keycloak. You also gained a basic understanding of how Keycloak leverages OpenID Connect to make this all happen in a standard and secure way. Together with what you learned in the first chapter of the book, you now have a solid foundation to start learning more about Keycloak.

In the next chapter, we will dive deeper into securing applications with Keycloak, giving you a better understanding of how it all works.

Questions

1. How does an application authenticate with Keycloak?

2. What do you need to configure in the Keycloak admin console in order to allow an application to authenticate with Keycloak?

3. How does an application securely invoke a protected backend service?

Section 2: Securing Applications with Keycloak

In this section, you will understand the options available in terms of how to secure different application types, including different strategies for authorization.

This section comprises the following chapters:

3
Brief Introduction to Standards

In this chapter, you will get a brief introduction to the **standards** that enable you to integrate your applications securely and easily with Keycloak. We very briefly cover **OAuth 2.0**, **OpenID Connect**, **JSON Web Tokens (JWT)**, and **SAML 2.0**. If you are new to these standards, this chapter will give you a gentle introduction without going too much into detail. Even if you are fairly familiar with these standards, you may still want to skim through this chapter.

By the end of this chapter, you will have a basic understanding of OAuth 2.0, OpenID Connect, JWT, and SAML 2.0, along with a decent understanding of what these standards can offer you.

In this chapter, we're going to cover the following main topics:

- Authorizing application access with OAuth 2.0
- Authenticating users with OpenID Connect
- Leveraging JWT for tokens
- Understanding why SAML 2.0 is still relevant

Authorizing application access with OAuth 2.0

OAuth 2.0 is by now a massively popular industry-standard protocol for authorization.

At the heart of OAuth 2.0 sits the OAuth 2.0 framework, which has enabled a whole ecosystem of websites to integrate with each other. Prior to OAuth 2.0 there was OAuth 1, as well as more bespoke solutions to allow third-party applications to access data on behalf of the user, but these approaches were complex or not easily interoperable. With OAuth 2.0, sharing user data to third-party applications is easy, doesn't require sharing user credentials, and allows control over what data is shared.

OAuth 2.0 is not only useful when dealing with *third-party applications*. It is also incredibly useful for *limiting access* to your own *applications*. Just as it wasn't uncommon for third-party applications to ask for your username and password to other sites, this was a common pattern within the enterprise as well. Applications would, for example, ask for your *LDAP username* and *password*, which would then be used to access other services within the enterprise. This could effectively mean that if one application is compromised, all services within the enterprise could also be compromised.

There are four roles defined in OAuth 2.0:

- **Resource owner**: This is typically the end user that owns the resources an application wants to access.
- **Resource server**: This is the service hosting the protected resources.
- **Client**: This is the application that would like to access the resource.
- **Authorization server**: This is the server issuing access to the client, which is the role of Keycloak.

In essence, in an OAuth 2.0 protocol flow, the client requests access to a resource on behalf of a resource owner from the authorization server. The authorization server issues a limited access to the resource in the form of an access token. After receiving the access token, the client can access the resource at the resource server by including the access token in the request.

Depending on the application type and use case, there are a number of different flows that can be used. To help you decide what flow type you should use for your application, you can use the following simple formula:

- If the application is accessing the resource on behalf of itself (the application is the resource owner), use the **Client Credentials flow**.

- If the application is running on a device without a browser or is input-constrained, use the **Device flow**. This could, for example, be a **smart TV** where it would be difficult for the user to enter the username and password.

- If none of the preceding conditions are applicable, use the **Authorization Code flow**.

In addition, there are two more flow types that are now legacy and should not be used:

- **Implicit flow**: This was a simplified flow for native applications and client-side applications, which is now considered insecure and should not be used.

- **Resource Owner Password Credentials flow**: In this flow, the application collects the user's credentials directly and exchanges them for an access token. It may be tempting to use this grant type for native applications, when a browser is not available, or simply because you want the login form to be directly integrated with your application. You should not be tempted, though. It is inherently insecure as you are exposing the user's credentials directly to the application, and you will also run into other problems in the long run, when you want your users to use stronger authentication than only a password, for example.

If you are not already familiar with the Authorization Code flow in OAuth 2.0, the following diagram will help you understand how it works:

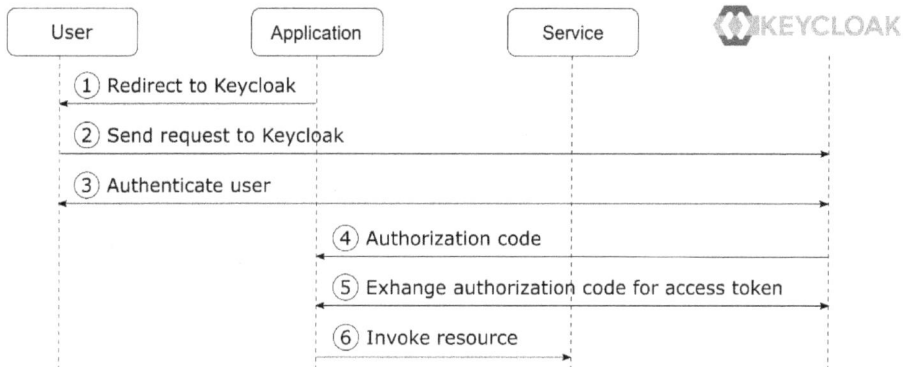

Figure 3.1 – OAuth 2.0 Authorization Code grant type simplified

In more detail, the steps in the diagram are as follows:

1. The **application** prepares what is called an **authorization request**, and requests the user's browser to be redirected to **Keycloak**.

2. The **user's** browser redirects the user to **Keycloak** at an endpoint called the **authorization endpoint**.

3. If the **user** is not already authenticated with **Keycloak**, **Keycloak** authenticates the user. Once authenticated, **Keycloak** asks the **user** to provide their consent to allow the application to access the service on their behalf.

4. The **application** receives an **authorization code** from **Keycloak** in the form of an **authorization response**.

5. The **application** exchanges the authorization code for an access token through an **access token request** to the **token endpoint** at **Keycloak**.

6. The **application** can now use the access token to invoke the protected resource.

Within an OAuth 2.0 flow there are two client types, which are **confidential** and **public** clients. **Confidential clients** are applications such as a server-side web application that are able to safely store credentials that they can use to authenticate with the authorization server. **Public clients**, on the other hand, are client-side applications that are not able to safely store credentials. As public clients are not able to authenticate with the authorization server, there are two safeguards in place:

- The authorization server will only send the authorization code to an application hosted on a pre-configured URL, in the form of a previously registered redirect URI.

- **Proof Key for Code Exchange** (**PKCE**, RFC 7636), which is an extension to OAuth 2.0, prevents anyone that intercepts an authorization code from exchanging it for an access token.

As access tokens are passed around from the application to services, they typically have a short lifetime. To allow applications to obtain new access tokens without going through the complete flow, a refresh token is used. A refresh token should be kept securely by the application and can be used by the application to obtain new access tokens.

In addition to the core OAuth 2.0 framework, there are a few additional specifications you should be aware of:

- **Bearer Tokens (RFC 6750)**: OAuth 2.0 does not describe the type of access token, or how it should be used. Bearer tokens are by far the most commonly used type of access tokens, and they are typically sent to resource servers through the HTTP Authorization header. They can also be sent in the form-encoded body, or as a query parameter. An important thing to note here is that sending bearer tokens as a query parameter has inherent security weaknesses and should be avoided.

- **Token Introspection (RFC 7662)**: In OAuth 2.0, the contents of access tokens are opaque to applications, which means the content of the access token is not readable by the application. The token introspection endpoint allows the client to obtain information about the access token without understanding its format.

- **Token Revocation (RFC 7009)**: OAuth 2.0 considers how access tokens are issued to applications, but not how they are revoked. This is covered by the token revocation endpoint.

There are also a number of best practices on how you should use OAuth 2.0. There are recommendations for **native applications, browser-based applications,** as well as security considerations and best practices. We will cover these in later chapters.

By now you should have a basic understanding of what OAuth 2.0 is and how you can leverage it in your applications. Don't worry if you don't fully understand all the details as we will come back to this subject later. In most cases, you will not be required to have a deep understanding of OAuth 2.0 in order to use it, as you should be using a library that hides its complexity from you and that helps you apply it in the correct way for your application.

One thing you may have noticed is that although OAuth 2.0 can grant access to resources, it does not cover the authentication of users. This is covered by an extension to OAuth 2.0 called **OpenID Connect**, which we will look at next.

Authenticating users with OpenID Connect

While OAuth 2.0 is a protocol for authorization, it does not cover authentication. OpenID Connect builds on top of OAuth 2.0 to add an authentication layer.

At the heart of OpenID Connect sits the **OpenID Connect Core specification**, which has enabled a whole ecosystem of websites to no longer need to deal with user management and authenticating users. In addition, it has significantly reduced the number of times a user has to authenticate, as well as the number of different passwords a user has to juggle, that is, if they care about using unique passwords for all websites they access. Just think about the endless number of websites that allow you to sign in using **Google**, or other social networks. I'm highlighting Google rather than other social networks here due to the fact that they are actually implementing OpenID Connect properly, which makes it incredibly easy to add sign-on with Google, compared to some other sites that have done their own tweaks to OAuth 2.0 rather than implement OpenID Connect according to the specifications.

OpenID Connect has not only enabled social login but is also, of course, very useful within the **enterprise** in order to have a centralized solution for authentication, supporting **single sign-on**. This also significantly increases security as applications don't have access to the **user credentials** directly. It also enables the use of **stronger authentication**, such as **OTP** or **WebAuthn**, without the need to support it directly within applications.

Not only does OpenID Connect enable easy authentication within the enterprise, but it also enables you to allow third parties such as employees at partner companies to access applications within your enterprise without having to create individual accounts within your enterprise.

Like OAuth 2.0, OpenID Connect defines a number of roles involved in the protocol:

- **End User**: This is the equivalent of the resource owner in OAuth 2.0. It is, of course, the human being that is authenticating.

- **Relying Party (RP)**: A somewhat confusing term for the application that would like to authenticate the end user. It is called the relying party, as it is a party that is relying on the OpenID Connect Provider to verify the identity of the user.

- **OpenID Provider (OP)**: The identity provider that is authenticating the user, which is the role of Keycloak.

In essence, in an OpenID Connect protocol flow, the Relying Party requests the identity of the end user from the OpenID Provider. As it builds on top of OAuth 2.0 at the same time as the identity of the user is requested, it can also obtain an access token.

OpenID Connect utilizes the *Authorization Code* grant type from OAuth 2.0. The main difference is that the client includes *scope=openid* in the initial request, which makes it an **authentication request**, rather than an **authorization request**.

While OAuth 2.0 calls the different flows grant types, OpenID Connect refers to them as flows. There are two flows in OpenID Connect that you should care about:

- **Authorization Code flow**: This uses the same flow as the OAuth 2.0 Authorization Code grant type and returns an authorization code like OAuth 2.0 that can be exchanged for an ID token, an access token, and a refresh token.

- **Hybrid flow**: In the Hybrid flow, the ID token is returned from the initial request alongside an authorization code.

Just like OAuth 2.0, OpenID Connect also defines the Implicit flow. However, we recommend that you do not use the Implicit flow at all.

OpenID Connect does not define equivalents to the Client Credential flow and the Device flow. This makes sense as neither of these flows requires authenticating users, instead just granting access to a service.

If you are not already familiar with the Authorization Code flow in OpenID Connect, the following diagram will help you understand how it works:

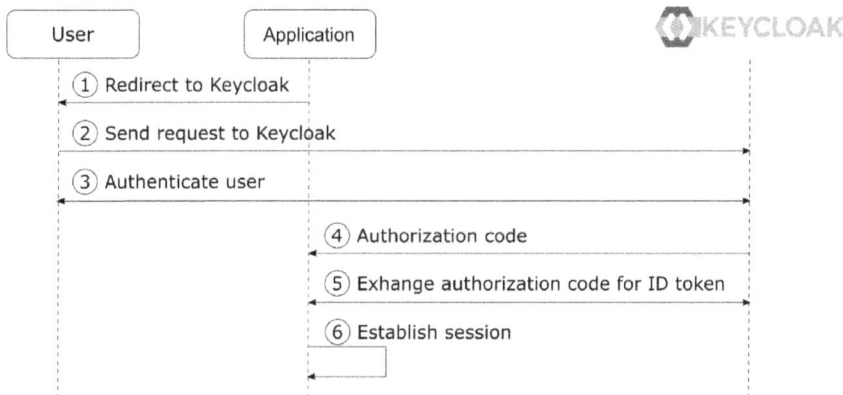

Figure 3.2 – OpenID Connect Authorization Code flow simplified

In more detail, the steps in the diagram are as follows:

1. The **application** prepares what is called an authentication request, and requests the **user's** browser to be redirected to **Keycloak**.

2. The **user's** browser redirects the user to **Keycloak** at an endpoint called the authorization endpoint.

3. If the **user** is not already authenticated with **Keycloak**, **Keycloak** authenticates the **user**.

4. The **application** receives an authorization code from **Keycloak** in the form of an authentication response.

5. The **application** exchanges the authorization code for an ID token and an access token through a token request to the token endpoint at **Keycloak**.

6. The **application** now has the ID token that it can use to discover the user's identity, and can establish an authenticated session for the user.

In addition to the OpenID Connect Core specification, there are a few additional specifications you should be aware of:

- **Discovery**: Allows clients to dynamically discover information about the OpenID Provider

- **Dynamic Registration**: Allows clients to dynamically register themselves with the OpenID Provider

- **Session Management**: Defines how to monitor the end user's authentication session with the OpenID Provider, and how the client can initiate a logout

- **Front-Channel Logout**: Defines a mechanism for single sign-out of multiple applications using embedded iframes

- **Back-Channel Logout**: Defines a mechanism for single sign-out for multiple applications using a back-channel request mechanism, which we will cover in the next chapter

OpenID Connect has two additional concepts on top of OAuth 2.0. It clearly specifies the format of the ID token by leveraging the JWT specification, which, unlike the access token in OAuth 2.0, is not opaque. It has a well-specified format, and the values (called claims) within the token can be directly read by the client. This allows the clients to discover information about the authenticated user in a standard way. In addition, it defines a **userinfo endpoint**, which can be invoked with an access token and returns the same standard claims as found in the ID token. In the next chapter, we will cover the userinfo endpoint in more detail, including how you can control what information is returned for a user.

For use cases where an increased level of security is required, there is a set of profiles from what is called the **Financial-grade API** working group. These are profiles that describe best practices of how OpenID Connect and related specifications should be used in high-risk scenarios. You should not get too hung up on the name Financial-grade API, as there is nothing specific to finance in these profiles.

By now, you should have a basic understanding of what OpenID Connect is and how you can leverage it in your applications. Don't worry if you don't fully understand all the details as we will come back to this later. In most cases, you will not be required to have a deep understanding of OpenID Connect in order to use it, as you should be using a library that hides its complexity from you and that helps you to apply it in the correct way for your application.

While OpenID Connect defines a standard format for the ID token, it also does not define any standard for the access token. In the next section, you will find out why Keycloak leverages JWT as the format for the default access tokens it issues.

Leveraging JWT for tokens

Keycloak has leveraged JWT as the format for access tokens from the very beginning of the project. This was a very conscious decision for interoperability as well as performance reasons.

Using a standard format, which is relatively easily consumable, makes it easier to integrate with Keycloak. As JWT is based on JSON, it can also easily be parsed and understood in any programming language.

In addition, as the resource servers are now able to directly read the value of the access token, they do not always have to make a request to the OAuth 2.0 token introspection endpoint, or the OpenID Connect UserInfo endpoint. This potentially eliminates two additional requests to Keycloak for a request to the resource server, reducing latency as well as significantly reducing the number of requests to Keycloak.

JWT comes from a family of specifications known as **JOSE**, which stands for **JavaScript Object Signing and Encryption**. The related specifications are as follows:

- **JSON Web Token (JWT, RFC 7519)**: Consists of two base64url-encoded JSON documents separated by a dot, a header, and a set of claims

- **JSON Web Signature (JWS, RFC 7515)**: Adds a digital signature of the header and the claims

- **JSON Web Encryption (JWE, RFC 7516)**: Encrypts the claims

- **JSON Web Algorithms (JWA, RFC 7518)**: Defines the cryptographic algorithms that should be leveraged for JWS and JWE

- **JSON Web Key (JWK, RFC 7517)**: Defines a format to represent cryptographic keys in JSON format

In addition to the preceding specifications, the OpenID Connect Discovery endpoint advertises an endpoint where the **JSON Web Key Set (JWKS)** can be retrieved, as well as what signing and encryption mechanisms from the JWA specification are supported.

When a resource server receives an access token, it is able to verify the token in the following ways:

- Retrieving the JWKS URL from the OpenID Connect Discovery endpoint.
- Downloading the public signing keys for the OpenID Provider from the JWKS URL endpoint. These are typically cached/stored at the Resource Server.
- Verifying the signature of the token using the public signing keys from the OpenID Provider.

There are some potential issues with the JWT specifications that can lead to unexpected vulnerabilities if care is not taken when validating a JWT. Let's take a look at two example vulnerabilities that can occur through the incorrect application of these specifications:

- **alg=none**: Interestingly enough, the JWS specification defines an algorithm value that is none. This basically means the JWS is unsigned. As this is a valid value, a JWT library could tell you a JWS is valid even though it has not actually been signed.
- **RSA to HMAC**: Another well-known issue is using the public RSA key, but setting the algorithm to HMAC. Some libraries blindly accept these types of tokens as they simply pick up the public RSA key and use it as the HMAC secret key.

These types of vulnerabilities can be avoided with a few relatively simple steps:

- Do not accept `alg=none`.
- Only use a key for the algorithm and the use (signing or encryption) it is intended for, and don't blindly trust the values in the JWT header.

In general, you would want to pick up a trusted JWT library and make sure you use it in the correct way. Or, even better, use an OpenID Connect/OAuth 2.0 library that supports JWT as the access token, which can do it properly for you. If neither options are available to you, it is very likely safer to use the token introspection endpoint than to try to validate the token yourself. We will cover this in more detail in *Chapter 5, Authorizing Access with OAuth 2.0*.

By now, you should have a basic understanding of OAuth 2.0, OpenID Connect, and JWT. In the next section, we will take a look at a significantly more mature specification, SAML 2.0.

Understanding why SAML 2.0 is still relevant

Security Assertion Markup Language 2.0 (SAML 2.0) is a mature and robust protocol for authentication and authorization. It is very widely used to enable *single sign-on* within enterprise and other domains, such as **education** and **government**. It was ratified as an *OASIS Standard* in March 2005, so has been around for a considerable amount of time.

SAML 2.0 is very widely available within enterprise applications, enabling you to easily allow your existing users to authenticate to new applications you wish to deploy. Not only is it available in self-hosted applications, but it is also available as an option for a large number of Software-as-a-Service solutions, such as Salesforce, Google Apps, and Office 365. For enterprises, this is a great option when choosing hosted solutions in the cloud as it quickly enables you to allow all your employees access to these solutions, without having to create accounts for each individual employee.

Even though SAML 2.0 is more mature and perhaps also more widely used, you may still want to favor OpenID Connect over SAML 2.0 for new applications. OpenID Connect has a stronger focus on modern architecture, such as single-page applications, mobile applications, REST APIs, and microservices, which means it is a better fit for the future. Developers will also often find that OpenID Connect is simpler to understand, due to OpenID Connect leveraging JSON and simple query parameters, while SAML 2.0 uses more complicated XML documents.

If you are unfamiliar with the details of OAuth 2.0, OpenID Connect, and SAML 2.0, we recommend starting by learning OAuth 2.0 and OpenID Connect. For this reason, we are not going to cover SAML 2.0 in this book.

That being said, SAML 2.0 is still important today. You will often find that SAML 2.0 is available to you as an option, while OpenID Connect is not. You may also find that SAML 2.0 is a better fit for your particular use case or, due to internal policies or compliance, you may be required to use SAML 2.0. The great thing about Keycloak is that both options are available to you. You can also seamlessly combine applications using OpenID Connect with applications using SAML 2.0 in the same single sign-on experience.

Summary

In this chapter, you learned how to use OAuth 2.0 to provide your applications, as well as third-party applications, with access to services without exposing credentials, as well as only giving applications exactly what access they need. You also learned how OpenID Connect can be leveraged for single sign-on to your applications, as well as allowing external users to access your applications. Finally, you learned how SAML 2.0 is still an important standard that you should be aware of, even though you may not want to choose it for your own applications.

In the next chapter, you will get a deeper understanding of OAuth 2.0 with a practical guide on how you can use Keycloak to leverage this standard in your applications.

Questions

1. How does OAuth 2.0 allow an application to access resources provided by a different application without asking for the user's username and password?

2. What does OpenID Connect add to OAuth 2.0?

3. What does JWT add to OAuth 2.0?

4
Authenticating Users with OpenID Connect

In this chapter, you will get a deeper understanding of how Keycloak enables you to authenticate users in your applications by leveraging the OpenID Connect standard. Through using a sample application that was written for this book, we will see the first-hand interaction between an application and Keycloak, including the contents of requests and responses.

By the end of this chapter, you will have a good understanding of OpenID Connect, including how to authenticate users, understanding the ID token, and how to deal with users logging out.

In this chapter, we're going to cover the following main topics:

- Running the OpenID Connect playground
- Understanding the Discovery endpoint
- Authenticating a user
- Understanding the ID token

- Invoking the UserInfo endpoint
- Dealing with users logging out

Technical requirements

To run the sample application included in this chapter you need to have Node.js (`https://nodejs.org/`) installed on your workstation.

You also need to have a local clone of the GitHub repository associated with the book. The GitHub repository is available at `https://github.com/PacktPublishing/Keycloak-Identity-and-Access-Management-for-Modern-Applications`.

Check out the following link to see the Code in Action video:

`https://bit.ly/3nQ8WZe`

Running the OpenID Connect playground

The **OpenID Connect** (**OIDC**) playground application was developed specifically for this book in order to make it as easy as possible for you to understand and experiment with OIDC in a practical way.

The playground application does not use any libraries for OIDC, but rather all OIDC requests are crafted by the application itself. One thing to note here is that this application is not implementing OIDC in a secure way, and is ignoring optional parameters in the requests that are important for a production application. There are two reasons for this. Firstly, it is so you can focus on understanding the general concepts of OIDC. Secondly, if you decide to implement your own application libraries for OIDC you should have a very good understanding of the specifications, and it is beyond the scope of this book to cover OIDC in that much detail.

Before continuing with reading this chapter, you should start the OIDC playground application, as it will be used throughout the rest of the chapter.

To run the OIDC playground application, open a terminal and run the following commands:

```
$ cd Keycloak-Identity-and-Access-Management-for-Modern-
Applications/ch4/
$ npm install
$ npm start
```

To verify the application is running, open `http://localhost:8000/` in your browser. The following screenshot shows the OIDC playground application page:

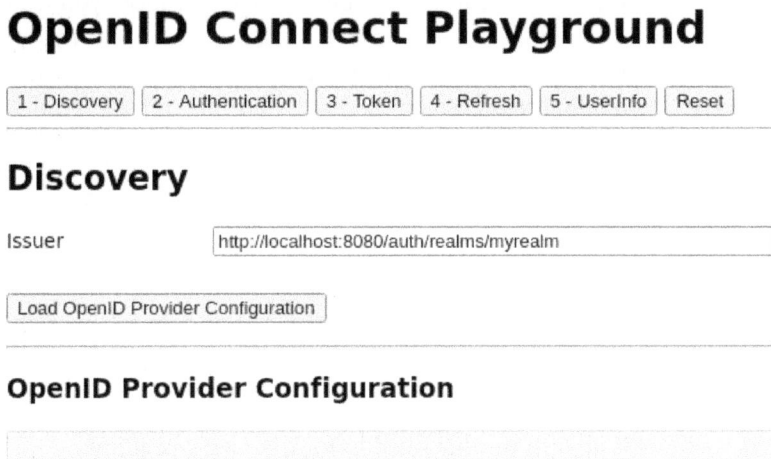

OpenID Connect Playground

| 1 - Discovery | 2 - Authentication | 3 - Token | 4 - Refresh | 5 - UserInfo | Reset |

Discovery

Issuer   `http://localhost:8080/auth/realms/myrealm`

Load OpenID Provider Configuration

OpenID Provider Configuration

Figure 4.1 – The OpenID Connect playground application

In order to be able to use the playground application you need Keycloak running, a realm with a user that you can log in with, and have a client with the following configuration:

- **Client ID**: `oidc-playground`
- **Access Type**: `public`
- **Valid Redirect URIs**: `http://localhost:8000/`
- **Web Origins**: `http://localhost:8000`

If you are unsure about how to do this you should refer to *Chapter 1*, *Getting Started with Keycloak*, and *Chapter 2*, *Securing Your First Application*.

In the next section, we will start taking a deeper look at OIDC by leveraging the playground application, starting with understanding how applications can discover information about an OpenID Provider.

Understanding the Discovery endpoint

The OIDC Discovery specification is an important aspect of both the interoperability and usability of OIDC Relying Party libraries. Without this specification, you would be required to do a lot of manual configuration in your applications to be able to authenticate with an OpenID Provider (more information on OpenID Providers can be found in *Chapter 3*, *Brief Introduction to Standards*).

It is an optional specification that an OpenID Provider can decide if it wants to implement or not. Luckily, most OpenID Providers, including Keycloak, implement this specification.

By simply knowing the base URL (often referred to as the issuer URL) for your OpenID Provider, a Relying Party can discover a lot of useful information about the provider. It does this by loading what is called the **OpenID Provider Metadata** from a standard endpoint, namely `<base URL>/.well-known/openid-configuration`.

To better understand the OpenID Provider Metadata, open the OIDC playground in your browser. You can see there is already a value filled in for the `issuer` input.

The value for the issuer URL that is already filled in is `http://localhost:8080/auth/realms/myrealm`. Let's break this URL apart and take a look at the parts of the issuer URL:

- `http://localhost:8080/auth`: This is the root URL for Keycloak. In a production system, this would obviously be a real domain name and would use HTTPS (for example, `https://auth.mycompany.com/`).
- `/realms/myrealm`: As Keycloak supports multi-tenancy, this is used to separate each realm in your Keycloak instance.

If you have Keycloak running on a different hostname, port, or have a different realm, you should change the `issuer` field. Otherwise, you can leave it as is.

Now click on **Load OpenID Provider Configuration**. When you click on this button, the playground application sends a request to `http://localhost:8080/auth/realms/myrealm/.well-known/openid-configuration` (assuming you left the `issuer` URL untouched) and receives a response in the form of the OpenID Provider Metadata for this Keycloak instance. The returned metadata is displayed in the **OpenID Provider Configuration** section of the playground application.

The following screenshot from the playground application shows an example of the loaded OpenID Provider Metadata:

OpenID Provider Configuration

```
{
  "issuer": "http://localhost:8080/auth/realms/myrealm",
  "authorization_endpoint": "http://localhost:8080/auth/realms/myrealm/protocol/openid-connect/auth
  "token_endpoint": "http://localhost:8080/auth/realms/myrealm/protocol/openid-connect/token",
  "introspection_endpoint": "http://localhost:8080/auth/realms/myrealm/protocol/openid-connect/toke
  "userinfo_endpoint": "http://localhost:8080/auth/realms/myrealm/protocol/openid-connect/userinfo"
  "end_session_endpoint": "http://localhost:8080/auth/realms/myrealm/protocol/openid-connect/logout
  "jwks_uri": "http://localhost:8080/auth/realms/myrealm/protocol/openid-connect/certs",
  "check_session_iframe": "http://localhost:8080/auth/realms/myrealm/protocol/openid-connect/login-
  "grant_types_supported": [
    "authorization_code",
    "implicit",
    "refresh_token",
    "password",
    "client_credentials"
  ],
  "response_types_supported": [
    "code",
    "none",
    "id_token",
    "token",
    "id_token token",
    "code id_token",
    "code token",
    "code id_token token"
  ],
```

Figure 4.2 – OpenID Provider Metadata for Keycloak

In the following list, we'll take a look at what some of these values mean:

- `authorization_endpoint`: The URL to use for authentication requests

- `token_endpoint`: The URL to use for token requests

- `introspection_endpoint`: The URL to use for introspection requests

- `userinfo_endpoint`: The URL to use for UserInfo requests

- `grant_types_supported`: The list of supported grant types

- `response_types_supported`: The list of supported response types

With all of this metadata, the Relying Party can make intelligent decisions about how to use the OpenID Provider, including what endpoints to send requests to and what grant types and response types it can use.

If you took an extra good look at the metadata, you may have noticed that Keycloak supports the `authorization_code` grant type and the `code` and `token` response types. This is good news since we'll use this grant type and these response types to authenticate the user in our playground application in the next section.

Authenticating a user

The most common way to authenticate a user with Keycloak is through the OpenID Connect authorization code flow.

In summary, to authenticate a user with this flow, an application redirects to Keycloak, which displays a login page to authenticate the user. After the user has authenticated, the application receives an ID token, which contains information about the user.

In the following diagram, the authorization code flow is shown in more detail:

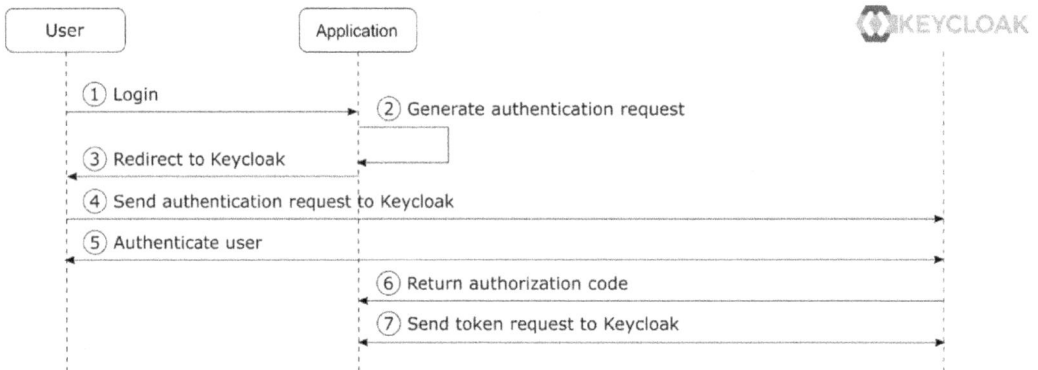

Figure 4.3 – The authorization code flow

The steps from the diagram are explained in more detail as follows:

1. The user clicks on a login button in the application.

2. The application generates an authentication request.

3. The authentication request is sent to the user in form of a 302 redirect, instructing the user-agent to redirect to the authorization endpoint provided by Keycloak.

4. The user-agent opens the authorization endpoint with the query parameters specified by the application via the authentication request.

5. Keycloak displays a login page to the user. The user enters their username and password and submits the form.

6. After Keycloak has verified the user's credentials, it creates an authorization code, which is returned to the application.

7. The application can now exchange the authorization code for the ID token, as well as a refresh token.

8. Let's give this a go by going back to the OIDC playground application. As you already loaded the OpenID Provider Metadata in the previous section, the playground application already knows where to send the authentication request. To send an authentication request, click on the button labelled **2 - Authentication**.

The form that is displayed has the following values that you should fill in:

- `client_id`: This is the client ID for the application registered with Keycloak. If you used a different value than `oidc-playground` when creating the client, you should change this value.

- `scope`: The default value is `openid`, which means we will be doing an OpenID request. Leave this as-is for now.

- `prompt`: This can be used for a few different purposes. For example, if you enter the value `none` in this field, Keycloak will not display a login screen to the user, but will instead only authenticate the user if the user already is logged in with Keycloak. You can also use the value `login` to require the user to log in again even if they are already logged in with Keycloak.

- `max_age`: This is the maximum number of seconds since the last time the user authenticated with Keycloak. If, for example, you set this field to `60`, it means that Keycloak will re-authenticate the user if it was more than 60 seconds since the user last authenticated.

- `login_hint`: If the application happens to know the username of the user that it wants to authenticate it can use this parameter to have the username filled in automatically on the login page.

Now let's take a look at what the authentication request will look like by clicking on the button labeled **Generate Authentication Request**. You will now see the actual request that the application will redirect the user-agent to in order to initiate the authentication.

The following screenshot from the playground application shows an example authentication request:

Authentication Request

```
http://localhost:8080/auth/realms/myrealm/protocol/openid-connect/auth

client_id=oidc-playground
response_type=code
redirect_uri=http://localhost:8000/
scope=openid
```

Figure 4.4 – Authentication request

This includes setting the `response_type` parameter to `code`, meaning that the application wants to receive an authorization code from Keycloak.

Next, click on the button labeled **Send Authentication Request**. You will now be redirected to the Keycloak login pages. Fill in the username and password for your user and click on **Log In**.

If you want to experiment a bit you can, for example, try the following steps:

- **Set prompt to login**: With this value, Keycloak should always ask you to re-authenticate.

- **Set max_age to 60**: With this value, Keycloak will re-authenticate you if you wait for at least 60 seconds since the last time you authenticated.

- **Set login_hint to your username**: This should prefill the username in the Keycloak login page.

If you try any of the preceding steps, don't forget to generate and send the authentication request again to see how Keycloak behaves.

After Keycloak has redirected back to the playground application, you will see the authentication response in the **Authentication Response** section. The code is what is called the **authorization code**, which the application uses to obtain the ID token and the refresh token.

Now that the application has the authorization code, you can go ahead and exchange it for some tokens.

Click on the button labeled **3 - Token**. You will see the authorization code has already been filled in on the form so you can go ahead and click on the button labeled **Send Token Request**.

Under **Token Request**, you can see the request the application sends to the token endpoint provided by Keycloak. It contains the authorization code and sets the `grant_type` to `authorization_code`, which means the application wants to exchange an authorization code for tokens.

An example **Token Request** is shown in the following screenshot from the playground application:

Token Request

```
http://localhost:8080/auth/realms/myrealm/protocol/openid-connect/token

grant_type=authorization_code
code=163c7414-8683-4820-adff-c08d1dae8c4d.d565bbda-a2ec-46c0-bde1-04308042c5f3.
client_id=oidc-playground
redirect_uri=http://localhost:8000/
```

Figure 4.5 – Token request

Under **Token Response**, you can see the response that Keycloak sent to the application. If you get the error with the value `invalid_grant`, it is most likely for one of the following two reasons:

- **You did the steps a bit too slowly**: The authorization code is only valid for one minute by default, so if it took more than one minute between receiving the authentication response from Keycloak and sending the token request, the request will fail.

- **You sent the token request more than once**: The authorization code is only valid once, so if it is included in more than one token request the request will fail.

The following screenshot shows an example successful token response from the playground application:

Token Response

```
{
  "access_token": "eyJhbGciOiJSUzI1NiIsInR5cCIgOiAiSldUIiwia2lkIiA6ICJpU3BBbjVm
  "expires_in": 300,
  "refresh_expires_in": 1800,
  "refresh_token": "eyJhbGciOiJIUzI1NiIsInR5cCIgOiAiSldUIiwia2lkIiA6ICI3ZThmNjM
  "token_type": "bearer",
  "id_token": "eyJhbGciOiJSUzI1NiIsInR5cCIgOiAiSldUIiwia2lkIiA6ICJpU3BBbjVmand1
  "not-before-policy": 0,
  "session_state": "d565bbda-a2ec-46c0-bde1-04308042c5f3",
  "scope": "openid profile email"
}
```

Figure 4.6 – Token response

Let's take a look at the values within this response:

- `access_token`: This is the access token, which in Keycloak is a JWS. We'll look more at this in the next chapter when we cover OAuth 2.0 in more detail.

- `expires_in`: As the access token is sometimes opaque, this will give the application a hint when the token expires.

- `refresh_token`: This is the refresh token, which we will look more at in the next section.

- `refresh_token_expires_in`: The refresh token is also opaque, and this gives the application a hint when the refresh token expires.

- `token_type`: This is the type of the access token, which in Keycloak is always bearer.

- `id_token`: This is the ID token, which we will look at in more detail in the next section.

- `session_state`: This is the ID of the session the user has with Keycloak.

- `scope`: The application requests a scope from Keycloak in the authentication request, but the actual returned scope of the tokens may not match the requested scope.

In the next section, we will take a deeper look at the ID token that the playground application just received from Keycloak.

Understanding the ID token

In the previous section, you received a token response, including an ID token from Keycloak, but we didn't take a good look at what's inside the ID token.

The ID token is by default a signed **JSON Web Token** (**JWT**), which follows this format:

```
<Header>.<Payload>.<Signature>
```

The header and the payload are Base64URL-encoded JSON documents.

If you take a look at the **Token Response** in the playground application, you can see the ID token in its encoded format. An example of the encoded ID token is also shown in the following screenshot from the playground application:

```
"token_type": "bearer",
"id_token": "eyJhbGci0iJSUzI1NiIsInR5cCIg0iAiSldUIiwia2lkIiA6ICJpU3BBBbjVmand1
"not-before-policy": 0,
```

Figure 4.7 – Encoded ID token

Under the **ID Token** section, you will see the decoded token broken into three parts. The header tells you what algorithm is used, the type of the payload, and the key ID of the key that was used to sign the token.

An example of a decoded **ID Token** is shown in the following screenshot from the playground application:

ID Token

Header

```
{
  "alg": "RS256",
  "typ": "JWT",
  "kid": "iSpAn5fjwuekOb_ysSloqMxcFoOmp9Uza_7CdBYCFvI"
}
```

Payload

```
{
  "exp": 1601317631,
  "iat": 1601317331,
  "auth_time": 1601316791,
  "jti": "83107dee-1c80-47da-9ef2-011df87cb0ae",
  "iss": "http://localhost:8080/auth/realms/myrealm",
  "aud": "oidc-playground",
  "sub": "67855660-fd6e-4416-96d1-72c99db5e525",
  "typ": "ID",
  "azp": "oidc-playground",
  "session_state": "d565bbda-a2ec-46c0-bde1-04308042c5f3",
  "at_hash": "1YAllhsd_LTejkEanCR9wQ",
  "acr": "0",
  "email_verified": false,
  "realm_access": {
    "roles": [
      "myrole"
    ]
  },
  "name": "Bob Foo",
  "preferred_username": "st",
  "myotherclaim": "myotherclaim",
  "given_name": "Bob",
  "family_name": "Foo",
  "email": "bob@bob"
}
```

Signature

```
fcjhWbPfqiBz3iPXVt8NT7EwoDR248MKHqNV2Oo6B6VEmiNjREghBIU8S9Iaul9vIzHXHuSerZA0uXgrKuE
```

Figure 4.8 – Decoded ID token

Let's take a look at some of the claims (values) within the ID token:

- `exp`: When the token expires.
- `iat`: When the token was issued.
- `auth_time`: When the user last authenticated.
- `jti`: The unique identifier for this token.
- `aud`: The audience of the token, which must contain the Relying Party that is authenticating the user.
- `azp`: The party the token was issued to.
- `sub`: The unique identifier for the authenticated user. When referring to a user it is recommended to use this instead of a username or email, as they may change over time.

> **Information**
>
> All times in JWT tokens are represented in Unix epoch time (seconds since January 1, 1970). It's not all that readable to human beings, but great for computers, and takes very little space compared to other formats. You can find a handy tool to convert epoch times to human-readable dates at `https://www.epochconverter.com/`.

In addition to the claims listed previously, there is information about the user such as the given name, family name, and preferred username.

If you take a look at the `exp` value for the ID token with `https://www.epochconverter.com/`, you will notice that the token expires in only a few minutes.

Usually, ID tokens have a short duration in order to mitigate the risk of tokens being leaked. This doesn't mean that the application has to re-authenticate the user, rather there is a separate refresh token that can be used to obtain an updated ID token. The refresh token has a much longer expiration, and can only be used directly with Keycloak, which means Keycloak can validate the token is still valid.

Next, let's try to refresh the ID token. Click on the button labeled **4 – Refresh**, then click on the button labeled **Send Refresh Request**.

In the **Refresh Request** window, you will see the request sent by the playground to the Keycloak Token endpoint. It uses the grant type `refresh_token`, and includes the refresh token and the client ID.

The following screenshot from the playground applications shows an example refresh request:

Refresh Request

```
http://localhost:8080/auth/realms/myrealm/protocol/openid-connect/token

grant_type=refresh_token
refresh_token=eyJhbGciOiJIUzI1NiIsInR5cCIgOiAiSldUIiwia2lkIiA6ICI3ZThmNjM2MyllMmM0OL
client_id=oidc-playground
scope=openid
```

Figure 4.9 – Refresh request

Under the **Refresh Response** you will see the response Keycloak sent to the playground. It is pretty much the same as the response for the original token request.

The following screenshot from the playground applications shows an example refresh response:

Refresh Response

```
{
    "access_token": "eyJhbGciOiJSUzI1NiIsInR5cCIgOiAiSldUIiwia2lkIiA6ICJpU3BBbjVmand1
    "expires_in": 300,
    "refresh_expires_in": 1800,
    "refresh_token": "eyJhbGciOiJIUzI1NiIsInR5cCIgOiAiSldUIiwia2lkIiA6ICI3ZThmNjM2Myl
    "token_type": "bearer",
    "id_token": "eyJhbGciOiJSUzI1NiIsInR5cCIgOiAiSldUIiwia2lkIiA6ICJpU3BBbjVmand1ZWtP
    "not-before-policy": 0,
    "session_state": "d565bbda-a2ec-46c0-bde1-04308042c5f3",
    "scope": "openid profile email"
}
```

Figure 4.10 – Refresh response

One thing to notice here is that the refresh response also includes a refresh token. It is important that the application uses this updated refresh token the next time it wants to refresh the ID token. This is important for a few reasons, including the following:

- **Key rotation**: Keycloak may rotate its signing keys, and it relies on clients receiving new refresh tokens signed with the new keys.

- **Session idle**: A client (or a session) has a feature called session idle, which means a refresh token may have shorter expiration than the associated session.

- **Refresh token leak detection**: To discover leaked refresh tokens, Keycloak will not allow the re-use of refresh tokens. This feature is currently disabled by default in Keycloak.

Finally, under **ID Token** you may notice that the token has more or less the same values except the expiration time (`exp`), the issue time (`iat`), and the token ID (`jti`) have changed.

Another benefit of refreshing the token is that your application can update information about the user from Keycloak without having to re-authenticate. We'll now experiment a bit with this.

For the next few sections, you should keep the playground application open. In a new browser window open the Keycloak Admin Console, click on **Users** and locate the user you used when authenticating to the playground application.

First, let's try to update the user profile.

Updating the user profile

Change the email, first name, and last name of the user. Then go back to the playground application and click on the **Send Refresh Request** button. You will now notice that the user profile was updated.

Now that you have tried updating the user profile, let's try to add a custom property to the user.

Adding a custom property

Let's take a look at the steps to add a custom property:

1. Going back to the Keycloak Admin Console window, which should still have the user open, click on **Attributes**.

2. In the table that is displayed, set the key to `myattribute` and the value to `myvalue`, then click on **Add**. You have now added a custom attribute to the user, but this is still not available to the application.

3. We will now create what is called a **client scope**. A client scope allows creating re-usable groups of claims that are added to tokens issued to a client. In the menu on the left-hand side, click on **Client Scopes**, then click on **Create**. For the name in the form, enter `myclaim`. Leave everything else as-is and click **Save**.

4. Now we'll add the custom attribute to the client scope by creating a mapper. Click on **Mappers**, then click on **Create**.

    Fill in the form with the following values:

    - **Name**: `myattribute`

    - **Mapper Type**: `User Attribute`

    - **User Attribute**: `myattribute`

    - **Token Claim Name**: `myattribute`

    - **Claim JSON Type**: `String`

    Make sure **Add to ID Token** is turned on, then click on **Save**. Next, we will add your newly created client scope to the client.

5. In the menu on the left-hand side, click on **Clients** and locate the `oidc-playground` application. Select **Client Scopes**; then, in the **Optional Client Scopes** window, select **myclaim** and click on **Add selected**.

    As we added this claim to the optional client scopes for the client, it means that the client has to explicitly request this scope. If you had added it to the default client scopes, it would have always been added for the client.

    We're doing this as we want to show how a client can request different information from Keycloak using the `scope` parameter. This allows the client to only request the information it needs at any given time, which is especially useful when the user is required to consent to access from the application, which we will take a look at in the next chapter.

6. Now go back to the playground application and again click on the **Send Refresh Request** button. You will notice that your custom attribute has not been added to the ID token.

> Tip
>
> If you get an error when refreshing the token, it is probably because your **Single-Sign On (SSO)** session with Keycloak has expired. By default, an SSO session expires if there is no activity for 10 minutes. Later in the book, we will look at how to change this.

Now let's send a new authentication request, but this time we'll include the `myclaim` scope. In the playground application, click on **2 – Authentication**. In the `scope` field, set the value to `openid myclaim`. Make sure you leave `openid` in there because, otherwise, Keycloak will not send you an ID token. Now go through these steps again to obtain a new token:

1. Click on **Generate Authentication Request**.

2. Click on **Send Authentication Request**.

3. Click on **3 – Token**.

4. Click on **Send Token Request**.

In the payload for the ID token, you will now notice the custom claim that you just added to the client.

Now that you have added a custom attribute, let's add roles to the ID token.

Adding roles to the ID token

By default, roles are not added to the ID token. You can change this behavior by going to **Client Scopes**, then selecting the **roles** client scope. Click on **Mappers**, then select **realm roles**. Turn on **Add to ID Token**, and click **Save**.

Assuming that the user you are using was the user you created during *Chapter 1, Getting Started with Keycloak*, the user should have a realm role associated with it. If it's a different user, make sure it does have a realm role associated with it.

Go back to the playground application and refresh the token again. You will now see `realm_access` within the ID token.

By default, all roles are added to all clients. This is not ideal as you want to limit what access each individual client has. This has less impact on the ID token as it is only used to authenticate the user to a specific client, while it has a bigger impact on the access token, which is used to access other services.

By now you should have a reasonably good understanding of how an application uses the ID token in order to authenticate the user, as well as discover information about the user. If you want to experiment some more with client scopes, now would be a good time since the playground application will allow you to play with scopes and see the result in the ID token.

In the next section, we will take a look at a different way an application can discover information about the authenticated user.

Invoking the UserInfo endpoint

In addition to being able to find information about the authenticated user from the ID token, it is also possible to invoke the UserInfo endpoint with an access token obtained through an OIDC flow.

Let's try this out by opening the playground application. You may at this point have to send new authentication and token requests, as it may be that your SSO session has expired.

If you're a quick reader (or you obtained new tokens), then click on **5 – UserInfo**. Under **UserInfo Request**, you will see that the playground application is sending a request to the Keycloak UserInfo endpoint, including the access token in the authorization header.

The following screenshot from the playground application shows an example **UserInfo Request**:

UserInfo Request

```
http://localhost:8080/auth/realms/myrealm/protocol/openid-connect/userinfo

Authorization: Bearer eyJhbGciOiJSUzI1NiIsInR5cCIgOiAiSldUIiwia2lkIiA6ICJpU3BBbjVman
```

Figure 4.11 – UserInfo request

Under **UserInfo Response** you will see the response Keycloak sent. You may notice that this does not have all the additional fields in the ID token, but rather is just a simple JSON response including only the user attributes.

The following screenshot from the playground application shows an example **UserInfo Response**:

UserInfo Response

```
{
    "sub": "67855660-fd6e-4416-96d1-72c99db5e525",
    "email_verified": false,
    "name": "Stian Thorgersen",
    "preferred_username": "st",
    "myotherclaim": "myotherclaim",
    "given_name": "Stian",
    "family_name": "Thorgersen",
    "email": "st@localhost"
}
```

Figure 4.12 – UserInfo response

Just as you can configure what information Keycloak returns in the ID token through client scopes and protocol mappers, you can also configure what information is returned in the UserInfo endpoint. Further, you can control what information is returned to the client that is invoking the UserInfo endpoint, and not the client that obtained the access token. This means that if a single access token is sent to two separate resource servers, they may see different information in the UserInfo endpoint for the same access token.

Let's try to add some custom information to the UserInfo endpoint. This time, instead of using a client scope, we'll add a protocol mapper directly to the client. Open the Keycloak Admin Console, then under clients locate the oidc-playground client. Click on **Mappers**, then click on **Create**, and fill in the form with the following values:

- **Name**: myotherclaim
- **Mapper Type**: Hardcoded claim
- **Token Claim Name**: myotherclaim
- **Claim value**: My Other Claim
- **Claim JSON Type**: String

Make sure **Add to userinfo** is turned on then click on **Save**. Go back to the playground application and send a new UserInfo request using the **Send UserInfo Request** button. You will now see the additional claim myotherclaim in the response.

One thing to remember about the UserInfo endpoint is that it can only be invoked with an access token obtained through an OIDC flow. We can try this out by going to the playground application, then clicking on the **2 – Authentication button**.

In the scope field, remove openid. Then click on **Generate Authentication Request** and **Send Authentication Request**.

Now click on **3 – Token**, then on **Send Token Request**. You will notice now that in the **Token Response** there is no id_token value, which is why there is no ID token displayed in the **ID Token** section.

Now, if you go to **5 – UserInfo** and click on the **Send UserInfo Request** button you will also notice that the **UserInfo Request** fails.

In the next section, we will take a look at how you can deal with users logging out.

Dealing with users logging out

Dealing with logout in a SSO experience can actually be a quite difficult task, especially if you want an instant logout of all applications a user is using.

Initiating the logout

A logout can for example be initiated by the user through clicking on a logout button in the application. When the logout button is clicked, the application would send a request to the OpenID Connect RP-Initiated logout.

The application redirects the user to the Keycloak End Session endpoint, which is registered in the OpenID Provider Metadata as `end_session_endpoint`. The endpoint takes the following parameters:

- `id_token_hint`: A previously issued ID token. This token is used by Keycloak to identify the client that is logging out, the user, as well as the session that the client wants to log out of.

- `post_logout_redirect_uri`: If the client wants Keycloak to redirect back to it after the logout, it can pass the URL to Keycloak. The client has to previously have registered the logout URL with Keycloak.

- `state`: This allows the client to maintain state between the logout request and the redirect. Keycloak simply passes this parameter when redirecting to the client.

- `ui_locales`: The client can use this parameter to hint to Keycloak what locale should be used for the login screen.

When Keycloak receives the logout request, it will notify other clients in the same session about the logout. Then it will invalidate the session, which effectively makes all tokens invalid.

Leveraging ID and access token expiration

The simplest and perhaps most robust mechanism for an application to discover if a logout has taken place is simply to leverage the fact that ID and access token usually have a short expiration. As Keycloak invalidates the session on logout, a refresh token can no longer be used to obtain new tokens.

This strategy has a downside that it may be a few minutes from the user having logged out until all applications are effectively logged out, but in many cases, this is more than sufficient.

This is also a good strategy for public clients. As they don't usually provide a service directly themselves, but rather leverage the access token to invoke other services, they will quickly realize the session is no longer valid.

In cases where tokens have a long validity, it is still good practice to invoke the Token Introspection endpoint to check token validity periodically, which we will look at in the next chapter.

Leveraging OIDC Session Management

Through OIDC Session Management, an application can discover if a session has been logged out without the need for any request to Keycloak, or for Keycloak to send any requests to it.

This works by monitoring the state of a special session cookie that Keycloak manages. As the application is usually hosted on a different domain than Keycloak, it is not able to read this cookie directly. Instead, a hidden HTML iframe tag loads a special page with Keycloak that monitors the cookie value and sends an event to the application when it observes the session state has changed.

This is an effective strategy, especially if the application is currently open. If the application is not open, it does mean that the application would not observe the logout until it is next opened. If, for example, a workstation was compromised, there is also a chance that a malicious party could prevent the session iframe from doing its job, leaving the application session still open. However, this can relatively easily be mitigated. One option is to only keep the application session open while the application is open. The Keycloak JavaScript adapter does exactly this by only storing tokens in the window state. It is also, of course, mitigated by having a short expiration time for tokens.

The OIDC Session Management approach is sadly becoming less relevant today, as many browsers have started blocking access to third-party content. This effectively means the hidden session iframe is no longer able to access the session cookie in some browsers. As such it is not a good idea to leverage this approach in new applications, and you will most likely want to migrate away from this approach in applications that are already using this approach.

Leveraging OIDC Back-Channel Logout

Through OIDC Back-Channel Logout, an application can register an endpoint to receive logout events.

When a logout is initiated with Keycloak, it will send a logout token to all applications in the session that have a back-channel logout endpoint registered.

The logout token is similar to an ID token, so it is a signed JWT. On receiving the logout token, the application verifies the signature and can now log out of the application session associated with the Keycloak session ID.

For server-side applications, using the back-channel logout is fairly effective. It does, however, become a bit complex to deal with for clustered applications with session stickiness. A common approach to scaling a stateful application is to distribute application session among the instances of the application, and there is no guarantee the logout request from Keycloak is sent to the same application instance that is actually holding the application session. It is not trivial to configure a load balancer to route the logout request to the correct session, so this is usually something that has to be dealt with at the application level.

For stateless server-side applications, a logout request is also hard to handle, as usually the session is stored in a cookie in this case. In this case, the application would have to remember the logout request until the next time a request is made to the application for the given session, or the application session expires.

A note on OIDC Front-Channel Logout

The OpenID Connect Front-Channel Logout renders a hidden iframe for each application that has registered a front-channel logout endpoint on a logout page at the OpenID Provider. This, in theory, would be a nice way to log out of stateless server-side applications, as well as client-side applications. However, in practice, it can be unreliable. There is no effective way for the OpenID Provider to discover that the application was successfully logged out, so using this approach is a bit hit and miss.

In addition, the OIDC Front-Channel logout approach also suffers from browsers blocking third-party content, which means that when the OpenID Provider opens the logout endpoint in an iframe there is no access to any application-level cookies, leaving the application unable to access the current authentication session.

How should you deal with logout?

In summary, the simplest approach is simply to rely on relatively short application sessions and token expiration. As Keycloak will keep the user logged in, it is possible to effectively use short application sessions without requiring users to frequently re-authenticate.

In other cases, or where logout has to be instant, you should leverage OIDC Back-Channel logout.

Summary

In this chapter, you experienced first-hand the interactions in an OIDC authentication flow. You learned how the application prepares an authentication request and then redirects the user-agent to the Keycloak authorization endpoint for authentication. Then you learned how the application obtains an authorization code, which it exchanges for an ID token. By inspecting the ID token, you then learned how an application can find out information about the authenticated users. You also learned how to leverage client scopes and protocol mappers in Keycloak to add additional information about users. Finally, you learned how to deal with not only single sign-on, but also single sign-out.

You should now have a basic understanding of OpenID Connect and how it can be used to secure your own applications. We will build on this knowledge later in the book to get you ready to start securing all your applications with Keycloak.

In the next chapter, you will get a deeper understanding of OAuth 2.0, with a practical guide on how you can use Keycloak to use this standard in your applications.

Questions

1. How does the OpenID Connect Discovery specification make it easier for you to switch between different OpenID Providers?

2. How does an application discover information about the authenticated user?

3. How do you add additional information about the authenticated user?

Further reading

Refer to the following links for more information on topics covered in this chapter:

*   OpenID Connect Core specification: `https://openid.net/specs/openid-connect-core-1_0.html`

*   OpenID Connect Discovery specification: `https://openid.net/specs/openid-connect-discovery-1_0.html`

*   OpenID Connect Session Management specification: `https://openid.net/specs/openid-connect-session-1_0.html`

*   OpenID Connect Back-Channel Logout specification: `https://openid.net/specs/openid-connect-backchannel-1_0.html`

5
Authorizing Access with OAuth 2.0

In this chapter, you will get a deeper understanding of how Keycloak enables you to authorize access to REST APIs and other services by leveraging the OAuth 2.0 standard. Through using a sample application that was written for this book, you will see first hand the interaction between an application and Keycloak to retrieve an access token that can be used to securely invoke a service.

We will start by getting the playground application up and running, before using the playground application to obtain a token from Keycloak that can be used to securely invoke a REST API. Then, we'll build on this knowledge to look at obtaining consent from a user before granting access to the application, as well as how to limit the access provided to the application. Finally, we'll look at how a REST API validates a token to verify whether access should be granted.

By the end of this chapter, you will have a good understanding of OAuth 2.0, including how to obtain an access token, understanding the access token, and how to use the access token to securely invoke a service.

In this chapter, we're going to cover the following main topics:

- Running the OAuth 2.0 playground

- Obtaining an access token

- Requiring user consent

- Limiting the access granted to access tokens

- Validating access tokens

Technical requirements

To run the sample application included in this chapter, you need to have **Node.js** (`https://nodejs.org/`) installed on your workstation.

You also need to have the GitHub repository associated with the book checked out locally. The GitHub repository is available at `https://github.com/PacktPublishing/Keycloak-Identity-and-Access-Management-for-Modern-Applications`.

Check out the following link to see the Code in Action video:

`https://bit.ly/3fcHEbV`

Running the OAuth 2.0 playground

The **OAuth 2.0** playground was developed specifically for this book in order to make it as easy as possible for you to understand and experiment with OAuth 2.0 in a practical way.

It does not use any libraries for OAuth 2.0, but rather all OAuth 2.0 requests are crafted by the application itself. One thing to note here is that this application does not implement OAuth 2.0 in a secure way, and ignores optional parameters in the requests that are important for a production application. There are two reasons for this. Firstly, this is done so that you can focus on understanding the general concepts of OAuth 2.0. Secondly, if you decide to implement your own libraries for OAuth 2.0, you should have a very good understanding of the specifications, and it is beyond the scope of this book to cover OAuth 2.0 in that much detail.

Before continuing with reading this chapter, you should start the OAuth 2.0 playground application, as it will be used throughout the rest of the chapter.

There are two parts to the playground application: a frontend application and a backend application.

To run the playground application, open a terminal and run the following commands to start the frontend part:

```
$ cd Keycloak-Identity-and-Access-Management-for-Modern-
Applications/ch5/frontend/
$ npm install
$ npm start
```

Then, in a new terminal window, run the following commands to start the backend part:

```
$ cd Keycloak-Identity-and-Access-Management-for-Modern-
Applications/ch5/backend/
$ npm install
$ npm start
```

To verify that the application is running, open http://localhost:8000/ in your browser. The following screenshot shows the OpenID Connect Playground application:

OAuth 2.0 Playground

| 1 - Discovery | 2 - Authorization | 3 - Invoke Service | Reset |

Discovery

Issuer   http://localhost:8080/auth/realms/myrealm

Load OAuth 2.0 Provider Configuration

OAuth 2.0 Provider Configuration

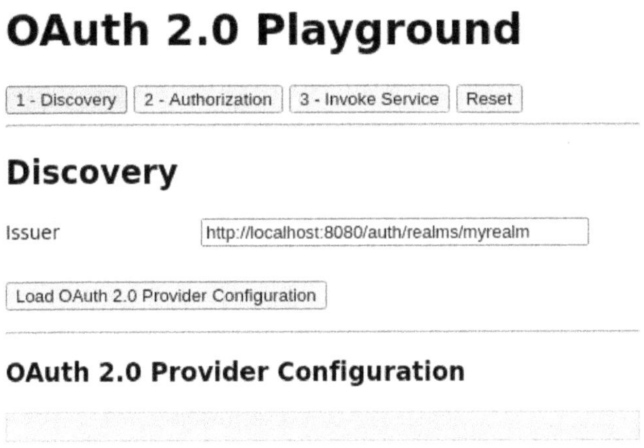

Figure 5.1 – The OAuth 2.0 Playground application

In order to be able to use the playground application, you need Keycloak to be running, as well as to have a realm with a user with the myrole global role and a client with the following configuration:

- **Client ID**: oauth-playground
- **Access Type**: public
- **Valid Redirect URIs**: http://localhost:8000/
- **Web Origins**: http://localhost:8000

If you are unsure about how to do this, you should refer to *Chapter 1*, *Getting Started with Keycloak*, and *Chapter 2*, *Securing Your First Application*.

In the next section, we will start to take a deeper look into OAuth 2.0 by leveraging the playground application.

Obtaining an access token

The most common way to obtain an **access token** that can be used to, for example, invoke a secure REST API is through the OAuth 2.0 Authorization Code grant type.

In summary, to obtain an access token, an application redirects to Keycloak, which authenticates the user and optionally prompts the user to grant the application access or not, before returning an access token to the application. The application can then include the access token in the requests it sends to the REST API, allowing the REST API to verify whether access should be provided.

In the following diagram, the authorization code grant type is shown in more detail:

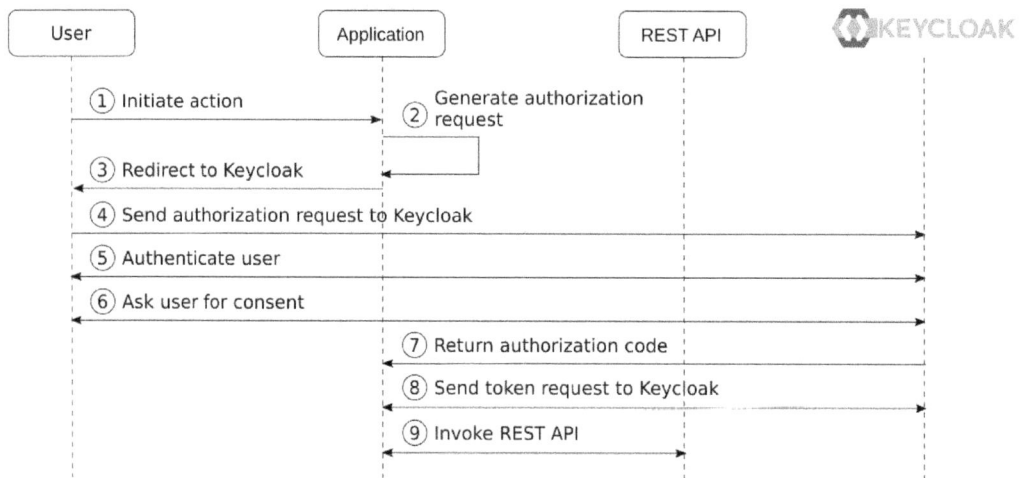

Figure 5.2 – The authorization code grant type

The steps in the diagram in more detail are as follows:

1. The user performs an action that requires sending a request to an external REST API.

2. The application generates an authorization request.

3. The authorization request is sent to the user agent in the form of a 302 redirect, instructing the user agent to redirect to the authorization endpoint provided by Keycloak.

4. The user agent opens the authorization endpoint with the query parameters specified by the application in the authorization request.

5. If the user is not already authenticated with Keycloak, a login page is displayed to the user.

6. If the application requires consent to access the REST API, a consent page is displayed to the user asking whether the user wants to provide access to the application.

7. Keycloak returns an authorization code to the application.

8. The application exchanges the authorization code for an access token, as well as a refresh token.

9. The application can now use the access token to invoke the REST API.

Let's give this a go with the OAuth 2.0 Playground application. Open the playground application at `http://localhost:8000`. First, you need to load the OAuth 2.0 provider configuration by clicking on the button labeled **Load OAuth 2.0 Provide Configuration**. After you've done this, click on the button labeled **2 – Authorization**. You can leave the **client_id** and **scope** values as they are, then click on the button labeled **Send Authorization Request**.

You will be redirected to the Keycloak login pages. Log in with the user you created in the first chapter. After you have logged in and have been redirected back to the playground application, the access token is displayed in the **Access Token** section. As Keycloak uses **JSON Web Token (JWT)** for its default token format, the playground application is able to directly parse and view the contents of the access token.

In the OpenID Connect Playground application that you experimented with in the previous chapter, you generated an authentication request, received an authorization code, then manually exchanged the authorization code for an ID token. As you've already experimented with this part, and it is completely the same flow for an OAuth 2.0 Authorization Code grant type, this flow has been simplified to a single step in the OAuth 2.0 Playground application.

The following screenshot shows an example access token from the playground application:

Access Token

Header

```
{
  "alg": "RS256",
  "typ": "JWT",
  "kid": "iSpAn5fjwuekOb_ysSloqMxcFoOmp9Uza_7CdBYCFvI"
}
```

Payload

```
{
  "exp": 1602524985,
  "iat": 1602524685,
  "auth_time": 1602523924,
  "jti": "234ec6c0-6eed-4ed1-a11f-a1deb56f8da3",
  "iss": "http://localhost:8080/auth/realms/myrealm",
  "aud": "account",
  "sub": "67855660-fd6e-4416-96d1-72c99db5e525",
  "typ": "Bearer",
  "azp": "oauth-playground",
  "session_state": "b5563148-da83-4884-9b66-e5cf700e09fe",
  "acr": "0",
  "allowed-origins": [
    "http://localhost:8000"
  ],
  "realm_access": {
    "roles": [
      "offline_access",
      "uma_authorization",
      "myrole"
    ]
  },
  "resource_access": {
    "account": {
      "roles": [
        "manage-account",
        "manage-account-links",
        "view-profile"
      ]
    }
  },
  "scope": "profile email",
  "email_verified": false,
  "name": "Stian Thorgersen",
  "preferred_username": "st",
  "given_name": "Stian",
  "family_name": "Thorgersen",
  "email": "st@localhost"
}
```

Figure 5.3 – Example access token displayed in the playground application

Let's take a look at some of the values within the access token:

- aud: This is a list of services that this token is intended to be sent to.

- realm_access: This is a list of global roles the token provides access to. It is a union of the roles a user has been granted, and the roles an application is allowed to access.

- resource_access: This is a list of client roles the token provides access to.

- scope: This is the scope included in the access token.

Now that the playground application has obtained an access token, let's try to invoke the REST API. Click on the button labeled **3 – Invoke Service**, then click on **Invoke**. You should now see a response that says **Secret message!**, as shown in the following screenshot:

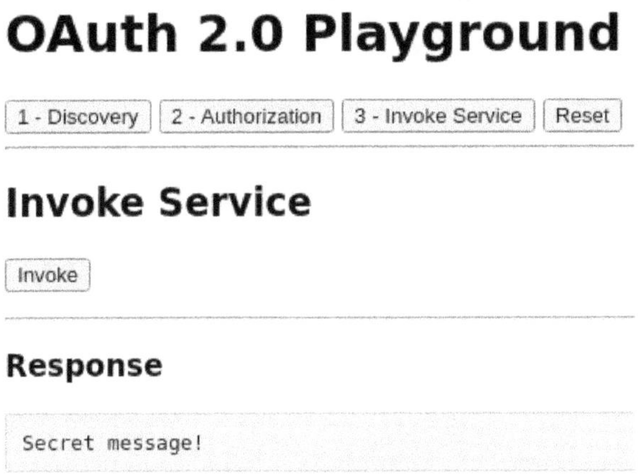

OAuth 2.0 Playground

| 1 - Discovery | 2 - Authorization | 3 - Invoke Service | Reset |

Invoke Service

| Invoke |

Response

```
Secret message!
```

Figure 5.4 – Successful response from the playground application backend

You should now have a good understanding of how OAuth 2.0 can be leveraged to issue an access token to an application that allows the application to access resources on behalf of users.

In the next section, we will take a look at how the user can consent to grant the application access.

Requiring user consent

When an application wants access to a third-party service on behalf of a user, the user will usually be asked whether they want to grant access to the application. Without this step, a user would not know what kind of access the application is getting, and if the user is already authenticated with the authorization server, the user may not even observe the application getting access.

In Keycloak, applications can be configured to either require consent or to not require consent. For an external application you should always require consent, but for an application you know and trust, you may choose to not require consent, which in essence means that you as an admin are trusting the application and are granting it access on behalf of users.

To try this out yourself, open the Keycloak admin console and navigate to the **oauth-playground** client. Then, turn on the **Consent Required** option, as shown in the following screenshot:

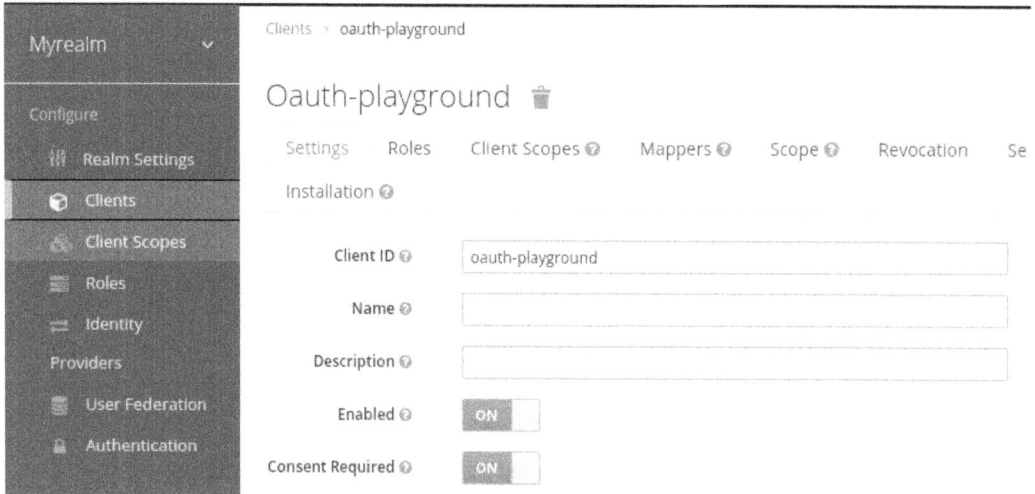

Figure 5.5 – Requiring consent for a client

Once you have this enabled, go back to the playground application and obtain a new token by clicking on the button labeled **2 – Authorization**, followed by the button labeled **Send Authorization Request**. You should now see a similar screen to what is displayed in the following screenshot:

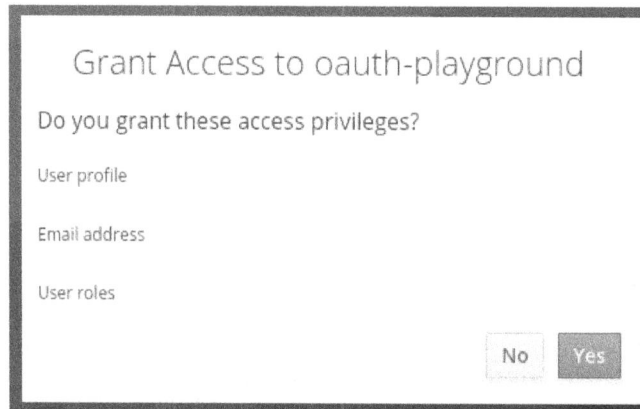

Figure 5.6 – Granting access

What type of access privileges the application is requesting is controlled by what scopes the application is requesting.

One interesting aspect of scopes is that an application can initially ask for limited access. As the user is starting to use more features within the application, the application can ask for additional access as needed. Doing this may be less intimidating to the user as it is clearer to the user why your application is asking for that access.

Let's give this a go by creating a new client scope and request this additional scope in the playground application.

Go back to the Keycloak admin console and click on **Client Scopes** in the menu on the left-hand side. Then, click on **Create**. Fill in the form with the following values:

- **Name**: albums
- **Display On Consent Screen**: **ON**
- **Consent Screen Text**: View your photo albums

The following screenshot shows the client scope that you should create:

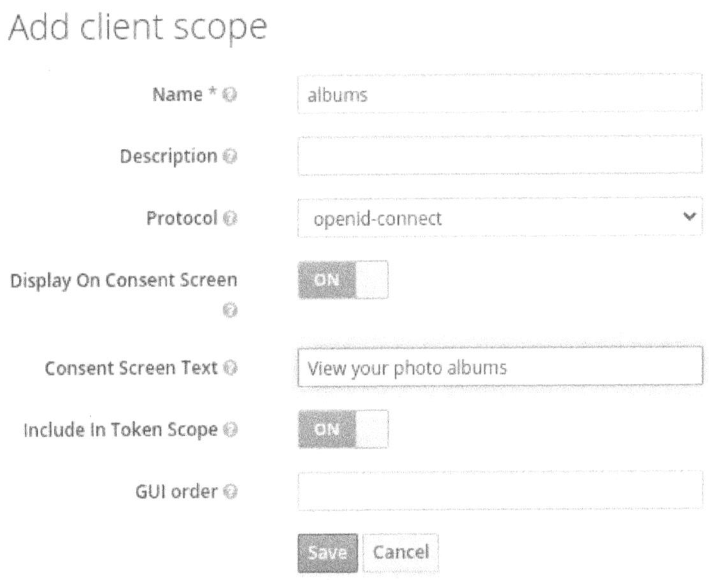

Figure 5.7 – Creating a client scope

You can leave the other values as is, then click on **Save**. Now, navigate to the **oauth-playground** client again, then click on **Client Scopes**. From the **Optional Client Scopes** section in **available client scopes**, select **albums** and click on **Add selected**.

Now, return to the playground application again, then click on the button labeled
2 – **Authorization**. In the scope field, enter albums, then click on **Send Authorization Request**. This time, you should be prompted to grant access to view photo albums as shown in the following screenshot:

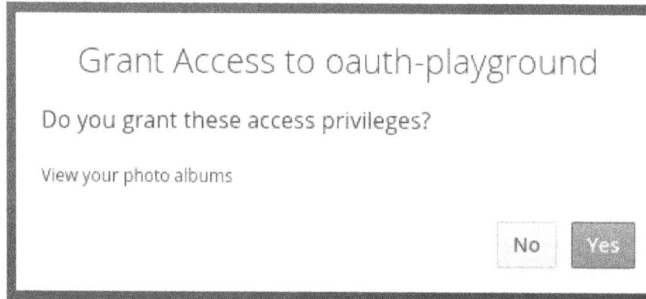

Figure 5.8 – Granting access to photo albums

Keycloak remembers what consent a user has given to a particular application, which means the next time the application asks for the same scope, the user will not be prompted again.

> **Tip**
> Through the account console, a user can remove access to an application if they wish. You can try this out by going to the account console, navigating to **Applications**, then revoking the access for the **oauth-playground** application. The next time you try to obtain an access token again through the playground application, Keycloak will again ask you to provide access to **oauth-playground**.

You should now have a good understanding of how an admin can grant access to trusted applications on behalf of users, as well as how third-party applications can be required to ask the user for consent prior to getting access.

In the next section, we will look at strategies for scoping access tokens, which in essence means controlling what access a token provides to the application.

Limiting the access granted to access tokens

As access tokens get passed around from the application to services, it is important to limit the access granted. Otherwise, any access token could potentially be used to access any resource the user has access to.

There are a few different strategies that can be used to limit access for a specific access token. These include the following:

- **Audience**: Allows listing the resource providers that should accept an access token.

- **Roles**: Through controlling what roles a client has access to, it is possible to control what roles an application can access on behalf of the user.

- **Scope**: In Keycloak, scopes are created through client scopes, and an application can only have access to a specific list of scopes. Furthermore, when applications require consent, the user must also grant access to the scope.

Let's go through these one at a time and see exactly how this can be done with Keycloak, starting with audience.

Using the audience to limit token access

At the moment, access tokens issued to the frontend part of the playground application do not actually include the backend in the audience. The reason this works is that the backend part has not been configured to check the audience in the token.

Let's start with configuring the backend to check the audience. Stop the backend part, then open the `Keycloak-Identity-and-Access-Management-for-Modern-Applications/ch5/backend/keycloak.json` file in a text editor. Change the value of the `verify-token-audience` field to `true`, as shown in the following screenshot:

```
1 {
2   "realm": "myrealm",
3   "bearer-only": true,
4   "auth-server-url": "${env.KC_URL:http://localhost:8080/auth}",
5   "resource": "oauth-backend",
6   "verify-token-audience": true
7 }
```

Figure 5.7 – Enabling verifying the token audience for the backend

One thing to notice in this file is the `resource` field, which is the value the backend will look for in the audience field to know whether it should accept the token.

Start the backend part again. Once started, go back to the playground application and obtain a new access token. If you look at the values for the access token, you will see the `aud` field, and you will also notice that `oauth-backend` is not included.

If you now try to invoke the service through the playground application, you will get a response telling you that access was denied. The backend is now rejecting the access token.

In Keycloak, there are two different ways to include a client in the audience. It can be done manually by adding a specific client to the audience with a protocol mapper (added directly to the client, or through a client scope), or it can be done automatically if a client has a scope on another client role from another client.

Let's try to add the audience manually with a protocol mapper. Open the Keycloak admin console and navigate to **Clients**. Create a new client with the **Client ID** value set as **oauth-backend**.

Then, click on **Save**. After it has been saved, change **Access Type** to **bearer-only**, and click **Save** again.

Now go back to the client list and open the **oauth-playground** client. Click on **Mappers**, then click on **Create**. Fill in the form with the following values:

- **Name**: backend audience
- **Mapper Type**: **Audience**
- **Included Client Audience**: **oauth-backend**
- Then, click on **Save**.
- Go back to the playground application and obtain a new access token. Now **oauth-backend** is included in the aud field, and if you again try to invoke the service through the playground application, you will get a successful response.

When looking at the aud field of the access token, you may have noticed that account was included. The reason this is included is that by default, a client has a scope on all roles, and by default, a user has a few client roles for the account client that provide the user access to the Keycloak account console. In the next section, we will take a closer look at how roles work.

Using roles to limit token access

Keycloak has built-in support for roles, which can be used to grant users permissions. Roles are also a very useful tool to limit the permissions for an application as you can configure what roles are included in the access token for a given application.

A user has role mappings on a number of roles granting the user the permissions that the role provides. A client, on the other hand, does not have roles assigned directly to it but instead has a scope on a set of roles, which controls what roles can be included in the tokens sent to the client. This means that the roles included in tokens are the intersection between the roles a user has and the roles a client is allowed to use, as shown in the following diagram:

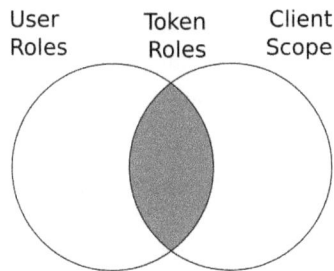

Figure 5.8 – Roles included in tokens

Let's try this out in the playground application. Before making any changes, obtain a new access token and take a look at the aud, realm_access, and resource_access claims. The following shows an example access token with all non-relevant claims removed:

```
{
  "aud": [
    "oauth-backend",
    "account"
  ],
  "realm_access": {
    "roles": [
      "offline_access",
      "uma_authorization",
      "myrole"
    ]
  },
  "resource_access": {
    "account": {
      "roles": [
        "manage-account",
        "manage-account-links",
        "view-profile"
```

```
        ]
      }
    }
  }
```

Within the aud claim, you can see two clients. The oauth-backend client is included as we explicitly included this client in the audience in the previous section. The account client, on the other hand, is included as the token includes roles for the account client, which by default results in the client automatically being added to the audience of the token as we can assume that if the token includes roles specifically for a client, the token is intended to be used to access this client.

You can also see that the token includes all roles granted to the user. By default, all roles for a given user are included in the token. This is for convenience when getting started with Keycloak and you should not include all roles in a production scenario.

Now, let's try to limit the role scope for the **oauth-playground** client to limit what is included in the token. Open the Keycloak admin console and navigate to the **oauth-playground** client. Then, click on the tab labeled **Scope**. You will notice that it has the **Full Scope Allowed** option turned on. This is the feature that by default includes all roles for a user in the tokens sent to this client.

Turn off **Full Scope Allowed**, then return to the playground application and obtain a new access token. In the new access token, you will notice that there are no longer any roles in the token and the aud claim now only includes the **oauth-playground** client. If you now try to invoke the service with this token, you will get an access denied message. This is because the service only permits requests that include the myrole role.

Go back to the Keycloak admin console and again open the scope tab for the **oauth-playground** client. Under **Realm Roles**, select the **myrole** role and click on **Add selected**. Return to the playground application and obtain a new access token, and you will now see that the myrole role is included in the realm_access claim, as shown in the following access token snippet:

```
{
  "aud": "oauth-backend",
  "realm_access": {
    "roles": [
      "myrole"
    ]
  }
}
```

It is also possible to add scope through a client scope that is attached to a client. This may be a bit confusing as the term scope is somewhat overused within Keycloak. The following list tries to clarify this potential confusion:

- **A client has a scope on roles**: This is configured through the **Scope** tab for a client.

- **A client can access one or more client scopes**: This is configured through the **Client Scopes** tab for a client.

- **A client scope can also have a scope on roles**: When a client has access to a client scope that in turn has a scope on roles, the client has a scope on the roles that the client scope has.

As this may still be a bit confusing, let's experiment a bit with this in practice by leveraging the playground application.

Before continuing, you should first remove the scope that the oauth-playground client has on the myrole role. To do this, return to the Keycloak admin console, navigate to the oauth-playground client, and click on the **Scope** tab. Then, select the **myrole** role from the **Assigned Roles** section and click on **Remove selected**.

Now the tokens sent to the oauth-playground client no longer include the myrole role, which is exactly what we want as we will now add this through a client scope instead of directly to the client.

Open the Keycloak admin console and go to **Client Scopes**. Click on **Create** to create a new client scope. For the name, enter myrole and leave everything else as is, then click on **Save**. Now, select the tab labeled **Scope**. This is where you control what roles are included in the token when this client scope is included. Select the **myrole** role from **Available Roles** and click on **Add selected**.

You have now created a client scope that has a scope on the myrole role. Next, let's add this client scope as an optional client scope to the oauth-playground client. Navigate to the oauth-playground client and click on **Client Scopes**. In the **Optional Client Scopes** section, select **myrole** and click on **Add selected**.

As you added the myrole client scope as an optional client scope, it means the myrole role is only included in the token if the oauth-playground client explicitly requests the myrole scope.

Return to the playground application and obtain a new access token. You will see that the `myrole` role is not yet included in the `realm_access` claim. In fact, the `realm_access` claim should not be included at all since the client does not at this point have a scope on any global roles. In the **Scope** field, set the value to `myrole`, and click on **Send Authorization Request** to obtain a new access token that includes this scope. This results in the playground application requesting the `myrole` scope, which in turn will add the `myrole` role to the token.

In the next section, we will take a look at how scopes on their own can be leveraged to limit the access granted by a token.

Using the scope to limit token access

The default mechanism in OAuth 2.0 to limit the permissions for an access token is through scopes directly. Using scopes is especially useful with third-party applications where users should consent to giving applications access to resources on their behalf.

Within Keycloak, a scope in OAuth 2.0 is mapped to a client scope. If you only want to have a scope that the application can request that is then used by a resource provider to provide limited access to resources, you can simply define an empty client scope that has no protocol mappers and doesn't have access to any roles.

While defining scopes, it is important to not go overboard and to limit the number of scopes you define, and consider how scope is represented to an end user, who should understand what giving permissions to that scope implies, and not be confused by an application requesting a large number of scopes.

Scopes should usually also be unique within all applications in your organization, so you may want to prefix the scope with the name of the service, or even consider using the URL of the service as a prefix.

Here are some example scopes to give you an idea:

- `albums:view`
- `albums:create`
- `albums:delete`
- `https://api.acme.org/bombs/bombs.purchase`
- `https://api.acme.org/bombs/bombs.detonate`

There is no standard for defining scopes, so you need to define your own. What can be useful is looking at scopes defined by Google, GitHub, Twitter, and so on for inspiration. One thing to bear in mind in these cases is that with GitHub and Twitter, they, in a way, have a dedicated authorization server for a single service, which means they do not have to worry as much about prefixing scopes with the service. On the other hand, Google uses the same authorization server for multiple services.

Here are some example scopes defined by Google:

- `https://www.googleapis.com/auth/gmail.compose`
- `https://www.googleapis.com/auth/photoslibrary.readonly`
- `https://www.googleapis.com/auth/calendar.events`

Here are some example scopes defined by GitHub:

- `repo`
- `write:org`
- `notifications`

Let's give this a go with the playground application by imagining that we have a photo album service that provides access to view albums, create albums, and delete albums. We'll also pretend that the playground application offers functionality to view and manage photo albums.

Start by creating the following three client scopes through the Keycloak admin console:

- `albums:view`
- `albums:create`
- `albums:delete`

We have already covered how to create client scopes previously, but in summary, the steps you need to create a client scope are as follows:

1. Open **Client Scopes** in the Keycloak admin console.
2. Click on the button labeled **Create**.
3. Enter the name from the preceding list, and enter some value for the **Consent Screen Text** field that describes to a user what permissions are given (for example, `View photo albums`).
4. Click on the button labeled **Save**.

After you have created the three client scopes, navigate to the `oauth-playground` client and click on **Client Scopes**. In the **Default Client Scopes** section, select **albums:view** and click on **Add selected**. Then, in the **Optional Client Scopes** section, select **albums:create** and **albums:delete**, then click on **Add selected**.

We added the scope to view permissions as a default scope as we're assuming that the playground application always requires viewing albums. On the other hand, we set the ability to create and delete albums as optional. This is sometimes referred to as incremental authorization, where the application requests additional permissions only when the user starts using a part of an application that requires the additional permissions. This approach makes it a lot more intuitive to the user why the application is requesting the permissions.

Before continuing, make sure the `oauth-playground` client requires consent by selecting the **Settings** tab and then checking that **Consent Required** is turned on.

Now, return to the playground application and remove any value in the **Scope** field before clicking on the **Send Authorization Request** button. Keycloak should now ask you to grant the `oauth-playground` application access to view photo albums, as shown in the following screenshot:

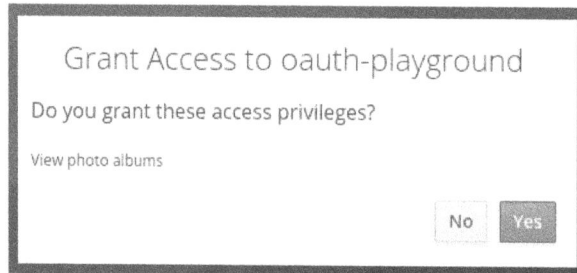

Figure 5.11 – Granting oauth-playground access to view photo albums

After clicking on **Yes**, the access token displayed within the playground application will include `albums:view` in the scope claim. Let's now imagine that the user would like to create a new photo album through the playground application, so it must have access to also create albums. Set the value of the scope field to **albums:create** and click on **Send Authorization Request** again. This time, you will be prompted to grant access to create photo albums. After clicking **Yes**, this time you will see that the scope claim in the access token now includes both `albums:view` and `albums:create`.

By now, you should have a good understanding of the different techniques for limiting the access provided by a given access token. In the next section, we will take a look at how an application can validate an access token.

Validating access tokens

You have two choices to validate an access token, either by invoking the token introspection endpoint provided by Keycloak, or by directly verifying the token.

Using the token introspection endpoint is the simplest approach, and it also makes your applications less tied to Keycloak being the authorization server. OAuth 2.0 does not define a standard format for access tokens and these should be considered opaque to the application. Instead, it defines a standard token introspection endpoint that can be used to query the authorization server for the state of a token as well as claims associated with the token. This also enables tokens to not be self-contained, meaning that not all relevant information about the token is encoded into the token, but rather the token only serves as a reference to the information.

One downside of using the token introspection endpoint is that it introduces extra latency in processing the request as well as additional load on the authorization server. A common technique here is to have a cache that remembers previously verified tokens preventing the service from re-validating already verified tokens within a configurable amount of time. The time between re-validating the token should be fairly short, usually in terms of a few minutes only.

You can try to invoke the token introspection endpoint by using `curl` or any other tool that lets you send an HTTP request.

First, we need two things: the credentials for the `oauth-backend` client and an encoded access token.

To get the credentials for the `oauth-backend` client, go to the Keycloak admin console and navigate to the `oauth-backend` client. Then, click on **Credentials** and copy the value of the **Secret** field.

Open a terminal and set the secret to an environment variable as shown in the following example:

```
$ export SECRET=b1e0073d-3f2b-4ea4-bec0-a35d1983d5b6
```

Keep this terminal open, then open the playground application and obtain a new access token. At the bottom of the field, in the **Encoded** section, you will see the encoded access token. Copy this value, then set an environment variable in the terminal you opened previously as shown in the following example:

```
$ export TOKEN=eyJhbGciOiJSUzI1NiIsInR5c...
```

Now, you can invoke the token introspection endpoint by running the following command in the same terminal:

```
$ curl --data "client_id=oauth-backend&client_
secret=$SECRET&token=$TOKEN" http://localhost:8080/auth/realms/
myrealm/protocol/openid-connect/token/introspect
```

The endpoint will return a JSON document with the state of the token, and associated information for the token, as shown in the following screenshot:

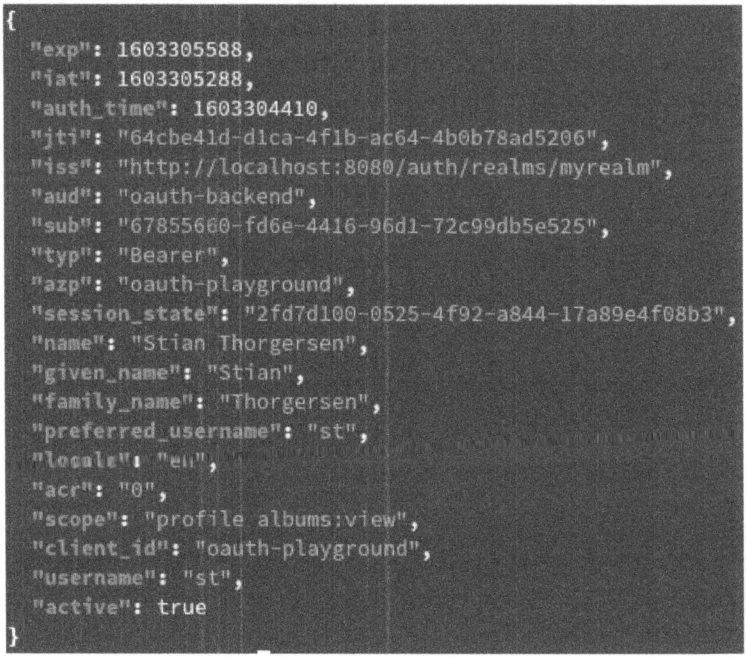

```
{
    "exp": 1603305588,
    "iat": 1603305288,
    "auth_time": 1603304410,
    "jti": "64cbe41d-d1ca-4f1b-ac64-4b0b78ad5206",
    "iss": "http://localhost:8080/auth/realms/myrealm",
    "aud": "oauth-backend",
    "sub": "67855660-fd6e-4416-96d1-72c99db5e525",
    "typ": "Bearer",
    "azp": "oauth-playground",
    "session_state": "2fd7d100-0525-4f92-a844-17a89e4f08b3",
    "name": "Stian Thorgersen",
    "given_name": "Stian",
    "family_name": "Thorgersen",
    "preferred_username": "st",
    "locale": "en",
    "acr": "0",
    "scope": "profile albums:view",
    "client_id": "oauth-playground",
    "username": "st",
    "active": true
}
```

Figure 5.12 – Token introspection endpoint response

The other approach to verifying access tokens issued by Keycloak is validating them directly in the application. As Keycloak uses JWT as its access token format, this means you can parse and read the contents directly from your application, as well as verifying that the token was issued by Keycloak as it is signed by Keycloak using its private signing keys. We're not going to go into detail on how to do this though, as there are quite a lot of mistakes you can make when verifying a token yourself and you should have a very good understanding of JWT as well as the information within the token before you consider implementing this approach yourself.

All Keycloak client libraries, which are referred to as application adapters by Keycloak, verify tokens directly without the token introspection endpoint. There are also a number of good libraries available for different programming languages you can use. To give you an idea though to verify an access token, you would need to do the following:

- Retrieve the public signing keys from the JWKS endpoint provided by Keycloak.

- Verify the signature of the access token.

- Verify that the access token has not expired.

- Verify the issuer, audience, and type of the token.

- Verify any other claims that your application cares about.

You should now have a good idea of how a service can verify a token either by using the token introspection endpoint or by directly verifying the token if it is a JWT.

Summary

In this chapter, you experienced first hand how to obtain access tokens using the OAuth 2.0 Authorization Code grant type. You learned how an admin can grant access to internal applications on behalf of a user, and how users themselves can grant access to third-party applications. You learned about various different techniques on how you can limit the access provided by a specific access token. Finally, you learned how a service can directly read and understand the contents of an access token issued by Keycloak, as it is using JWT-based tokens. You also learned how the token introspection endpoint can be leveraged to validate and discover information about an access token in a more standard and portable way.

You should now have a basic understanding of OAuth 2.0 and how it can be used to secure your own applications. We will build on this knowledge later in the book to get you ready to start securing all your applications with Keycloak.

In the next chapter, you will learn about how to use Keycloak to secure a range of different application types.

Questions

1. How does an application invoke a protected REST API by leveraging OAuth 2.0?

2. What are the three different techniques you can use to limit the access provided by an access token?

3. How can a service validate an access token to decide whether permission should be granted?

Further reading

Refer to the following links for more information on the topics covered in this chapter:

*   OAuth 2.0 Authorization Code grant specification: `https://oauth.net/2/grant-types/authorization-code/`

*   OAuth 2.0 token introspection specification: `https://oauth.net/2/token-introspection/`

*   OAuth scopes: `https://oauth.net/2/scope/`

6
Securing Different Application Types

In this chapter, we will first begin by understanding whether the application we want to secure is an internal or external application. Then, we will look at how to secure a range of different application types, including web, native, and mobile applications. We will also look at how to secure REST APIs and other types of services with bearer tokens.

By the end of this chapter, you will have learned the principles and best practices behind securing different types of applications. You will understand how to secure web, mobile, and native applications, as well as how bearer tokens can be used to protect any type of service, including REST APIs, gRPC, WebSocket, and other types of services.

In this chapter, we're going to cover the following main topics:

- Understanding internal and external applications
- Securing web applications
- Securing native and mobile applications
- Securing REST APIs and services

Technical requirements

To run the sample application included in this chapter, you need to have Node.js (`https://nodejs.org/`) installed on your workstation.

You also need to have a local copy of the GitHub repository associated with the book. If you have Git installed, you can clone the repository by running this command in a terminal:

```
$ git clone https://github.com/PacktPublishing/Keycloak-
Identity-and-Access-Management-for-Modern-Applications.git
```

Alternatively, you can download a ZIP of the repository from `https://github.com/PacktPublishing/Keycloak-Identity-and-Access-Management-for-Modern-Applications/archive/master.zip`.

Check out the following link to see the Code in Action video:

`https://bit.ly/3b5R0F2`

Understanding internal and external applications

When securing an application, the first thing to consider is whether the application is an internal application or an external application.

Internal applications, sometimes referred to as first-party applications, are applications owned by the enterprise. It does not matter who developed the application, nor does it matter how it is hosted. The application could be an off-the-shelf application, and it can also be a **Software as a Service** (**SaaS**)-hosted application, while still being considered an internal application.

For an internal application, there is no need to ask the user to grant access to the application when authenticating to the user, as this application is trusted and the administrator that registered the application with Keycloak can pre-approve the access on behalf of the user. In Keycloak, this is done by turning off the **Consent Required** option for the client, as shown in the following screenshot:

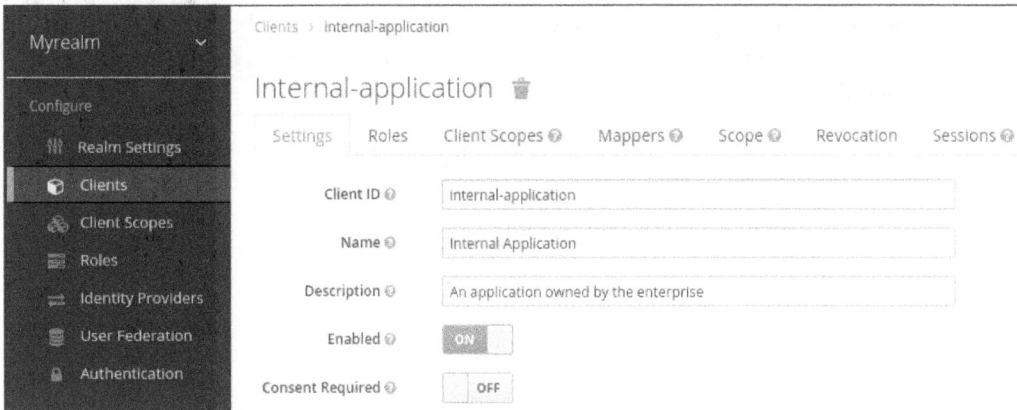

Figure 6.1 – Internal application configured to not require consent

When a user authenticates or grants access to an internal application, the user is only required to enter the username and password. For external applications, on the other hand, a user must also grant access to the application.

External applications, sometimes referred to as third-party applications, are applications that are not owned and managed by the enterprise itself, but rather by a third party. All external applications should have the **Consent Required** option enabled, as shown in the following screenshot:

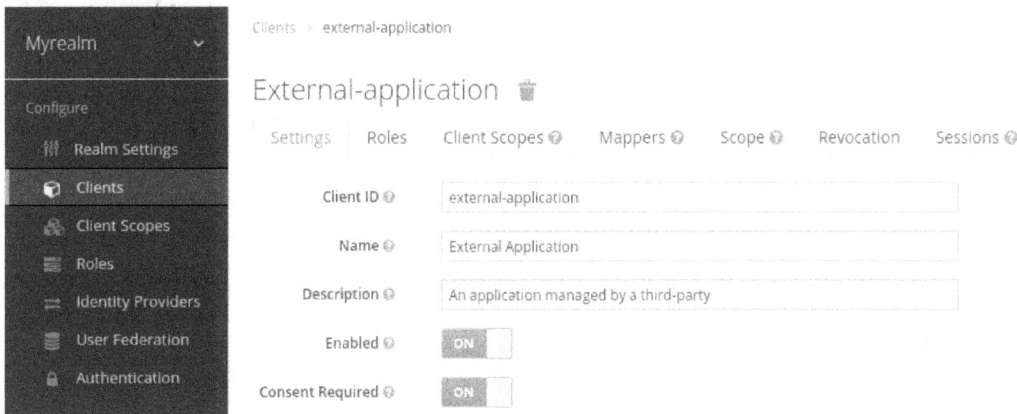

Figure 6.2 – External application configured to require consent

When a user authenticates or grants access to an external application, the user is required to not only enter the username and password but also to grant access to the application, as shown in the following screenshot:

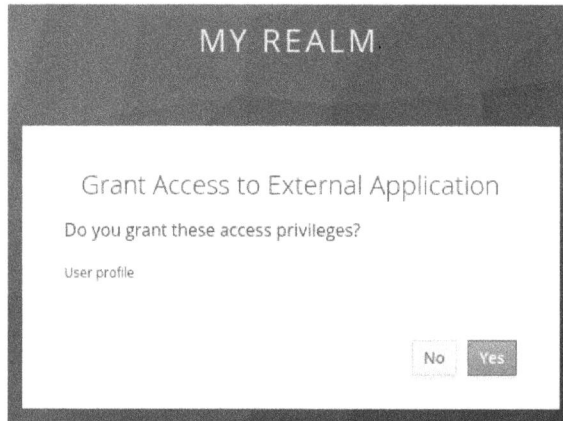

Figure 6.3 – User granting access to an external application

You should now understand the difference between an internal and an external application, including how to require users to grant access to external applications. In the next section, we will look at how to secure web applications with Keycloak.

Securing web applications

When securing a web application with Keycloak, the first thing you should consider is the architecture of the application as there are multiple approaches:

- First and foremost, is your web application a traditional web application running on the server side or a modern **single-page application** (**SPA**) running in the browser?

- The second thing to consider is whether the application is accessing any REST APIs, and if so, are the REST APIs a part of the application or external?

If it is a SPA-type application invoking external APIs, then there are two further options to consider. Does the application invoke the external REST API directly, or through a dedicated REST API hosted alongside the application?

Based on this, you should determine which of the following matches the architecture of the application you are securing:

- **Server side**: If the web application is running inside a web server or an application server.

- **SPA with dedicated REST API**: If the application is running in the browser and is only invoking a dedicated REST API under the same domain.

- **SPA with intermediary API**: If the application is running in the browser and invokes external REST APIs through an intermediary API, where the intermediary API is hosted under the same domain as the application

- **SPA with external API**: If the application is running in the browser and only invokes APIs hosted under different domains.

Before we take a look at details specific to these different web application architectures, let's consider what is common among all architectures.

Firstly, and most importantly, you should secure your web application using the Authorization Code flow with the **Proof Key for Code Exchange** (**PKCE**) extension. If you are not sure what the Authorization Code flow is, you should read *Chapter 4, Authenticating Users with OpenID Connect*, before continuing with this chapter. The PKCE extension is an extension to OAuth 2.0 that binds the authorization code to the application that sent the authorization request. This prevents abuse of the authorization code if it is intercepted. We are not covering PKCE in detail in this book, as we recommend you use a library. If you do decide not to use a library, you should refer to the specifications on how to implement support for OAuth 2.0 and OpenID Connect yourself.

When porting existing applications to use Keycloak, it may be tempting to keep the login pages in the existing application, then exchanging the username and password for tokens, by using the Resource Owner Password Credential grant to obtain tokens. This would be similar to how you would integrate your application with an LDAP server.

However, this is simply something that you should not be tempted to do. Collecting user credentials in an application effectively means that if a single application is compromised, an attacker would likely have access to all applications that the user can access. This includes applications not secured by Keycloak, as users often reuse passwords. You also do not have the ability to introduce stronger authentication, such as two-factor authentication. Finally, you do not get all the benefits of using Keycloak with this approach, such as **single sign-on** (**SSO**) and social login.

As an alternative to keeping the login pages within your existing applications, you may be tempted to embed the Keycloak login page as an iframe within the application. This is also something that you should avoid doing. With the login page embedded into the application, it can be affected by vulnerabilities in an application, potentially allowing an attacker access to the username and password.

As the login page is rendered within an iframe, it is also not easy for users to see where the login pages are coming from, and users may not trust entering their passwords into the application directly. Finally, with third-party cookies being frequently used for tracking across multiple sites, browsers are becoming more and more aggressive against blocking third-party cookies, which may result in the Keycloak login pages not having access to the cookies it needs to function.

In summary, you should get used to the fact that an application should redirect the user to a trusted identity provider for authentication, especially in SSO scenarios. This is also a pattern that most of your users will already be familiar with as it is widely in use nowadays. The following screenshot shows an example of the Google and Amazon login pages, where you can see that they are not embedded in the applications themselves:

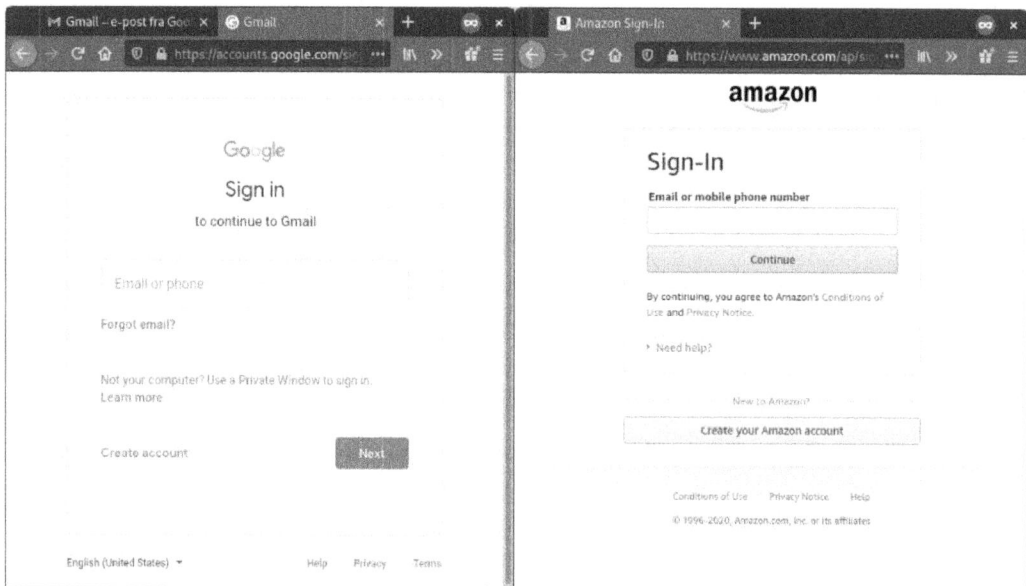

Figure 6.4 – Example from Google and Amazon showing external login pages

You should now have a good, basic understanding of how to go about securing a web application with Keycloak. In the next section, we will start looking at how to secure different types of web applications, starting with server-side web applications.

Securing server-side web applications

When securing a server-side web application with Keycloak, you should register a confidential client with Keycloak. As you are using a confidential client, a leaked authorization code can't be leveraged by an attacker. It is still good practice to leverage the PKCE extension as it provides protection against other types of attacks.

You must also configure applicable redirect URIs for the client as otherwise, you are creating what is called an open redirect. An open redirect can be used, for example, in a spamming attack to make a user believe they are clicking on a link to a trusted site. As an example, if a spammer sends the `https://trusted-site.com/...?redirect_uri=https://attacker.com` URL to a user in an email, the user may only notice the domain name is to a trusted site and click on the link. If you have not configured an exact redirect URI for your client, Keycloak would end up redirecting the user to the site provided by the attacker.

With a server-side web application, usually, only the ID token is leveraged to establish an HTTP session. The server-side web application can also leverage an access token if it wants to invoke external REST APIs under the context of the user.

The following diagram shows the flow for a server-side web application:

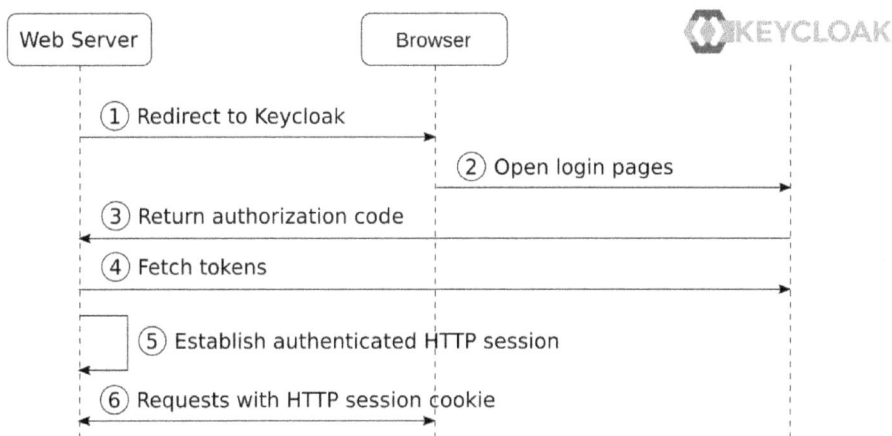

Figure 6.5 – Server-side web application

In more detail, the steps in the diagram are as follows:

1. The **web server** redirects the browser to the **Keycloak** login pages using the **Authorization Code** flow

2. The user authenticates with Keycloak.

3. The authorization code is returned to the server-side web application.

4. The application exchanges the authorization code for tokens, using the credentials registered with the client in Keycloak.

5. The application retrieves the ID token directly from Keycloak as it does not need to verify the token, and can directly parse the ID token to find out information about the authenticated user, and establish an authenticated HTTP session.

6. Requests from the browser now include the HTTP session cookie.

In summary, the application leverages the Authorization Code flow to obtain an ID token from Keycloak, which it uses to establish an authenticated HTTP session.

For server-side web applications, you can also choose to use SAML 2.0, rather than using OpenID Connect. As OpenID Connect is generally easier to work with, it is recommended to use OpenID Connect rather than SAML 2.0, unless your application already supports SAML 2.0.

You should now have a good understanding of how to secure a server-side web application with Keycloak. In the next section, we will look at web applications running on the client side, starting with SPAs that have their own dedicated REST API backend.

Securing a SPA with a dedicated REST API

A SPA that has a dedicated REST API on the same domain should be secured with Keycloak in the same way as a server-side web application. As the application has a dedicated REST API, it should leverage the Authorization Code flow with a confidential client for the highest level of security, and use an HTTP session to secure the API requests from the client side to the dedicated REST API.

The following diagram shows the flow for a SPA with a dedicated REST API:

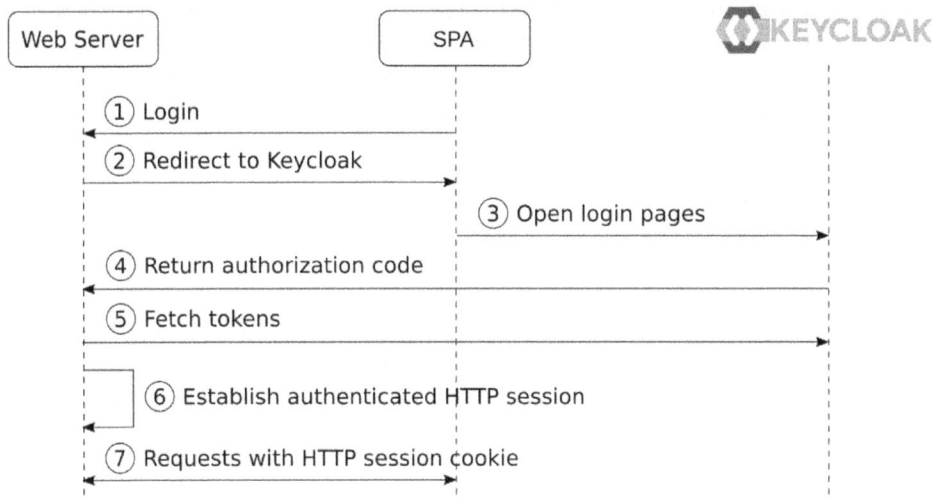

Figure 6.6 – A SPA with a dedicated REST API

In more detail, the steps in the diagram are as follows:

1. The user clicks on the login link in the application, which sends a request to the web server.

2. The web server redirects to the Keycloak login pages.

3. The user authenticates with Keycloak.

4. The authorization code is returned to the web server.

5. The web server exchanges the authorization code for tokens.

6. As the application retrieves the ID token directly from Keycloak, it does not need to verify the token, and can directly parse the ID token to find out information about the authenticated user, and establish an authenticated HTTP session.

Requests from the SPA to the dedicated REST API include the HTTP session cookie. In summary, the application leverages the Authorization Code flow to obtain an ID token from Keycloak, which it uses to establish an authenticated HTTP session, which enables the SPA to securely invoke the REST API provided by the web server.

You should now have a good understanding of how to go about securing a SPA when there is a dedicated REST API hosted on the same domain. In the next section, we will look at a SPA where an external REST API is invoked, but it is done through a backend REST API hosted on the same domain as the SPA.

Securing a SPA with an intermediary REST API

The most secure way to invoke external REST APIs from a SPA is through an intermediary API hosted on the same domain as the SPA. By doing this, you are able to leverage a confidential client and tokens are not directly accessible in the browser, which reduces the risk of tokens, especially the refresh token, being leaked.

This type of SPA is often referred to as the backend for frontends patterns. Not only does it have increased security, but it also makes your SPA more portable and may make it easier to develop. This is due to the application not having to directly deal with external APIs, but rather a dedicated REST API built specifically to service the frontend SPA.

Further, by default, browsers do not allow a SPA to invoke a REST API on a different domain unless **Cross-Origin Resource Sharing (CORS)** is enabled. CORS enables a REST API to return special HTTP headers that tell the browser a request from a different origin is permitted. As the SPA is making the requests through an intermediary REST API on the same domain, you don't need to deal with CORS in this case.

The following diagram shows the flow for a SPA with an intermediary REST API:

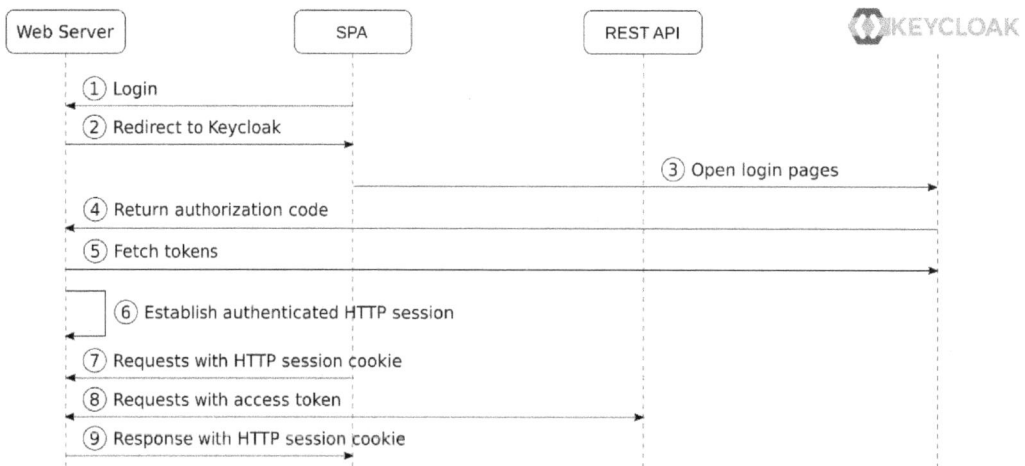

Figure 6.7 – SPA with an intermediary REST API

In more detail, the steps in the diagram are as follows:

1. The user clicks on the login link in the application, which sends a request to the web server.

2. The web server redirects to the Keycloak login pages.

3. The user authenticates with Keycloak.

4. The authorization code is returned to the web server.

5. The web server exchanges the authorization code for tokens.

6. As the web server retrieves the ID token directly from Keycloak, it does not need to verify the token, and can directly parse the ID token to find out information about the authenticated user, and establish an authenticated HTTP session. The refresh token and access token are stored within the HTTP session.

7. Requests from the SPA to the dedicated REST API includes the HTTP session cookie.

8. The web server retrieves the access token from the HTTP session and includes it in requests to the external REST API.

9. The web server returns the response to the SPA, including the HTTP session cookie.

In summary, the application leverages the Authorization Code flow to obtain an ID token from Keycloak, which it uses to establish an authenticated HTTP session, which enables the SPA to securely invoke the web server, which in turn proxies the request to the external REST API.

You should now have a good understanding of how to secure a SPA with an intermediary API hosted on the same domain, which is leveraged to invoke external REST APIs. In the next section, we will look at a SPA where there is no REST API hosted on the same domain.

Securing a SPA with an external REST API

The simplest way to secure a SPA with Keycloak is by doing the Authorization Code flow directly from the SPA itself with a public client registered in Keycloak. This is a somewhat less secure approach as the tokens, including the refresh token, are exposed directly to the browser. For very critical applications, such as financial applications, this is not an approach you want to use. However, there are a number of techniques that can be leveraged to provide a good level of security for this approach, such as the following:

- Have a short expiration for the refresh token. In Keycloak, this is configured by setting the client session timeouts for the client. This makes it possible to configure a client to for example have refresh tokens that are valid for 30 minutes, while the SSO session can be valid for several days.

- Rotate refresh tokens. In Keycloak, this is configured by enabling **Revoke Refresh Token** for the realm, which results in previously used refresh tokens being invalidated. If an invalid refresh token is used, the session is invalidated. This would result in a leaked refresh token being quickly invalidated as both the SPA and the attacker would try to use the refresh token, resulting in it being invalidated.

- Use the PKCE extension. For a public client, using the PKCE extension is required; otherwise, there is a high chance that a leaked authorization code can be used by an attacker to obtain tokens.

- Store tokens in the window state or HTML5 storage session, and avoid using easily guessable keys such as `window.sessionStorage.accessToken`.

- Protect the SPA from **Cross-Site Scripting (XSS)** and other attacks by following best practices from the **Open Web Application Security Project (OWASP)**.

- Be careful when using third-party scripts in your application.

At the end of the day, this is a trade-off that you will have to decide for yourself. Are you comfortable with the risk of tokens being leaked, and have you made sure your SPA is secure? If so, then using this approach provides you with a simpler solution and also removes the need to have a dedicated backend for your SPA, which also reduces the cost of maintaining the application.

The following diagram shows the flow for a SPA with an external REST API:

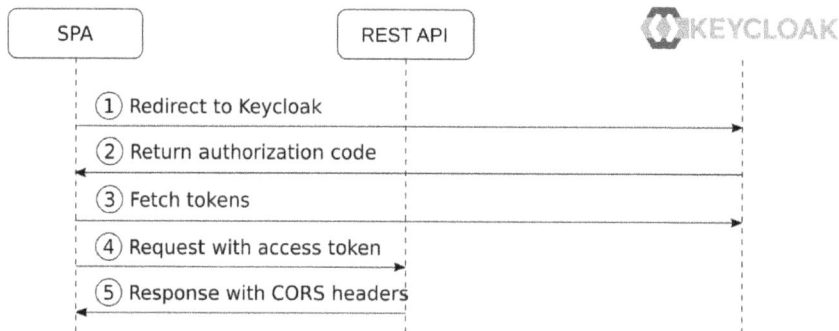

Figure 6.8 – A SPA with an external REST API

In more detail, the steps in the diagram are as follows:

1. The SPA redirects to the Keycloak login pages.

2. After the user has authenticated, the authorization code is returned to the SPA.

3. The SPA exchanges the authorization code for tokens. As the SPA is running in the browser, it does not have a way to secure credentials for the client and for this reason, it uses a public client registered in Keycloak.

4. The SPA has direct access to the access token and includes this in requests to the REST API.

5. The REST API is required to include CORS headers in the response. Otherwise, the browser would block the SPA from reading the response.

In summary, the SPA uses the Authorization Code flow directly to obtain tokens from Keycloak, which results in the tokens being available directly in the browser, which has a higher risk of tokens being leaked.

You should now have a good understanding of how to secure different types of web applications, such as traditional server-side web applications, and more modern client-side applications. You have learned that the best practice for securing any web application is redirecting to the Keycloak login pages through the Authorization Code flow, with the PKCE extension. Finally, you also learned that although a SPA can obtain tokens directly from Keycloak, it may not be secure enough for highly sensitive applications.

In the next section, we will look at how to secure mobile applications with Keycloak.

Securing native and mobile applications

Securing a web application with Keycloak is more straightforward than securing a native or mobile application. Keycloak login pages are essentially a web application and it is more natural to redirect a user to a different web application when they are already within the browser.

You may be tempted to implement login pages within the application itself to collect the username and password, then leverage the OAuth 2.0 Resource Owner Password Credential grant to obtain tokens. However, this is simply something that you should not be tempted to do. As mentioned in the previous section, applications should never have direct access to the user credentials, and this approach also means you miss out on a lot of features provided by Keycloak.

To secure a native or mobile application, you should use the Authorization Code flow with the PKCE extension instead. This is more secure, and at the same time gives you the full benefits of using Keycloak.

Effectively, this means that your native or mobile application must use a browser to authenticate with Keycloak. In this regard, there are three options available depending on the type of application:

- Use an embedded web view.
- Use an external user agent (the user's default browser).
- Use an in-app browser tab without the application, which is supported on some platforms, such as Android and iOS.

Using an embedded web view may be tempting as it provides a way to place the login pages within the application. However, this option is not recommended as it is open to vulnerabilities where the credentials may be intercepted. It also does not enable SSO as there are no shared cookies between multiple applications.

Using an in-app browser tab is a decent approach as it enables leveraging the system browser while displaying the login pages with the application. However, it is possible for a malicious application to render a login page within the application that looks like an in-app browser tab, allowing the malicious application to collect the credentials. For users that are concerned about this, they can open the page in the external browser instead.

The following screenshot shows the Keycloak login page in an in-app browser tab on Android:

Figure 6.9 – Keycloak login pages displayed in an in-app browser tab on Android

In all the options, the Keycloak login pages are opened in a browser to authenticate the user. After the user is authenticated, the authorization code is returned to the application, which can then obtain tokens from Keycloak. The following diagram shows the steps involved:

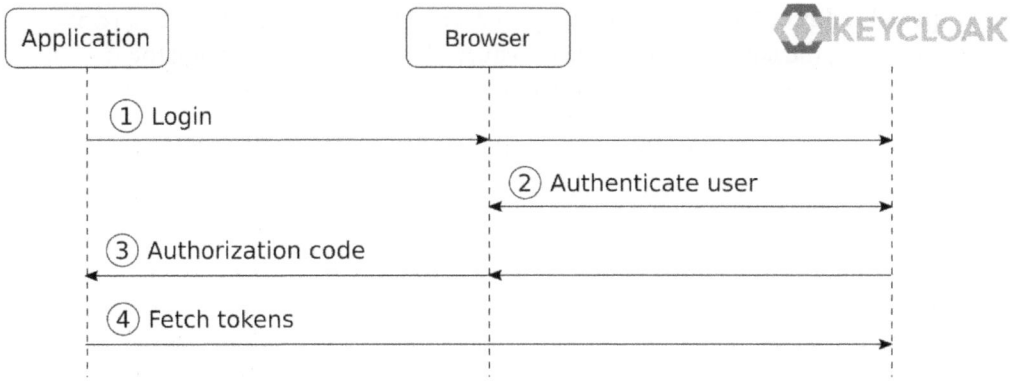

Figure 6.9 – Native application

In more detail, the steps in the diagram are as follows:

1. The application opens the login page in an external browser or using an in-app browser tab.

2. The user authenticates with Keycloak through the external browser.

3. The authorization code is returned to the application.

4. The application exchanges the authorization code for tokens.

To return the authorization code to the application, there are four different approaches using special redirect URIs defined by OAuth 2.0:

- **Claimed HTTPS scheme**: Some platforms allow an application to claim an HTTPS scheme (a URL starting with `https://`), which opens the URI in the application instead of the system browser. For example, the `https://app.acme.org/oauth2callback/provider-name` redirect URI could be claimed by an application called Acme App, resulting in the callback being opened in the Acme App rather than in the browser.

- **Custom URI scheme**: A custom URI scheme is registered with the application. When Keycloak redirects to this custom URI scheme, the request is sent to the application. The custom URI scheme should match the reverse of a domain that is owned by the application developer. For example, the `org.acme.app://oauth2/provider-name` redirect URI matches the domain name `app.acme.org`.

- **Loopback interface**: The application can open a temporary web server on a random port on the loopback interface, then register the `http://127.0.0.1/oauth2/provider-name` redirect URI, which will send the request to the web server started by the application.

- **A special redirect URI**: By using the special `urn:ietf:wg:oauth:2.0:oob` redirect URI, the authorization code is displayed by Keycloak, allowing the user to manually copy and paste the authorization code into the application.

When available, the claimed HTTPS scheme is the recommended approach, as it is more secure. In cases when neither a claimed HTTPS scheme nor a custom scheme can be used, for example, in a CLI, the loopback interface option is a good approach.

To give you a better understanding of how a native application is secured with Keycloak, there is an example application included with this chapter that you can try. The example is showing a CLI that uses the system browser to obtain the authorization code. Before running the example, you need to register a new client with Keycloak with the following settings:

- **Client ID**: `cli`
- **Access Type**: `public`
- **Standard Flow Enabled**: ON
- **Valid Redirect URIs**: `http://localhost/callback`

After you have registered the client, you can run the sample in a terminal by running the following commands:

```
$ cd Keycloak-Identity-and-Access-Management-for-Modern-
Applications/ch6/
$ npm install
$ node app.js
```

When you run the example CLI, it starts a temporary web server on a random port, then it opens the authorization request in the system browser. After you have logged in to Keycloak, it redirects to the web server provided by the application, including the authorization code. The application now has access to the authorization code and can exchange it for an access token.

When running the example CLI, you should see the following output:

```
Listening on port: 40437
Authorization Code: 32ab30d2…
Access Token: eyJhbGciOiJSUzI1NiIsInR3GOMibcto…
```

There are also, of course, cases where a browser is not available – for example, running a terminal within a server that does not have a graphical interface. In these cases, the Device Code grant type is a good option.

In summary, the Device Code grant type works by the application showing a short code that a user enters into a special endpoint at the authorization server in a different device with a browser. After entering the code, the user will be asked to log in if they are not already logged in. After completion, the application is able to retrieve the authorization code from the authorization server.

You should now have a good understanding of how to secure native and mobile applications with Keycloak by using the Authorization Code flow through an external browser. In the next section, we will look at how to secure REST APIs with Keycloak.

Securing REST APIs and services

When an application wants to invoke a REST API protected by Keycloak, it first obtains an access token from Keycloak, then includes the access token in the authorization header in requests it sends to the REST API:

```
Authorization: bearer eyJhbGciOiJSUzI1NiIsInR5c…
```

The REST API can then verify the access token to decide whether access should be granted.

This approach makes it easy to provide a REST API that can be leveraged by many applications, even making the REST API available as a public API on the internet for third-party applications to consume.

In *Chapter 5*, *Authorizing Access with OAuth 2.0*, we covered how the application obtains an access token from Keycloak, then includes the access token in requests it makes to REST APIs so that the REST API can verify whether access should be granted. We also covered various strategies for limiting the access provided by a specific access token, as well as how an access token is verified by the REST API.

With microservices, using tokens to secure the services is especially useful as it enables propagating the authentication context when a service invokes another service, making it easy to provide full end-to-end authentication of the user, as shown in the following diagram:

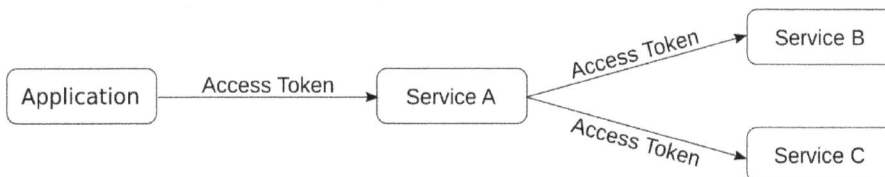

Figure 6.10 – End-to-end user authentication for microservices

In this example, the application includes an access token when it invokes Service A. Service A is then able to invoke both Service B and Service C with the same access token, resulting in all the services using the same authentication context.

Keycloak also has support for service accounts, which allows a service to obtain an access token on behalf of itself by using the Client Credential grant type. Let's give this a go by opening the Keycloak admin console and creating a new client. Use the following values when creating the client:

- **Client ID**: `service`
- **Client Protocol: openid-connect**
- **Access Type: confidential**
- **Standard Flow Enabled: OFF**
- **Implicit Flow Enabled: OFF**
- **Direct Access Grants Enabled: OFF**
- **Service Accounts Enabled: ON**

The following screenshot shows the client you should create:

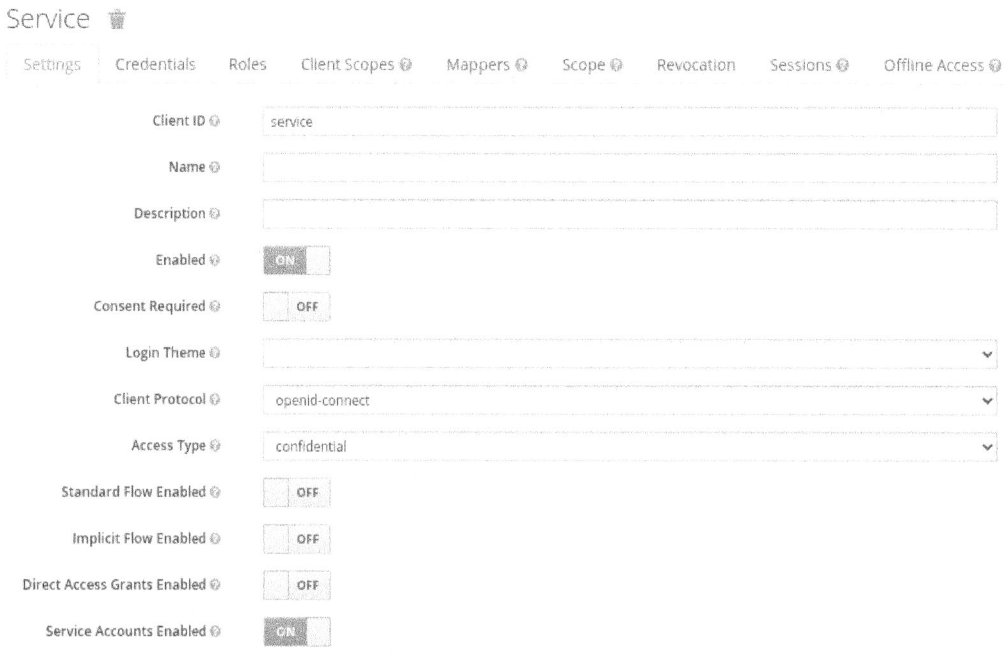

Figure 6.11 – Service account client in Keycloak

As you have turned off the **Standard Flow Enabled** option for this client, it is not able to obtain tokens using the Authorization Code flow, but as it has **Service Accounts Enabled** turned on, it can use the Client Credential flow instead. The Client Credential flow allows a client to obtain tokens on behalf of itself by using the credentials for the client.

To obtain an access token, the client makes a POST request to the Keycloak token endpoint with the following parameters:

- client_id
- client_secrent
- grant_type=client_credentials

Let's try to use curl to get an access token. First, you need to go to the **Credentials** tab for the client you just created and copy the secret for the client. Then, you can open a terminal and run the following command:

```
$ export SECRET=<insert secret from Keycloak Admin Console>
$ curl --data "client_id=service&client_secret=$SECRET&grant_
type=client_credentials" http://localhost:8080/auth/realms/
myrealm/protocol/openid-connect/token
```

Keycloak will return an access token response, which is a JSON document that, among other things, includes the access token:

```
{
    "access_token": "eyJhbGciOiJSUzI1NiIsI…",
    "expires_in": 299,
    "token_type": "bearer",
    "scope": "profile email",
    …
}
```

It is not only REST APIs that can leverage tokens. **Simple Authentication and Security Layer** (SASL), which is a popular protocol for authentication for a range of protocols, also include support for bearer tokens. gRPC and WebSockets can also leverage bearer tokens for secure invocation.

In this section, you have learned how by including a bearer token in the request to a service, the service is able to verify whether the request should be accepted by verifying the token either directly or through the token introspection endpoint.

Summary

In this chapter, you learned the difference between an internal and an external application, where external applications require asking the user for consent to grant access, while internal applications do not. You then learned how different web application architectures are secured with Keycloak, and why it is more secure to have a backend for a SPA that obtains tokens from Keycloak, instead of directly obtaining tokens in the SPA itself. You then learned how Keycloak can be used to secure other types of applications, such as native and mobile applications. Finally, you learned that bearer tokens can be used to secure a range of different services, including REST APIs, microservices, gRPC, WebSockets, and a range of other protocols.

You should now have a good understanding of the principles and best practices for securing your application with Keycloak. In the next chapter, we will look at what options are available to integrate all your applications with Keycloak.

Questions

1. What is the best way to secure the invocations from a SPA to a REST API?

2. Can OAuth 2.0 and bearer tokens only be used to secure web applications and REST APIs?

3. How should you secure a native or mobile application with Keycloak?

Further reading

For more information on the topics covered in this chapter, refer to the following links:

- OAuth 2.0 for browser-based apps: `https://oauth.net/2/browser-based-apps/`

- OAuth 2.0 for mobile and native apps: `https://oauth.net/2/native-apps/`

- AppAuth: `https://appauth.io/`

7
Integrating Applications with Keycloak

So far, you have been presented with the main concepts and configuration options in Keycloak. In this chapter, you finally will learn how to apply them so that you can configure your applications and let them integrate with Keycloak.

Through some selected integration scenarios and coding examples, you will learn which integration approach works best for you according to the technology stack your applications are using and the platform they are running on. You will be presented with different integration options for applications using GoLang, Java, JavaScript, Node.js, and Python. If none of the options work for you, then don't worry – you will learn how to integrate with Keycloak using a reverse proxy that sits in front of your application.

By the end of this chapter, you will have a good understanding of some of the available integration options for you, depending on the characteristics of your applications and their runtime, as well as what you should consider if none of the options herein mentioned work for you and you need to look for alternatives.

In this chapter, we are going to cover the following topics and integrations:

- Choosing an integration architecture
- Choosing an integration option
- Integrating with Golang applications
- Integrating with Java applications
- Integrating with JavaScript applications
- Integrating with Node.js applications
- Integrating with Python applications
- Using a reverse proxy
- Try not to implement your own integration

> **Note**
> We are not opinionated about the integrations in this chapter, and the focus is to show you how to integrate Keycloak with practically any type of application.

Technical requirements

The example code for this chapter can be find in the GitHub repository associated with this book. If you have Git installed, you can clone the repository by running this command in a terminal:

```
$ git clone https://github.com/PacktPublishing/Keycloak-
Identity-and-Access-Management-for-Modern-Applications.git
```

Alternatively, you can download a ZIP of the repository from https://github.com/PacktPublishing/Keycloak-Identity-and-Access-Management-for-Modern-Applications/archive/master.zip.

After cloning or extracting the repository, take a look at the ch7 directory, which is where all the examples are located.

Before we begin, you need to run Keycloak on a different port. For that, start the server, as follows:

```
$ cd $KC_HOME
$ bin/standalone.sh -Djboss.socket.binding.port-offset=100
```

If you are using Docker, you should run the following command to start the server:

```
$ docker run -e KEYCLOAK_USER=admin \
             -e KEYCLOAK_PASSWORD=admin \
             -p 8180:8080 \
             quay.io/keycloak/keycloak
```

We are running Keycloak in a different port because the example applications we are about to run will be listening on port `8080`, the default port used by Keycloak. The server should be available at `http://localhost:8180/auth`.

Now that the server has been started, create a new realm called `myrealm`.

Since we are going to integrate Keycloak with different types of applications, we need to create a client in the `myrealm` realm for each of them.

Let's start by creating the `mybrowserapp` client, which we will use to protect browser-based apps:

- **Client ID**: `mybrowserapp`
- **Root URL**: `http://localhost:8080`

For protecting server-side web applications, we will use a `mywebapp` client:

- **Client ID**: `mywebapp`
- **Root URL**: `http://localhost:8080`

After creating the `mywebapp` client in Keycloak, change the following settings on the client details page:

- **Access Type**: `Confidential`

Let's create the client we will be using to protect the backend application:

- **Client ID**: `mybackend`
- **Root URL**: `http://localhost:8080`

After creating the `mybackend` client in Keycloak, change the following settings on the client details page:

- **Access Type**: `Confidential`
- **Direct Access Grants Enabled**: ON

> **Note**
>
> As you will see in later chapters, the **Direct Access Grants Enabled** option should be disabled for clients. The only reason we are doing this here is to make the examples easier to follow when an access token needs to be obtained in any way other than using a browser.

The last client we are going to create will be used by a reverse proxy running in front of an application. Create a client with the following settings:

- **Client ID**: `proxy-client`
- **Root URL**: `http://localhost`

After creating the `proxy-client` client in Keycloak, change the following settings on the client details page:

- **Access Type**: `Confidential`

Finally, create a user in Keycloak:

- **Username**: `alice`
- **Password**: `alice`

Regardless of the type of application we are about to integrate with, the configuration you just created will not change due to the interoperable nature of Keycloak.

Before we dive into the different integrations, let's understand how they are grouped into two main architectural styles, as well as how they impact how your application integrates with Keycloak.

Check out the following link to see the Code in Action video:

`https://bit.ly/2PRIqSM`

Choosing an integration architecture

There are two main integration styles, depending on where the integration code and configuration are located:

- Embedded
- Proxied

Integrations that are **embedded** into your technology stack are usually provided by a third-party library, framework, web container, or application server. In this style, your application talks directly with Keycloak and is responsible for making requests and processing OAuth2 and OpenID Connect responses. Applications using this style usually need to implement some code or provide some form of configuration to enable support for these protocols. Any setting you need to change will require you to redeploy your application:

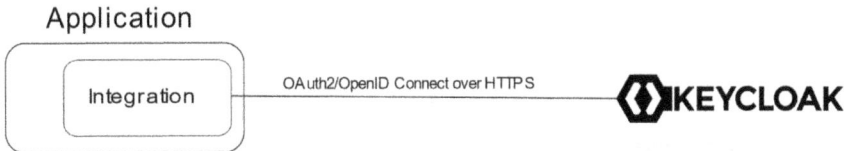

Application

OAuth2/OpenID Connect over HTTPS

KEYCLOAK

Integration

Figure 7.1 – Embedded integration style

On the other hand, in the **proxied** style, there is a layer of indirection where the integration is managed by a service running in front of your application, which, in turn, relies on HTTP headers to fetch tokens or any other security-related data associated with a request. The integration code and configuration are outside your application's boundaries and are managed through the external service:

Platform

OAuth2/OpenID Connect over HTTPS

KEYCLOAK

Integration

HTTP(S)

Application

Figure 7.2 – Proxied integration style

There is no rule of thumb when selecting the best integration style. And sometimes, you may be constrained to use a specific one. They are not mutually exclusive, though, and it is perfectly fine to have both within your application's ecosystem.

The proxied style is a good fit if you do not have control over the application code (for example, legacy code) or if your application is behind a reverse proxy or API gateway and you want to leverage its capabilities. It also gives you the ability to control and manage the integration with Keycloak from a single place.

On the other hand, embedding the integration into your code is simpler as it does not require managing an external service, giving you more control over the integration. Your application is self-contained and, if the framework or library you are using provides good support for OpenID Connect and OAuth2, the integration is usually just a matter of writing a few lines of code or providing some configuration files.

In this section, you learned about the two main architectural styles you can use to integrate with Keycloak.

In the next section, we will cover different integration options based on the styles that have been presented.

Choosing an integration option

In addition to choosing between the two architectural styles we've just mentioned, we should also understand some key points when it comes to choosing an integration.

There are quite a lot of client-side implementations for OpenID Connect and sometimes, you may find hard to choose which one works better for you. If none of the options suggested here work for you, it is important to be aware of how to choose alternatives.

As a rule of thumb, the decision for a good integration should be based on implementations that do the following:

- Are widely adopted, actively maintained, and backed by a strong community of developers.
- Are up to date with the latest versions of the OAuth2 and OpenID Connect specifications.
- Are aligned with the security best practices for OAuth2 and OpenID Connect.
- Provide a good user experience, a simple configuration, and a deployment model.
- Hide details from developers as much as possible while still providing good defaults to make your application aligned with security best practices.
- Avoid vendor lock-in and keep your application compliant with OAuth2 and OpenID Connect as much as possible. Keycloak can integrate with any client that's compliant with these specifications.

Ideally, you should be using whatever comes for free from the technology stack and platform on which your applications are deployed.

You may also consider looking at the OpenID Connect website for a list of certified implementations. The list is available at `https://openid.net/developers/certified/`.

In the next section, we are going to look at how to integrate Keycloak using different technology stacks.

> **Note**
>
> The code examples provided in this chapter are not targeted at being run in production; instead, they demonstrate how to integrate Keycloak with different types of applications.

Integrating with Golang applications

Go applications can integrate with Keycloak using whatever library you prefer, as long as it complies with the OpenID Connect or OAuth2 specifications.

For the sake of simplicity and to provide a generic example of how to integrate with Keycloak, we are going to use the `https://github.com/coreos/go-oidc` package. The code examples for this section are available in the following directory:

```
$ cd Keycloak-Identity-and-Access-Management-for-Modern-
Applications/ch7/golang
```

In the preceding directory, you will find a `main.go` file that contains all the code you will need to follow and run the examples.

In the next section, we are going to start looking at how to enable a web application that can authenticate users using Keycloak.

Configuring a Golang client

First, you need to create a provider using a base URL that the OpenID Connect Discovery Document will be fetched from. This will set up the necessary endpoints that your application will be talking to when you're authenticating users and obtaining tokens from Keycloak. The following code creates a new provider using the discovery document available at `http://localhost:8180/realms/myrealm/.well-known/openid-configuration`:

```
func createOidcProvider(ctx context.Context) *oidc.Provider {
    provider, err := oidc.NewProvider(ctx, "http://
localhost:8180/realms/myrealm")
```

```
    if err != nil {
        log.Fatal("Failed to fetch discovery document: ",
err)
    }

    return provider
}
```

You also need to provide information about the client in Keycloak that the application will use to access Keycloak. For that, we need to set the client ID and secret like so:

```
func createConfig(provider oidc.Provider) (oidc.Config, oauth2.
Config) {
    oidcConfig := &oidc.Config{
        ClientID: "mywebapp",
    }

    config := oauth2.Config{
        ClientID:     oidcConfig.ClientID,
        ClientSecret: CLIENT_SECRET,
        Endpoint:     provider.Endpoint(),
        RedirectURL: "http://localhost:8080/auth/callback",
        Scopes:       []string{oidc.ScopeOpenID, "profile",
"email"},
    }

    return *oidcConfig, config
}
```

> **Note**
>
> You should change the reference to CLIENT_SECRET in the preceding code with the secret generated by Keycloak for the mywebapp client. For that, go the mywebapp client details page in Keycloak and click on the **Credentials** tab. The client secret should be available from the **Secret** field in this tab.

The next step is to change your application so that it redirects users to Keycloak when they try to access the application. In the following code, we have set a cookie to track the value of the state parameter and redirect users to Keycloak:

```go
func redirectHandler(w http.ResponseWriter, r *http.Request) {
state := addStateCookie(w)
    http.Redirect(w, r, oauth2Config.AuthCodeURL(state), http.
StatusFound)
}
```

Note, however, that, as a developer, you are responsible for implementing how users are redirected to Keycloak using the `oauth2Config.AuthCodeuRL` function. We are also implementing the necessary logic to generate the `state` parameter, as well as how we can store it as an HTTP cookie, so that we can associate the original authorization request with a response from Keycloak once the user is authenticated. Depending on the library you are using, you do not need to perform any of these steps in your code as they might be performed transparently by the library.

Finally, let's implement the callback URL that Keycloak is going to redirect users to right after a successful authentication attempt:

```go
func callbackHandler(resp http.ResponseWriter, req *http.
Request) {
    err := checkStateAndExpireCookie(req, resp)


    if err != nil {
        http.Error(resp, err.Error(), http.StatusBadRequest)
        return
    }
    tokenResponse, err := exchangeCode(req)
    if err != nil {
        http.Error(resp, "Failed to exchange code", http.
StatusBadRequest)
        return
    }
    idToken, err := validateIDToken(tokenResponse, req)
    if err != nil {
        http.Error(resp, "Failed to validate id_token", http.
StatusUnauthorized)
        return
```

```
    }
        handleSuccessfulAuthentication(tokenResponse, *idToken,
resp)
}
```

The callback handler is responsible for the following:

- Checking whether the state is the same as the one that was originally sent when you performed the authorization request to Keycloak.

- Exchanging the code that was returned from Keycloak to obtain the ID token, access token, and refresh token.

- Verifying the ID token's validity in terms of signature, audience, and expiration date.

> **Note**
>
> A proper integration would avoid reusing the same `state` value, as well as managing local sessions once the user has been authenticated for the very first time. In fact, clients should prefer using **Proof Key for Code Exchange (PKCE)** to prevent **Cross-Site Request Forgery (CSRF)** and code replay attacks. We are using the state due to the lack of PKCE support from the `go-oidc` package. To use PKCE, you will need to implement it by yourself or use some third-party package.

Let's start the application by running the following command at the root directory of your project:

```
$ cd Keycloak-Identity-and-Access-Management-for-Modern-
Applications/ch7/golang
$ go run main.go
```

Your application should start and be available at `http://localhost:8080`. Now, try to access that URL and log into Keycloak using the credentials for the user we created at the beginning of this chapter.

If the integration is working properly, you should be redirected to Keycloak to authenticate. After providing these user credentials, you should be redirected back to the application, now as an authenticated user, and a page will appear that contains the tokens that have been issued by the server.

In this section, you learned about the basics of to how integrate a GoLang application with Keycloak. The `go-oidc` package is a well-known package that provides OpenID Connect capabilities for client applications. It provides a good baseline for integrating with Keycloak and allows you to enable authentication for your application. However, it requires additional work from the developer to get it done right, as well as to maintain the code.

If you are using a framework, such as Gin, or if you know about any other package that do not require you to understand the integration internals while providing a rich set of features and configuration, you should use that instead.

There are also quite a few third-party libraries you can find that are targeted at integrating with Keycloak. Unfortunately, we cannot recommend any of them since they are not in conformance with some of the recommendations that were mentioned at the beginning of this chapter – mainly the fact they are not backed by a strong community but by individuals.

In the next section, we are going to look at more integration options that use other programming languages.

Integrating with Java applications

Frameworks, web containers, and application servers that provide support for OpenID Connect and OAuth2 as part of their offerings should make your life a lot easier, since the integration is already available to your application and there is no need to add any other dependencies.

Leveraging what is already in your technology stack is usually the best choice. But that will not always be the case.

Keycloak also provides client-side implementations that have support for some of the most common frameworks, web containers, and application servers available. Also known as Keycloak adapters, these implementations are targeted at people looking for a deeper integration with Keycloak.

In the next few sections, we will look at the different options you can choose from so that you can pick the one that works best for your applications.

Using Quarkus

Quarkus provides an OpenID Connect compliant extension called `quarkus-oidc`. It provides a simple and rich configuration model that can protect both frontend and backend applications. Quarkus has built-in support for the most common **Integrated Development Environments (IDEs)**, such as IntelliJ and Eclipse, and you should be able to quickly create or configure an existing project in order to integrate it with Keycloak.

> **Tip**
>
> If you are new to Quarkus or just want to protect your applications using OpenID Connect and Keycloak, please look at the guides available at `https://quarkus.io/guides`. Most of these guides and code examples use Keycloak as an OpenID Provider and will help you quickly get started. Search for guides using `OpenID Connect` as a keyword to filter all the available guides related to integrating with Keycloak.

In summary, the `quarkus-oidc` extension allows you to protect two main types of applications: `web-app` and `service`.

The `web-app` type represents applications that authenticate using Keycloak through the browser, using the authorization code grant type. These are frontend applications.

On the other hand, the `service` type represents applications that rely on bearer tokens issued by a Keycloak server to authorize access to their protected resources. These are backend applications.

To use the `quarkus-oidc` extension in your project, add the following dependency to the application's `pom.xml` file:

```
<dependency>
    <groupId>io.quarkus</groupId>
    <artifactId>quarkus-oidc</artifactId>
</dependency>
```

Now that we've added the `quarkus-oidc` dependency, it is time to decide on the type of application.

The code examples for this section are available in this book's GitHub repository at the following link:

```
$ cd Keycloak-Identity-and-Access-Management-for-Modern-
Applications/ch7/quarkus
```

In the preceding directory, you will find a frontend directory and a backend directory, both of which contain all the code you will need to follow and run the upcoming examples.

In the next section, we are going to start looking at how to enable a web application so that we can authenticate users using Keycloak.

Creating a Quarkus client

In this section, we will be looking at the code examples that are available from the following directory:

```
$ cd Keycloak-Identity-and-Access-Management-for-Modern-
Applications/ch7/quarkus/frontend
```

Let's start by configuring a web-app application by adding the following properties to the src/main/resources/application.properties file:

```
quarkus.oidc.auth-server-url=http://localhost:8180/auth/realms/
myrealm
quarkus.oidc.client-id=mywebapp
quarkus.oidc.client-secret=CLIENT_SECRET
quarkus.oidc.application-type=web-app
quarkus.http.auth.permission.authenticated.paths=/*
quarkus.http.auth.permission.authenticated.policy=authenticated
```

From a configuration perspective, the main configuration options are as follows:

- The quarkus.oidc.auth-server-url property defines the URL that the application should fetch the OpenID Connect Discovery document from.

- The quarkus.oidc.client-id property maps a client in Keycloak with this application. For this application, we are going to use the mywebapp client, which we created at the beginning of this chapter.

- The quarkus.oidc.client-secret property is the secret that was generated by Keycloak when the client was created.

- The quarkus.oidc.application-type property defines that this application is a web application.

- The quarkus.http.auth.permission.authenticated.paths and quarkus.http.auth.permission.authenticated.policy properties define that all the paths in the applications require an authenticated user.

> **Note**
>
> You should change the reference to `CLIENT_SECRET` in the `src/main/resources/application.properties` file with the secret that was generated by Keycloak for the **mywebapp** client. For that, go to the **mywebapp** client details page in Keycloak and click on the **Credentials** tab. The client secret should be available from the **Secret** field in this tab.

Let's start the application by running the following command at the root directory of your project:

```
$ cd Keycloak-Identity-and-Access-Management-for-Modern-
Applications/ch7/quarkus/frontend
$ ./mvnw quarkus:dev
```

Your application should start and be available at `http://localhost:8080`. Try to access that URL and log into Keycloak using the credentials for the user we created at the beginning of this chapter.

If the integration is working properly, you should be redirected to Keycloak to authenticate. After providing the necessary user credentials, you should be redirected back to the application, now as an authenticated user.

> **Note**
>
> By default, Quarkus is going to set a cookie that will expire based on the expiration time of the token issued by Keycloak. If you are experiencing the user not redirected to Keycloak to authenticate, you might want to clear your browser cookies. This behavior is something you can configure. For more details, look at the **quarkus-oidc** extension documentation.

In this section, you learned about how to configure a web application in order to authenticate users using Keycloak. At this point, you should be able to create your own application or configure an existing one to authenticate users using Keycloak.

In the next section, we will look at how to configure a backend application to authorize access to resources based on tokens issued by Keycloak.

Creating a Quarkus resource server

The code examples that will be presented in this section are available from the following GitHub repository:

```
$ cd Keycloak-Identity-and-Access-Management-for-Modern-
Applications/ch7/quarkus/backend
```

For backend applications that have been protected using a OAuth2 Bearer Token, the configuration is similar to configuring frontend applications, except for changing `quarkus.oidc.application-type` to `service`, as well as `quarkus.oidc.client-id` so that it maps to a different client in Keycloak:

```
quarkus.oidc.auth-server-url=http://localhost:8180/auth/realms/
myrealm
quarkus.oidc.client-id=mybackend
quarkus.oidc.credentials.secret=CLIENT_SECRET
quarkus.oidc.application-type=service
quarkus.http.auth.permission.authenticated.paths=/*
quarkus.http.auth.permission.authenticated.policy=authenticated
```

> **Note**
>
> You should change the reference to CLIENT_SECRET in the `src/main/resources/application.properties` file with the secret that was generated by Keycloak for the **mybackend** client. For that, go the **mybackend** client details page in Keycloak and click on the **Credentials** tab. The client secret should be available from the **Secret** field in this tab.

The `quarkus.oidc.application-type` property, which is now set to `service`, indicates that this application should authorize access based on bearer tokens.

Let's start the application by running the following command at the root directory of your project:

```
$ cd Keycloak-Identity-and-Access-Management-for-Modern-
Applications/ch7/quarkus/backend
$ ./mvnw quarkus:dev
```

Your application should start and be available at `http://localhost:8080`. To access the resources at the running application, you will need an access token. To obtain one, use the following command:

```
$ export access_token=$(\
    curl -X POST http://localhost:8180/auth/realms/myrealm/
protocol/openid-connect/token \
    --user mybackend:CLIENT_SECRET\
    -H 'content-type: application/x-www-form-urlencoded' \
    -d 'username=alice&password=alice&grant_type=password' | jq
--raw-output '.access_token' \
 )
```

Once you have run this command, an access token will be saved in an `access_token` environment variable, and you can now access the application:

```
$ curl -X GET \
  http://localhost:8080/hello \
  -H "Authorization: Bearer "$access_token
```

As a result, you should expect the following output from that command:

```
$ Hello RESTEasy
```

Now, if you try to access the application without a `Bearer` token or use an invalid one, you should get a 401 status code, indicating that your request was forbidden:

```
$ curl -v -X GET \
  http://localhost:8080/hello
```

The `quarkus-oidc` extension validates tokens based on whether they represent a **JSON Web Token** (**JWT**) or not. If the token is a JWT, the extension will try to validate the token locally by checking its signatures, audience, and expiration date. Otherwise, if the token is opaque and the format is unknown, it will invoke the token's introspection endpoint at Keycloak to validate it. For Quarkus applications, the `quarkus-oidc` extension is the best option you have. It provides an amazingly simple configuration while providing a lot of other options you can use to customize its behavior.

We only covered the main steps of setting up the `quarkus-oidc` extension here so that you can authenticate your users through Keycloak. There is lot more you can do with this extension, such as leverage capabilities for logout, obtain information about the subject into your beans, multi-tenancy, and so on. For more details, please check out the extension's documentation at `https://quarkus.io/guides/security#openid-connect`.

In the next section, we will look at how to integrate with Spring Boot applications.

Using Spring Boot

Spring Boot applications can integrate with Keycloak by leveraging Spring Security's OAuth2/OpenID libraries. Spring Boot also has built-in support for the most common IDEs, such as IntelliJ and Eclipse, so you should be able to quickly create or configure an existing project so that it can be integrated with Keycloak.

There are two main libraries, where each is targeted by a specific type of application: clients and resource servers.

The code examples in this section are available from the following GitHub repository:

```
$ cd Keycloak-Identity-and-Access-Management-for-Modern-
Applications/ch7/springboot
```

In the preceding directory, you will find a frontend directory and a backend directory containing all the code you will need to follow and run the examples.

In the next section, we are going to start looking at how to enable a web application so that we can authenticate users using Keycloak.

Creating a Spring Boot client

The code examples presented in this section are available from the following GitHub repository:

```
$ cd Keycloak-Identity-and-Access-Management-for-Modern-
Applications/ch7/springboot/frontend
```

First, add the following dependencies to your project to enable OAuth2/Open ID Connect support:

```
<dependency>
    <groupId>org.springframework.boot</groupId>
    <artifactId>spring-boot-starter-oauth2-client</artifactId>
</dependency>
<dependency>
    <groupId>org.springframework.boot</groupId>
    <artifactId>spring-boot-starter-security</artifactId>
</dependency>
```

You should now change the src/main/resources/application.yaml file so that you can configure the application, as follows:

```
spring:
  security:
    oauth2:
      client:
        registration:
          myfrontend:
            provider: keycloak
            client-id: mywebapp
            client-secret: CLIENT_SECRET
```

```
                    authorization-grant-type: authorization_code
                    redirect-uri: "{baseUrl}/login/oauth2/code/"
                    scope: openid
              provider:
                keycloak:
                    authorization-uri: http://localhost:8180/auth/
realms/myrealm/protocol/openid-connect/auth
                    token-uri: http://localhost:8180/auth/realms/
myrealm/protocol/openid-connect/token
                    jwk-set-uri: http://localhost:8180/auth/realms/
myrealm/protocol/openid-connect/certs
```

> **Note**
>
> You should change the reference to CLIENT_SECRET in the preceding configuration with the secret generated by Keycloak for the **mywebapp** client. For that, go the **mywebapp** client details page in Keycloak and click on the **Credentials** tab. The client secret should be available from the **Secret** field in this tab.

Let's start the application by running the following command at the root directory of your project:

```
$ cd Keycloak-Identity-and-Access-Management-for-Modern-
Applications/ch7/springboot/frontend
$ ./mvnw spring-boot:run
```

Your application should start and be available at http://localhost:8080. Try to access that URL and log into Keycloak using the credentials for the user we created at the beginning of this chapter.

If the integration is working properly, you should be redirected to Keycloak to authenticate. After providing the user credentials, you should be redirected back to the application, now as an authenticated user.

In this section, you learned about how to configure a web application to authenticate users using Keycloak. With that, you should be able to create your own application or configure an existing one to authenticate users using Keycloak.

In the next section, we will look at how to configure a backend application to authorize access to resources based on tokens issued by Keycloak.

Creating a Spring Boot resource server

The code examples presented in this section are available from the following GitHub repository:

```
$ cd Keycloak-Identity-and-Access-Management-for-Modern-
Applications/ch7/springboot/backend
```

First, add the following dependencies to your project to enable OAuth2/Open ID Connect support:

```
<dependency>
    <groupId>org.springframework.boot</groupId>
    <artifactId> spring-boot-starter-oauth2-resource-server</
artifactId>
</dependency>
<dependency>
    <groupId>org.springframework.boot</groupId>
    <artifactId>spring-boot-starter-security</artifactId>
</dependency>
```

For backend applications protected using a OAuth2 Bearer Token, the configuration is similar to configuring frontend applications. But here, the application is going to act as a resource server that validates JWT tokens:

```
spring:
  security:
    oauth2:
      resourceserver:
        jwt:
          issuer-uri: http://localhost:8180/auth/realms/myrealm
```

Let's start the application by running the following command at the root directory of your project:

```
$ cd Keycloak-Identity-and-Access-Management-for-Modern-
Applications/ch7/springboot/backend
$ ./mvnw spring-boot:run
```

Your application should start and be available at `http://localhost:8080`. For accessing resources at the running application, you now need an access token. To obtain one, use the following command:

```
$ export access_token=$(\
    curl -X POST http://localhost:8180/auth/realms/myrealm/
protocol/openid-connect/token \
    --user mybackend:CLIENT_SECRET\
    -H 'content-type: application/x-www-form-urlencoded' \
    -d 'username=alice&password=alice&grant_type=password' | jq
--raw-output '.access_token' \
 )
```

> **Note**
> You should change the reference to `CLIENT_SECRET` in the preceding command with the secret generated by Keycloak for the **mybackend** client. For that, go the **mybackend** client details page in Keycloak and click on the **Credentials** tab. The client secret should be available from the **Secret** field in this tab.

Once you run this command, an access token will be saved in an `access_token` environment variable, and you can now access the application:

```
$ curl -X GET \
  http://localhost:8080 \
  -H "Authorization: Bearer "$access_token
```

As a result, you should expect the following output from that command:

```
$ Greetings from Spring Boot!
```

Now, if you try to access the application without a `Bearer` token or use an invalid one, you should get a 401 status code, indicating that your request was forbidden:

```
$ curl -v -X GET \
  http://localhost:8080
```

In this section, you learned about how to use Spring Security's OAuth2/OpenID libraries to integrate with Keycloak. We only covered the main steps for setting up Spring Security here so that you can authenticate your users through Keycloak. For more details, please check out the Spring Security documentation at `https://docs.spring.io/spring-security-oauth2-boot/docs/current/reference/html5/`.

In the next section, we are going to look at Keycloak adapters, which we can use as an alternative in case none of the integration options we've presented so far work for you.

Using Keycloak adapters

In addition to the Keycloak server itself, there are several client libraries under the Keycloak umbrella that provide integration with different languages, frameworks, web containers, and application servers.

Also known as Keycloak adapters, these client implementations are meant for integrating with Keycloak, so you should not expect from them to work with other OAuth2 and OpenID Connect servers.

By being specific to Keycloak, you should expect a deeper integration from Keycloak adapters with Keycloak where specific features or capabilities can't be found in any other standard compliant client implementation.

> **Tip**
> It may sound like these adapters are the best you can get for integrating with Keycloak, but you should always prefer using generic OpenID Connect libraries, as well as whatever comes for free from the stack you are using, as mentioned in the *Choosing an integration option* section.

We are not going to go deeper into all the Keycloak adapters. Instead, we will quickly iterate over each one and point you to their respective documentation and examples.

In general, these adapters rely on hooks provided by the underlying programming language, framework, web container, and application server they are related to, so you should expect differences when using each adapter. However, regardless of the adapter you choose, you will be using a `keycloak.json` file to configure the adapter and how your application will be interacting with Keycloak to authenticate, authorize, and log out users.

From a configuration perspective, you should expect the same configuration experience across the different adapters. However, you may experience some gaps in some of them due to limitations and constraints from the underlying runtime.

In the following sections, you are going to learn about the different types of adapters and the types of applications they are meant for. We are not going to deep dive into the details because you will find the comprehensive documentation and examples for all the supported adapters in the Keycloak Securing Applications documentation at `https://www.keycloak.org/docs/latest/securing_apps/` and in the Keycloak Quickstarts repository at `https://github.com/keycloak/keycloak-quickstarts`.

Using WildFly and the Red Hat Enterprise Application Platform (EAP)

The Keycloak WildFly and EAP adapter are targeted at applications that have been deployed to the WildFly JEE application server or to the Red Hat EAP.

You can use this adapter by following two main patterns:

- Embedded configuration
- Managed configuration

The **embedded configuration** means that the adapter's configuration is defined in a `keycloak.json` file within your application.

In the **managed configuration**, the adapter's configuration is external to your application and managed through the Keycloak adapter subsystem.

The main difference between these two approaches is whether you need to redeploy your application due to configuration changes. In the managed configuration, changes to the configuration are made via the application server management interfaces.

However, the managed configuration is usually not in sync with the latest configuration options that you can set, and that makes the embedded configuration more appealing.

For more details about this adapter, check out the Keycloak WildFly and EAP adapter documentation:

`https://www.keycloak.org/docs/latest/securing_apps/#jboss-eap-wildfly-adapter`

Using JBoss Fuse

For more details about this adapter, check out the Keycloak Fuse adapter documentation:

`https://www.keycloak.org/docs/latest/securing_apps/#_fuse7_adapter`

Using a web container

For more details about this adapter, check out the following documentation:

- Keycloak Tomcat adapter documentation: `https://www.keycloak.org/docs/latest/securing_apps/#_tomcat_adapter`

- Keycloak Jetty adapter documentation: `https://www.keycloak.org/docs/latest/securing_apps/#_jetty9_adapter`

Desktop applications

The Keycloak desktop adapter is a handy library that leverages Keycloak's capabilities to authenticate users using a Java desktop application.

It relies on the system's default browser to redirect users to Keycloak to authenticate, and also allows you to have access to tokens issued by Keycloak once the user has been successfully authenticated.

By using this adapter, you should be able to authenticate your users using Kerberos tickets, where Keycloak acts a broker to your existing Kerberos infrastructure.

For more details about this adapter, check out the following Keycloak desktop adapter documentation:

`https://www.keycloak.org/docs/latest/securing_apps/#_installed_adapter.`

In this section, you learned about the different options for integrating and protecting your Java application with Keycloak. You learned how to leverage some of the capabilities provided by two common frameworks, Quarkus and Spring Boot, and that Keycloak provides client implementations for applications running on any of the supported web containers and application servers, as well as how to integrate Keycloak with desktop applications.

In the upcoming sections, we are going to look at more integration options when it comes to using different programming languages.

Integrating with JavaScript applications

You will find different OpenID Connect client implementations for JavaScript that you can use to integrate Keycloak with your **Single-Page Applications (SPA)**.

In this section, we are going to cover how to use the Keycloak JavaScript adapter, a client implementation provided by Keycloak that is targeted at JavaScript-based applications running in a browser, as well as for those using React.JS or React Native.

The code examples for this section are available from the following GitHub repository:

```
$ cd Keycloak-Identity-and-Access-Management-for-Modern-
Applications/ch7/keycloak-js-adapter
```

In the preceding directory, you will find all the code you'll need to follow and run the upcoming examples.

The first step to configuring your application with the Keycloak JS adapter is adding the keycloak.js library to your page:

```
<script type="text/javascript" src="KC_URL/js/keycloak.js"></
script>
```

Here, KC_URL is the URL where your Keycloak server is available, such as http://localhost:8180/auth if you are running it locally.

> **Tip**
> By fetching the library from the server as opposed to embedding it in your application, you are guaranteed to always be using the version of the library that is compatible with the Keycloak server your application is talking to.

Now that the library is available on your page, you need to create a keycloak object with the client's information and initialize it when the browser window is loaded:

```
keycloak = new Keycloak({ realm: 'myrealm', clientId:
'mybrowserapp' });
keycloak.init({onLoad: 'login-required'}).success(function () {
    console.log('User is now authenticated.');
    profile();
}).error(function () {
    window.location.reload();
});
```

Similarly, to other types of adapters provided by Keycloak, the client information can also be fetched from a keycloak.json file at the root path of your application.

The init method is responsible for bootstrapping the adapter and returning a promise that we can use to perform actions, based on whether the user is authenticated or when an error occurs during this process.

When your page is loaded for the first time, the adapter is going to check whether the user is already authenticated. If they aren't authenticated yet, the adapter is going to redirect the user to Keycloak. Once the user is successfully authenticated and returns to your application, the adapter will run the function defined by the success callback, which, in turn, is going to show a page with information about the user.

Now, let's start the application by running the following code:

```
$ cd Keycloak-Identity-and-Access-Management-for-Modern-
Applications/ch7/keycloak-js-adapter
$ npm install
$ npm start
```

Your application should start and be available at http://localhost:8080. Try accessing that URL and logging into Keycloak using the credentials for the user we created at the beginning of this chapter.

If the integration is working properly, you should be redirected to Keycloak to authenticate. After providing the user credentials, you should be redirected back to the application, now as an authenticated user.

If your application needs to access protected resources in some backend server using a bearer token, you can easily obtain the access token from the keycloak object and pass it over when you make HTTP requests:

```
function sendRequest() {
    var req = new XMLHttpRequest();
    req.onreadystatechange = function() {
        if (req.readyState === 4) {
            output(req.status + '\n\n' + req.responseText);
        }
    }
    req.open('GET', 'https://myservice.url', true);
    req.setRequestHeader('Authorization', 'Bearer ' + keycloak.
token);
    req.send();
}
```

The Keycloak JavaScript adapter allows you to quickly integrate with Keycloak. This library was built due to the lack of good JavaScript libraries for OpenID Connect at the time it was created, which does not hold true anymore due to the number of libraries available today. This adapter is actively maintained under the Keycloak umbrella and is well-documented, but still specific to integrating with Keycloak as opposed to being a generic and fully compliant OpenID Connect library.

> **Note**
>
> Using OpenID Connect and OAuth2 in browser-based applications is surrounded by security concerns due to their nature. When it comes to choosing a good library, you should follow the best practices as per the OAuth2 Security Best Practices for Browser-Based Apps, available at `https://tools.ietf.org/html/draft-ietf-oauth-browser-based-apps`.

We have only scratched the surface here and there is far more you can do with it, such as obtaining tokens issues from the server, refresh tokens or automatically doing this based on a certain period of time, and logouts.

For more details about the Keycloak JavaScript adapter, check out the documentation at `https://www.keycloak.org/docs/latest/securing_apps/#_javascript_adapter`.

In the next section, we are going to continue looking at how to integrate with Node.js applications.

Integrating with Node.js applications

For Node.js applications, Keycloak provides a specific adapter called Keycloak Node.js Adapter. Like other adapters, it is targeted at integration with Keycloak rather than a generic OpenID Connect client implementation.

The Keycloak Node.js adapter hides most of the internals from your application through a simple API that you can use to protect your application resources. The adapter is available as an npm package and can be installed into your project as follows:

```
$ npm install keycloak-connect
```

The code examples for this section are available from the following GitHub repository:

```
$ cd Keycloak-Identity-and-Access-Management-for-Modern-
Applications/ch7/nodejs
```

In the preceding directory, you will find a `frontend` directory and a `backend` directory, which contain all the code you'll need to follow and run the following examples.

Now that you have installed the `keycloak-connect` dependency on your application, we are going to look at how to configure your application as a client and as a resource server.

Creating a Node.js client

Once you've installed the `keycloak-connect` package, you need to change your application code so that it creates a `keycloak` object:

```
var keycloak = new Keycloak({ store: memoryStore });
```

Since we are protecting a frontend application, we want to create a local session for our users so that they are not redirected to Keycloak once they are authenticated. For that, note that the Keycloak object is created with a `memoryStore`:

```
var memoryStore = new session.MemoryStore();
```

Just like other Keycloak adapters, the configuration is read from a `keycloak.json` file containing the client configuration:

```
{
    "realm": "myrealm",
    "auth-server-url": "${env.KC_URL:http://localhost:8180}",
    "resource": "mywebapp",
    "credentials" : {
        "secret" : CLIENT_SECRET
    }
}
```

> **Note**
>
> You should change the reference to CLIENT_SECRET in the `keycloak.json` file with the secret that was generated by Keycloak for the **mywebapp** client. For that, go the **mywebapp** client details page in Keycloak and click on the **Credentials** tab. The client secret should be available from the **Secret** field in this tab.

The next step is to install the adapter as a middleware so that you can use it to protect the resources in your application:

```
app.use(keycloak.middleware());
```

Now that the middleware has been installed, protecting the resources in your application should be as simple as doing the following:

```
app.get('/', keycloak.protect(), function (req, res) {
    res.setHeader('content-type', 'text/plain');
    res.send('Welcome!');
});
```

The `keycloak.protect` method automatically adds the necessary capabilities to your endpoints, to check whether users are authenticated yet or not so that they can be redirected to Keycloak if not. After successful authentication, the middleware will automatically process the response from Keycloak and establish a local session for the user based on the tokens issued by the server.

Now, let's start the application:

```
$ cd Keycloak-Identity-and-Access-Management-for-Modern-
Applications/ch7/nodejs/frontend
$ npm install
$ npm start
```

Your application should start and be available at `http://localhost:8080`. Try to access that URL and log into Keycloak using the credentials for the user we created at the beginning of this chapter.

If the integration is working properly, you should be redirected to Keycloak to authenticate. After providing the user credentials, you should be redirected back to the application, now as an authenticated user.

Creating a Node.js resource server

The code examples presented in this server are available from the following GitHub repository:

```
$ cd Keycloak-Identity-and-Access-Management-for-Modern-
Applications/ch7/nodejs/backend
```

For backend applications, you can create a `keycloak` object as follows:

```
var keycloak = new Keycloak({});
```

Compared to frontend applications, we do not need to track user sessions; instead, we must rely on bearer tokens to authorize requests.

Similar to the previous example, we also need to update the `keycloak.json` file with the client configuration:

```
{
    "realm": "myrealm",
    "bearer-only": true,
    "auth-server-url": "${env.KC_URL:http://localhost:8180/
auth}",
    "resource": "mybackend"
}
```

In this configuration, we are explicitly marking this application so that it only accepts bearer tokens, forcing the adapter to check whether a request can access resources in the application by performing local validations and introspections on the token.

The next step is to install the adapter as a middleware so that you can use it to protect the resources in your application:

```
app.use(keycloak.middleware());
```

Now that the middleware has been installed, protecting the resources in your application should be as simple as doing the following:

```
app.get('/protected', keycloak.protect(), function (req, res) {
    res.setHeader('content-type', 'text/plain');
    res.send('Access granted to protected resource');
});
```

The `keycloak.protect` method automatically adds bearer token authorization to your endpoints so that requests containing an authorization header with a valid token can fetch the protected resources in your application.

Now, let's start the application:

```
$ cd Keycloak-Identity-and-Access-Management-for-Modern-
Applications/ch7/nodejs/backend
$ npm install
$ npm start
```

Your application should start and be available at http://localhost:8080. To access the resources at the running application, you will need an access token. To obtain one, use the following command:

```
$ export access_token=$(\
    curl -X POST http://localhost:8180/auth/realms/myrealm/
protocol/openid-connect/token \
    --user mybackend:CLIENT_SECRET\
    -H 'content-type: application/x-www-form-urlencoded' \
    -d 'username=alice&password=alice&grant_type=password' | jq
--raw-output '.access_token' \
  )
```

> **Note**
>
> You should change the reference to CLIENT_SECRET in the preceding command with the secret generated by Keycloak for the **mybackend** client. For that, go the **mybackend** client details page in Keycloak and click on the **Credentials** tab. The client secret should be available from the **Secret** field in this tab.

Once you've run that command, an access token will be saved in an access_token environment variable, which means you can now access the application:

```
$ curl -v -X GET \
  http://localhost:8080/protected \
  -H "Authorization: Bearer "$access_token
```

As a result, you should expect the following output:

```
$ Access granted to protected resource
```

Now, if you try to access the application without a `Bearer` token or use an invalid one, you should get a 403 status code, indicating that your request was forbidden:

```
$ curl -v -X GET \
  http://localhost:8080/protected
```

There is much more you can do with the Keycloak Node.js adapter in terms of configuration and usage. You should be able to use `keycloak.protect` to perform role-based access controls and obtain the tokens representing the authenticated subject.

The Keycloak Node.js adapter is actively maintained under the Keycloak umbrella, but it's still specific to integrating with Keycloak as opposed to being a generic and fully compliant OpenID Connect library.

For more details about the Keycloak JavaScript adapter, check out the available documentation at `https://www.keycloak.org/docs/latest/securing_apps/#_nodejs_adapter`.

In this section, you learned how to configure your Node.js application so that you can integrate with Keycloak using the `keycloak-connect` library. Next, you will learn how to integrate Python applications with Keycloak.

Integrating with Python applications

Python applications that use Flask can easily enable OpenID Connect and OAuth2 to applications through the Flask-OIDC library. It can be used to protect client as well as resource server applications.

> **Tip**
> If you are looking for a library to enable OpenID Connect support for command-line interfaces, there are different OpenID Connect client implementations you can use at `https://openid.net/developers/certified/`.

To install Flask-OIDC, run the following command:

```
$ pip install Flask-OIDC
```

The code examples for this section are available from the following GitHub repository:

```
$ cd Keycloak-Identity-and-Access-Management-for-Modern-
Applications/ch7/python
```

In the preceding directory, you will find a `frontend` directory and a `backend` directory containing all the code you will need to follow and run the following examples.

In the next section, we are going to start looking at how to enable a web application in order to authenticate users using Keycloak.

Creating a Python client

The code examples presented here are available from the following GitHub repository:

```
$ cd Keycloak-Identity-and-Access-Management-for-Modern-
Applications/ch7/python/frontend
```

To enable authentication to your web application, you will need a configuration file called `oidc-config.json` at the root path of your program that contains some metadata about the endpoints and client information from Keycloak:

```
{
  "web": {
    "client_id": "mywebapp",
    "client_secret":CLIENT_SECRET,
    "auth_uri": "http://localhost:8180/auth/realms/myrealm/
protocol/openid-connect/auth",
    "token_uri": "http://localhost:8180/auth/realms/myrealm/
protocol/openid-connect/token",
    "issuer": "http://localhost:8180/auth/realms/myrealm",
    "userinfo_uri": "http://localhost:8180/auth/realms/myrealm/
protocol/openid-connect/userinfo",
    "redirect_uris": [
      "http://localhost:8080/oidc/callback"
    ]
  }
}
```

> **Note**
> You should change the reference to `CLIENT_SECRET` in the preceding configuration with the secret generated by Keycloak for the **mywebapp** client. For that, go the **mywebapp** client details page in Keycloak and click on the **Credentials** tab. The client secret should be available from the **Secret** field in this tab.

Finally, create an application by creating an `app.py` file with the following content:

```python
from flask import Flask
app = Flask(__name__)
app.secret_key = 'change_me'
app.config['OIDC_CLIENT_SECRETS'] = 'oidc-config.json'
app.config['OIDC_COOKIE_SECURE'] = False
from flask_oidc import OpenIDConnect
oidc = OpenIDConnect(app)


@app.route('/')
@oidc.require_login
def index():
    if oidc.user_loggedin:
        return 'Welcome %s' % oidc.user_getfield('preferred_
username')
    else:
        return 'Not logged in'
```

To start the application, run Flask and configure it to run on port `8080`:

```
$ cd Keycloak-Identity-and-Access-Management-for-Modern-
Applications/ch7/python/frontend
$ flask run -p 8080
```

Your application should start and be available at `http://localhost:8080`. Try to access that URL and log into Keycloak using the credentials for the user we created at the beginning of this chapter.

If the integration is working properly, you should be redirected to Keycloak to authenticate. After providing the user credentials, you should be redirected back to the application, now as an authenticated user.

Creating a Python resource server

The code examples presented here are available from the following GitHub repository:

```
$ cd Keycloak-Identity-and-Access-Management-for-Modern-
Applications/ch7/nodejs/backend
```

To protect the resources in your application, you need to annotate your endpoints with @ oidc.accept_token():

```python
import json
from flask import Flask, g
app = Flask(__name__)
app.secret_key = 'change_me'
app.config['OIDC_CLIENT_SECRETS'] = 'oidc-config.json'
app.config['OIDC_RESOURCE_SERVER_ONLY'] = 'true'
from flask_oidc import OpenIDConnect
oidc = OpenIDConnect(app)


@app.route('/', methods=['POST'])
@oidc.accept_token(True)
def api():
    return json.dumps({'hello': 'Welcome %s' % g.oidc_token_
info['preferred_username']})
```

Create an oidc-config.json file at the root path of your program with some metadata about the endpoints and client information from Keycloak:

```json
{
  "web": {
    "client_id": "mybackend",
    "client_secret": CLIENT_SECRET,
    "auth_uri": "http://localhost:8180/auth/realms/myrealm/
protocol/openid-connect/auth",
    "token_uri": "http://localhost:8180/auth/realms/myrealm/
protocol/openid-connect/token",
    "issuer": "http://localhost:8180/auth/realms/myrealm",
    "token_introspection_uri": "http://localhost:8180/auth/
realms/myrealm/protocol/openid-connect/token/introspect",
    "redirect_uris": [
```

```
        "http://localhost:8080/oidc/callback"
    ]
  }
}
```

> **Note**
>
> You should change the reference to CLIENT_SECRET in the preceding
> configuration with the secret generated by Keycloak for the **mybackend** client.
> For that, go the **mybackend** client details page in Keycloak and click on the
> **Credentials** tab. The client secret should be available from the **Secret** field in
> this tab.

To start the application, run `flask` and configure it to run on port `8080`:

```
$ cd Keycloak-Identity-and-Access-Management-for-Modern-
Applications/ch7/python/backend
$ flask run -p 8080
```

Your application should start and be available at `http://localhost:8080`. To access
the resources at the running application, you will need an access token. To obtain one, use
the following command:

```
$ export access_token=$(\
    curl -X POST http://localhost:8180/auth/realms/myrealm/
protocol/openid-connect/token \
    --user mybackend:CLIENT_SECRET\
    -H 'content-type: application/x-www-form-urlencoded' \
    -d 'username=alice&password=alice&grant_type=password' | jq
--raw-output '.access_token' \
  )
```

> **Note**
>
> You should change the reference to CLIENT_SECRET in the preceding
> command with the secret generated by Keycloak for the **mybackend** client.
> For that, go the **mybackend** client details page in Keycloak and click on the
> **Credentials** tab. The client secret should be available from the **Secret** field in
> this tab.

Once you've run that command, an access token will be saved in an `access_token` environment variable, which means you can now access the application:

```
$ curl -v -X POST -d 'access_token='$access_token \
    -H "Content-Type: application/x-www-form-urlencoded" \
    http://localhost:8080
```

Now, if you try to access the application without a `Bearer` token or use an invalid one, you should get a 401 status code, indicating that your request was forbidden:

```
$ curl -v -X POST \
  http://localhost:8080
```

`@oidc.accept_token()` does not support bearer tokens sent via the Authorization HTTP header, as per RFC 6750 - Bearer Token Usage, but they can be sent as parameters when you're making `GET` and `POST` requests.

This is not in compliance with the standards and is not the best way to send tokens to applications, especially if you're using the `GET` HTTP method.

Flask-OIDC is one of the available options for integrating Python applications with Keycloak. It provides support for protecting applications acting as clients, as well as resource servers.

The fact that bearer tokens require HTTP requests to pass the token via parameters is probably something you want to change. This will help you follow the best practices surrounding bearer token authorization.

The library also supports methods that are specific to integrating with Keycloak, such as checking whether a token is carrying a specific client role.

In this section, you learned about the possibility to integrate Python applications with Keycloak using the Flask-OIDC library. If this library is not part of your technology stack, you can still leverage any other library or framework for the same purpose, as long it is compliant with the OpenID Connect specifications.

In the next section, we are going to look an integration option related to the proxied architectural style, which is useful if none of the options that have been presented so far are enough to address your requirements.

Using a reverse proxy

By running in front of your application, you can use reverse proxies to add additional capabilities to your application. The most common proxies provide support for OpenID Connect where enabling authentication is a matter of changing the proxy configuration.

Whether using a proxy is better than having the integration code and configuration within your application really depends on the use case and, depending on the circumstances, it might be your only option or the option that will save you precious time from implementing your own integration code, even if you have a library available for the technology stack your application is using.

Nowadays, OpenID Connect and OAuth2 support is a mandatory capability for proxies, and you find support for these protocols in most of them, regardless of whether they're open source or proprietary. As an example, two of the most popular proxies, Apache HTTP Server and Nginx, provide the necessary extensions for these protocols.

In this section, we are going to cover how to set up Apache HTTP Server in front of our application so that we can integrate it with Keycloak and authenticate users using mod_auth_oidc. The documentation on how to install it is available at https://github.com/zmartzone/mod_auth_openidc.

Once the module has been installed, we need to configure the server so that we can proxy our application and use the module to make sure users are authenticated through Keycloak:

```
LoadModule auth_openidc_module modules/mod_auth_openidc.so
ServerName localhost


<VirtualHost *:80>
    ProxyPass / http://localhost:8000/
    ProxyPassReverse / http://localhost:8000/


    OIDCCryptoPassphrase CHANGE_ME


    OIDCProviderMetadataURL http://localhost:8180/auth/realms/
myrealm/.well-known/openid-configuration


    OIDCClientID mywebapp
    OIDCClientSecret CLIENT_SECRET
    OIDCRedirectURI http://localhost/callback
```

```
    OIDCCookieDomain localhost
    OIDCCookiePath /
    OIDCCookieSameSite On

    <Location />
        AuthType openid-connect
        Require valid-user
    </Location>
</VirtualHost>
```

> **Note**
>
> You should change the reference to `CLIENT_SECRET` in the preceding configuration with the secret generated by Keycloak for the **mywebapp** client. For that, go the **mywebapp** client details page in Keycloak and click on the **Credentials** tab. The client secret should be available from the **Secret** field in this tab.

Now, let's start the application:

```
$ cd Keycloak-Identity-and-Access-Management-for-Modern-
Applications/ch7/reverse-proxy/app/
$ npm install
$ npm start
```

Your application should start and be available at `http://localhost`. Try to access that URL and log into Keycloak using the credentials for the user we created at the beginning of this chapter.

If the integration is working properly, you should be redirected to Keycloak to authenticate. After providing the user credentials, you should be redirected back to the application, now as an authenticated user.

Try not to implement your own integration

OAuth2 and OpenID Connect are simple protocols, and their simplicity is, in part, due to the effort that's been made to make the protocol easier to implement by client applications. You may feel tempted to write your own code to integrate with Keycloak, but this is usually a bad choice.

You should rely on well-known and widely used libraries, frameworks, or capabilities provided by the platform where your application is deployed. By doing that, you can focus on your business and, most importantly, delegate to people specialized and focused on these standards to keep their implementations always up to date with the latest versions of the specifications, as well as with any fixes for security vulnerabilities.

Also, remember that the more people there are using an implementation, the less likely it is that you will face bugs and security vulnerabilities that can impact not only your application, but also your organization.

Summary

In this chapter, you learned how to integrate Keycloak with different types of applications, depending on the technology stack they are using, as well as the platform they are running. You also learned about the importance of using well-known and established open standards and what that means in terms of interoperability. This means you are free to choose the OpenID Connect client implementation that better serves your needs, while still respecting compliance and keeping your applications up to date with the OAuth2 and OpenID Connect best practices and security fixes.

Finally, you learned why you should avoid implementing your own integration, as well as the things you should consider when you're looking for alternatives, if none of the other options work for you.

In the next chapter, you will learn about the different authorization strategies you can use to protect your application resources.

Questions

1. What is the best way to integrate with Keycloak?

2. Should I always consider using the Keycloak adapters if they fit into my technology stack?

3. How should you secure a native or mobile application with Keycloak?

4. What is the best integration option for cloud-native applications?

Further reading

For more information on the topics that were covered in this chapter, please refer to the following links:

- Certified OpenID Connect Implementations: `https://openid.net/developers/certified`
- OAuth 2.0 for Browser-Based Apps: `https://tools.ietf.org/html/draft-ietf-oauth-browser-based-apps-07`
- OAuth 2.0 Security Best Current Practice: `https://tools.ietf.org/html/draft-ietf-oauth-security-topics-16`
- Keycloak Quickstarts: `https://github.com/keycloak/keycloak-quickstarts`
- Securing Applications and Services Guide: `https://www.keycloak.org/docs/latest/securing_apps`

8
Authorization Strategies

In the previous chapter, you learned about the options for integrating with Keycloak using different programming languages, frameworks, and libraries. You learned how to obtain tokens from Keycloak and use these tokens to authenticate users.

This chapter will focus on the different authorization strategies you can choose from and how to leverage them to enable authorization to your applications using different access control mechanisms such as **role-based access control (RBAC)**, **group-based access control (GBAC)**, OAuth2 scopes, and **attribute-based access control (ABAC)**, as well as learning how to leverage Keycloak as a centralized authorization server to externalize authorization from your applications. You will also learn about the differences between these options and how to choose the best strategy for you.

By the end of this chapter, you will have a good understanding of how you can leverage Keycloak authorization capabilities and choose the right authorization strategy for your applications.

We will be covering the following topics in this chapter:

- Understanding authorization
- Using RBAC
- Using GBAC

- Using OAuth2 scopes
- Using ABAC
- Using Keycloak as a centralized authorization server

Understanding authorization

Any authorization system will try to help you to answer the question of whether a user can access a resource and perform actions on it.

The answer to this question usually involves questions such as the following:

- Who is the user?
- What data is associated with the user?
- What are the constraints for accessing the resource?

By having the answers to these three questions, we can then decide if access should be granted based on the data associated with the user, and the constraints that govern access to the resource.

As an identity provider, Keycloak issues tokens to your applications. As such, applications should expect authorization data from these tokens. Tokens issued by Keycloak carry information about the user and the context in which the user was authenticated; the context may contain information about the client the user is using or any other information gathered during the authentication process.

The constraints, however, may involve evaluating different types of data, from a single attribute the user has, to a set of one or more roles, or even data associated with the current transaction. By relying on the information carried by tokens, applications can opt for different access control mechanisms, depending on how they interpret the claims within a token when enforcing access to protected resources.

There are two main authorization patterns for implementing and enforcing the access constraints imposed on protected resources. The first, and probably the most common, is to enforce access control at the application level, either declaratively – using some metadata and configuration – or programmatically. On the other hand, applications can also delegate access decisions to an external service and enforce access control based on the decisions taken by this service, a strategy also known as centralized authorization. These two patterns are not mutually exclusive, though, and it is perfectly fine to use both in your applications. We are going to cover that in more detail later when understanding how to use Keycloak as a centralized authorization server.

As we will see in the following sections, Keycloak is very flexible and allows you to exchange any information you might need to protect resources at the application level using different access control mechanisms. It also allows you to choose from different authorization patterns for managing and enforcing access constraints.

In the next sections, we will be looking at how Keycloak can be used to enable different authorization strategies for your applications.

Using RBAC

Probably one of the most-used access control mechanisms, **RBAC** allows you to protect resources depending on whether the user is granted a **role**. As you learned in previous chapters, Keycloak has built-in support for managing roles, as well as for propagating those roles to your applications using tokens.

Roles usually represent a role a user has in either your organization or in the context of your application. As an example, users can be granted an **administrator** role to indicate they act as someone allowed to access and perform actions on any resource in your application. Or, they can be granted a **people-manager** role to indicate that they act as someone allowed to access and perform actions on resources related to their subordinates.

As you learned from previous chapters, Keycloak has two categories of roles: realm and client roles. Roles defined at the realm level are called **realm roles**. These roles usually represent the user's role within an organization, regardless of the different clients that co-exist in a realm.

On the other hand, **client roles** are specific to a client, and their meaning depends on the semantics used by the client.

The decision of when to define a role as a realm or client role depends on the scope the role has. If it spans multiple clients in a realm while keeping the same meaning, then a realm role makes sense. Otherwise, if only a specific client is supposed to interpret the role, having it as a client role makes more sense.

When using roles, you should also avoid role explosion. In other words, too many roles in your system makes things hard to manage. One way to avoid this is to create roles very carefully, having in mind the scope they are related to (realm- or client-wide) and the granularity of the permissions associated with them in your applications. The more fine-grained the scope of a role is, the more roles you will have in your system. As a rule of thumb, do not use roles for fine-grained authorization in your system. They are just not meant for that.

In Keycloak, you can grant roles to groups. That is a powerful capability where members of a group are automatically granted roles for the group they belong to. By leveraging this capability, you should be able to overcome some of the role management issues by avoiding granting privileges individually to many users.

Keycloak also provides the concept of **composite roles**, a special type of role that chains other roles, where a user granted a composite role is automatically granted any role in this chain (a regular role or even another composite role). Although it is a powerful and unique feature that Keycloak has, you should use it carefully to avoid performance issues – such as when chaining multiple composite roles – as well as manageability issues due to the proliferation of roles in your system and the granularity of the permissions associated with them. As a recommendation, if you need to grant multiple roles to your users, you should consider using groups and assigning roles to these groups. This is a more natural permission model than using composite roles.

The way you model your system roles also has an impact on the size of tokens issued by Keycloak. Ideally, tokens should contain the minimum set of roles the client needs to authorize their users either locally or when accessing another service that consumes these tokens.

> **Tip**
> Keep in mind that the more roles your system has, the more complex it will become to maintain and manage.

In this topic, you learned about the main concepts when using RBAC in Keycloak. You also learned about some recommendations and considerations when using roles that may impact your applications in terms of maintainability and performance.

In the next topic, we will be looking at how Keycloak helps you to implement GBAC and recommendations when using it in applications.

Using GBAC

Keycloak allows you to manage groups for your realms, where users are put into groups to represent their relationship with a specific business unit in your organization (mapping your organization tree) or just group users together according to their role in your applications, as when you want to have a specific group for users that can perform administrative operations.

Usually, groups and roles are usually used interchangeably, and this causes some confusion when defining a permission model. In Keycloak, there is a clear separation between these two concepts where, different than roles, groups are meant to organize your users and to grant permissions according to the roles associated with a group.

By allowing assigning roles to groups, Keycloak makes it a lot easier to manage roles for multiple users without forcing you to grant and revoke roles for each individual user in your realm.

Groups in Keycloak are hierarchical, and when tokens are issued, you can traverse the hierarchy by looking at the path of the group. For instance, suppose you have a **human resource** group. As a child of this group, you have a **manager** group. When Keycloak is including information about groups into tokens, you should expect this information in the following format: /human resource/manager. This information should be available for every token issued by the server where the subject (the user) is a member of the group.

Different from roles, group information is not automatically included in tokens. For that, you should associate a specific protocol mapper with your client (or a client scope with the same mapper).

In the next sections, you will learn how to include group information about users into tokens.

Mapping group membership into tokens

Different from roles, there is no default protocol mapper that automatically includes group information in tokens. To do that, we need to create a protocol mapper to your client.

> **Tip**
> Alternatively, you can also create a client scope and assign it to any client in your realm.

Let's start by creating the myclient client:

- **Client ID**: myclient

Now, create a user in Keycloak:

- **Username**: alice

Navigate to the **myclient** settings and click on the **Mappers** tab. In this tab, click on the **Create** button to create a new mapper:

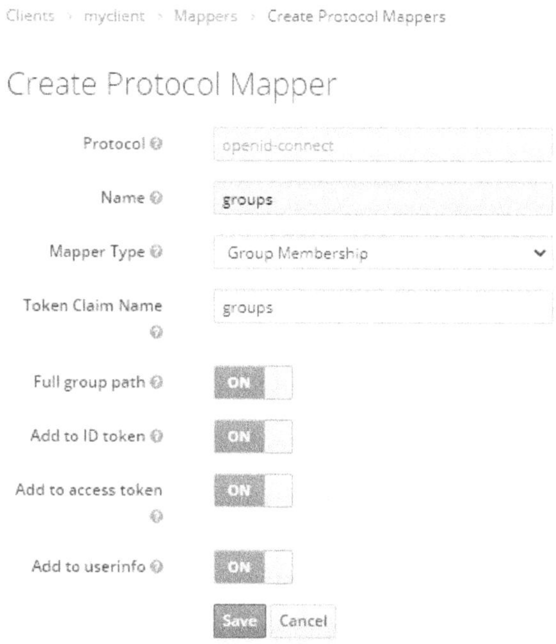

Figure 8.1 – Creating a group membership protocol mapper

On this page, create a new mapper with the following information:

- **Name**: groups
- **Mapper Type**: Group Membership
- **Token Claim Name**: groups

Now, click on the **Save** button to create the mapper. You should see the following:

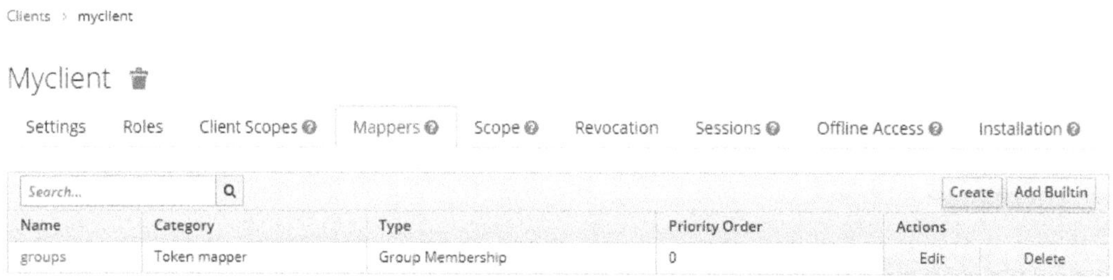

Figure 8.2 – Listing the mappers associated with a client

Let's now create a group for this user. For that, click on the **Groups** link in the left-hand menu:

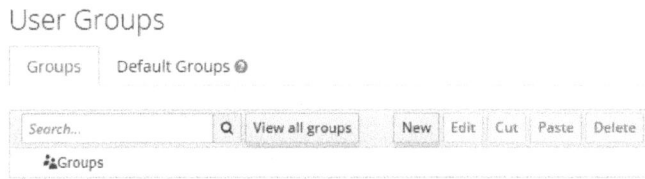

Figure 8.3 – Listing groups

To create a new group, click on the **New** button:

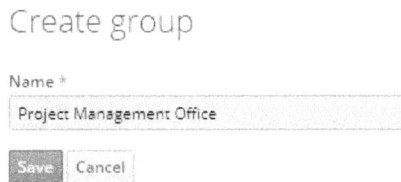

Figure 8.4 – Creating a new group

Let's create a group named **Project Management Office**. Type this name in the **Name** field and then click on the **Save** button.

Now, let's add the **alice** user as a member of this group. For that, navigate to the **alice** user details page and click on the **Groups** tab:

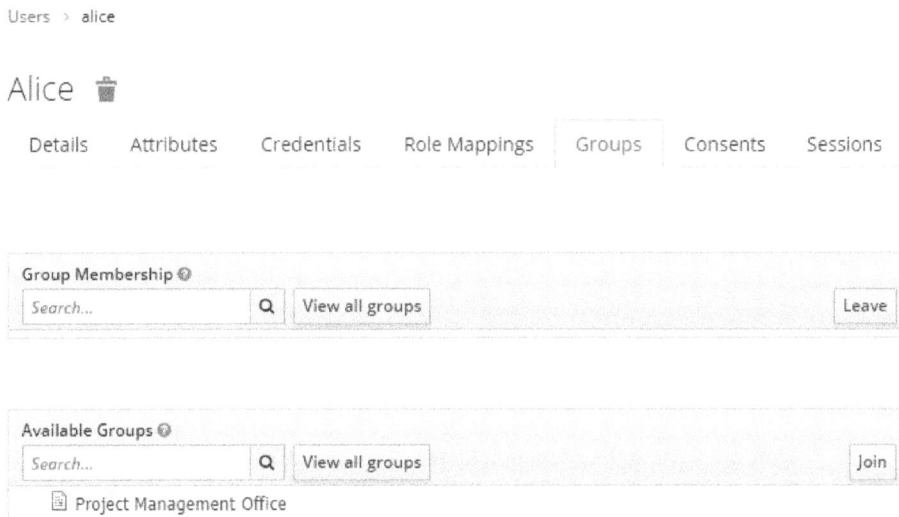

Figure 8.5 – Managing group membership for a user

From this page, you can look at the group hierarchy created for a realm and select the group that the user should be a member of. Let's choose the **Project Management Office** group from the **Available Groups** list and then click on the **Join** button to associate the user as a member of the group:

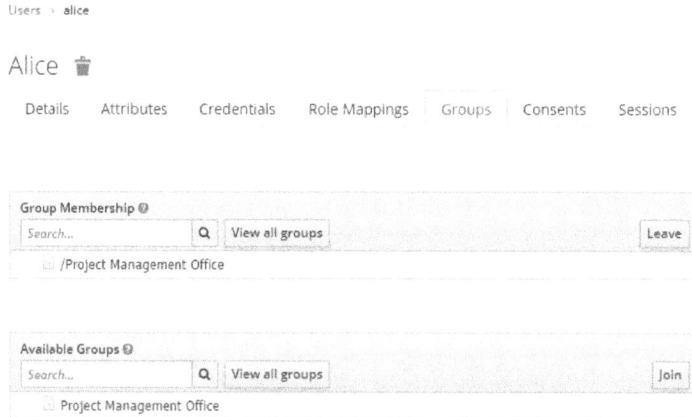

Figure 8.6 – Assigning users as a member of a group

The **alice** user is now a member of **Project Management Office**.

Let's now go back to the **myclient** details page and use the evaluation tool to see how group information will be added to tokens. Click on the **Client Scopes** tab. In this tab, click on the **Evaluate** sub-tab:

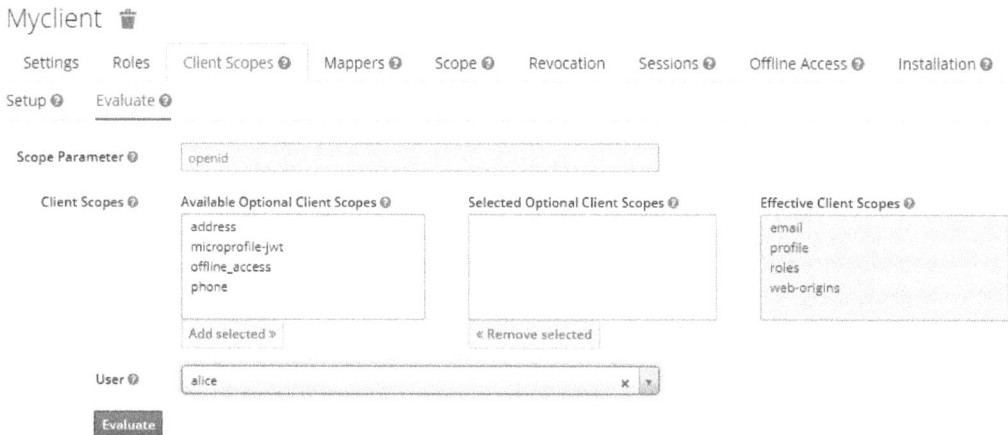

Figure 8.7 – Using the evaluation tool to check group information

Search for the `alice` user in the **User** field and then click **Evaluate**; once done, you should see the following:

Name	Parent Client Scope	Category	Type	Priority Order
allowed web origins	web-origins	Token mapper	Allowed Web Origins	0
full name	profile	Token mapper	User's full name	0
username	profile	Token mapper	User Property	0
updated at	profile	Token mapper	User Attribute	0
gender	profile	Token mapper	User Attribute	0
given name	profile	Token mapper	User Property	0
family name	profile	Token mapper	User Property	0
zoneinfo	profile	Token mapper	User Attribute	0

Effective Protocol Mappers ❷   Effective Role Scope Mappings ❷   Generated Access Token ❷

Figure 8.8 – Evaluation result

Click on the **Generated Access Token** tab at the bottom of the page to see if the generated token includes information about the groups that the user belongs to:

```
{
    ...
    "groups": [
       "/Project Management Office"
    ],
    ...
}
```

As you can see, the generated token now includes a `groups` claim with a list of groups the user is a member of. In this case, the user `alice` is a member of a single `Project Management Office` group.

In this section, you learned how to manage groups and how to make a user a member of a group. You also learned how to use a protocol mapper to include group information into tokens so that your application can use this information to enforce access control using the groups that a user belongs to.

In the next section, we are going to look at how your applications can use custom claims to enforce access to their resources.

Using OAuth2 scopes

At its core, Keycloak is an OAuth2 authorization server. In pure OAuth2, there are two main types of applications: clients and resource servers.

As you learned from previous chapters about OAuth2, access tokens are issued to clients so that they can act on behalf of a user, where these tokens are limited to a set of scopes based on the user consent.

On the other hand, resource servers are the consumers of access tokens, which they need to introspect to decide whether the client can access a protected resource on the resource server accordingly to the scopes granted by the user.

As you can see, authorization using OAuth2 scopes is solely based on user consent. It is the best strategy when you want third parties integrating with your APIs so that you delegate to your users the decision on whether a third-party application can access their resources. In this strategy, the main point is to protect user information rather than regular resources at the resource server. There is a fundamental difference between using OAuth2 scopes and the other authorization strategies you learned so far, mainly in terms of the entity you are protecting your system from. By using OAuth2 scopes, you are protecting your system from clients, whereas when using RBAC, for instance, you are protecting your system from users. In a nutshell, you are basically checking whether a client is allowed to perform some action or access a resource on behalf of the user, the usual delegation use case solved by OAuth2.

By default, clients in Keycloak are configured to not ask for user consent. The reason for that is that Keycloak is usually used in enterprise use cases. Different from the delegation use case, there is no need for user consent because clients are within the enterprise boundaries and the resources they need to access do not depend on any consent from users but on the permissions granted to them by a system administrator. Here, clients are more interested in authenticating users, where the scope of access is defined according to the roles, groups, or even specific attributes associated with a user.

In this topic, you learned about the concepts of authorizing access using OAuth2 scopes. You also learned that this authorization strategy is more suitable for allowing access from third parties to information about your users through your APIs.

In the next topic, we will look at how to authorize access based on claims mapped to tokens.

Using ABAC

When users authenticate through Keycloak, tokens issued by the server contain important information about the authentication context. Tokens contain information about the authenticated user and the client to which tokens were issued, as well as any other information that can be gathered during the authentication process. With that in mind, any information carried by a token can be used to authorize access to your applications. They are just claims mapped to tokens.

ABAC involves using the different attributes associated with an identity (represented by a token), as well as information about the authentication context, to enforce access to resources. It is probably the most flexible access control mechanism you can choose, with natural support for fine-grained authorization. Together with token-based authorization, applications using Keycloak can easily enable ABAC to protect their resources.

Token-based authorization is based on introspecting tokens and using the information there to decide whether access should be granted. This information is represented as a set of attributes, or claims, where their values can be used to enforce access.

Let's take as an example how roles are used to enforce access in your application. As you learned from the previous chapters and topics, roles are mapped to tokens using a specific set of claims. To enforce access using roles, your application only needs to use these claims to calculate what roles were granted to the user and then decide whether access should be granted to a particular resource.

This is no different from any other claim within a token, where your applications can use any claim and use it to enforce access. For each client, you can tailor what claims and assertions are stored in tokens. For that, Keycloak provides a functionality called protocol mappers. For more details, check out the Keycloak documentation at `https://www.keycloak.org/docs/latest/server_admin/#_protocol-mappers`.

In this topic, you learned about how to leverage claims mapped into tokens to perform ABAC. You also learned that Keycloak allows you to map any information you want to tokens so that they can be used to enforce access at the application level. Although ABAC is flexible enough to support multiple access control mechanisms, it is not easy to implement and manage.

In the next topic, we are going to look at how to leverage ABAC using Keycloak as a centralized authorization server.

Using Keycloak as a centralized authorization server

So far, you have been presented with authorization strategies that rely on a specific access control mechanism. Except for ABAC, these strategies rely on a specific set of data about the user to enforce access in applications. In addition to that, those strategies are tightly coupled with your applications, where changes to your security requirements would require changes in your application code.

As an example, suppose you have the following pseudo-code in your application:

```
If (User.hasRole("manager") {
    // can access the protected resource
}
```

In the preceding code, we have a quite simple check using RBAC where only users granted a manager role can access a protected resource. What would happen if your requirements changed and you also needed to give access to that same resource to a specific user? Or even grant access to that resource for users granted some other role? Or perhaps leverage ABAC to look at the different information about the context where a resource is being accessed?

At the very least, you would need to change your code and re-deploy your application, not to mention going through your continuous integration and delivery process to make sure the change is ready for production.

Centralized authorization allows you to externalize access management and decisions from your applications using an external authorization service. It allows you to use multiple access control mechanisms without coupling your application to them, and enforce access using the same semantics used by your applications to refer to the different resources that should be protected.

Let's take a look at the following code, which provides the same access check as the previous example:

```
If (User.canAccess("Manager Resource") {
    // can access the protected resource
}
```

As you can see from the preceding code snippet, there is no reference to a specific access control mechanism; access control is based on the resource you are protecting, and your application is only concerned with the permissions granted by an external authorization service. Changes to how `Manager Resource` can be accessed should not impact your application code, but changing the policies that govern access to that resource through the authorization service should.

Keycloak can act as a centralized authorization service through a functionality called **Authorization Services**. This functionality is based on a set of policies representing different access control mechanisms that you associate with the resources you want to protect. All this is managed through the Keycloak administration console and REST API.

The Keycloak Authorization Services functionality leverages ABAC to enable fine-grained authorization to your applications. By default, a set of policies representing different access control mechanisms are provided out of the box, with the possibility to aggregate these policies to easily support multiple authorization strategies when protecting resources. The Keycloak Authorization Services functionality also allows you to control access to specific actions and attributes associated with the resources you are protecting.

A common issue when using a centralized authorization server is the need for additional round trips to obtain access decisions. By leveraging token-based authorization, the Keycloak Authorization Services functionality allows you to overcome this issue by issuing tokens with all the permissions granted by the server, so that applications consuming these tokens do not need to perform additional network calls but introspect the token locally. It also supports incremental authorization, where tokens are issued a narrow set of permissions with the possibility to obtain new permissions as needed.

For more details about Keycloak Authorization Services, check the documentation at `https://www.keycloak.org/docs/latest/authorization_services/`.

In this section, you learned about centralized authorization and that Keycloak Authorization Services can be used to implement this form of authorization. You also learned that together with token-based authorization, Keycloak Authorization Services helps applications to enable fine-grained authorization to applications.

Summary

In this chapter, you learned about the different strategies you can choose from to authorize access to protected resources in your applications. By leveraging token-based authorization, applications should be able to introspect tokens – either locally or through the introspection endpoint – and use their claims to support different access control mechanisms such as RBAC, GBAC, and ABAC, or use the scopes granted by users to the client application acting on their behalf. You also learned that Keycloak can be used as a centralized authorization service to decouple authorization from applications, where access decisions are taken by Keycloak based on the resources and policies managed through the server.

In the next chapter, we are going to look at the main steps for running Keycloak in production.

Questions

1. How do you prevent tokens from becoming too big while still providing the necessary data to enforce access to resources at the application level?

2. How do you decide whether a role should be a realm or client role?

3. Is it possible to enforce access based on information gathered during authentication?

4. Is it possible to change how Keycloak maps roles into tokens?

5. Are those strategies mutually exclusive?

Further reading

For more information on the topics covered in this chapter, refer to the following links:

- Keycloak roles: `https://www.keycloak.org/docs/latest/server_admin/#roles`

- Keycloak groups: `https://www.keycloak.org/docs/latest/server_admin/#groups`

- Keycloak protocol mappers: `https://www.keycloak.org/docs/latest/server_admin/#_protocol-mappers`

- Keycloak client scopes: `https://www.keycloak.org/docs/latest/server_admin/#_client_scopes`

- Keycloak Authorization Services: `https://www.keycloak.org/docs/latest/authorization_services`

Section 3: Configuring and Managing Keycloak

In this section, you will understand how to configure Keycloak, making it ready for production use. A range of common use cases are covered, along with an explanation of how to achieve them with Keycloak.

This section comprises the following chapters:

9
Configuring Keycloak for Production

So far, you have learned how to use Keycloak, the key concepts, and how to start using it to secure your applications. In this chapter, you will be creating a pre-production Keycloak cluster to understand all the different aspects and steps when configuring it for production, such as if you were deploying it in bare metal or in a VM.

You should consider the same configuration aspects when running Keycloak as a container. Although, in this case, most of the configuration is done transparently by the container image, the concepts from this chapter are still useful to understand how containers are configured and what you should consider when deploying Keycloak on OpenShift or Kubernetes.

In the next sections, you will be introduced to each of these aspects and how they fit into a real production deployment of Keycloak. At the end of this chapter, you should be able to apply the same steps and recommendations provided herein to deploy Keycloak into your own production environment using a high-availability profile, and considering different non-functional aspects such as availability, performance, and failover.

For that, we will be covering the following topics:

- Setting the hostname for Keycloak
- Enabling TLS
- Configuring a database
- Enabling clustering
- Configuring a reverse proxy
- Testing your environment

Technical requirements

For this chapter, you need to have a local copy of the GitHub repository associated with the book. If you have Git installed, you can clone the repository by running this command in a terminal:

```
$ cd $KC_HOME
$ git clone https://github.com/PacktPublishing/Keycloak-
Identity-and-Access-Management-for-Modern-Applications.git
```

Alternatively, you can download a ZIP of the repository from the following URL:

```
https://github.com/PacktPublishing/Keycloak-Identity-and-
Access-Management-for-Modern-Applications/archive/master.zip
```

> **Note**
> Make sure to either clone or extract the repository into the Keycloak distribution directory.

To configure a reverse proxy, we are going to use a local domain name other than `localhost`. This domain name will be used as the public domain name where Keycloak is exposed for your users and applications.

If you are using Linux, you should be able to do that by changing your `/etc/hosts` file and including the following line:

```
127.0.0.1 mykeycloak
```

We are also going to need to run some CLI scripts to configure the server. For that, we are going to run the `jboss-cli.sh` script. This script is located in the `bin` directory of the Keycloak installation and can be executed as follows:

```
$ cd $KC_HOME
$ bin/jboss-cli.sh
```

Lastly, we are going to use HAProxy as a reverse proxy in front of multiple Keycloak instances. If you are using CentOS or Fedora Linux, you should be able to install HAProxy as follows:

```
$ sudo dnf -y install haproxy
```

Check out the following link to see the Code in Action video:

https://bit.ly/3b5W1gM

Setting the hostname for Keycloak

Keycloak exposes different endpoints to talk with applications as well as to allow managing the server itself. These endpoints can be categorized into three main groups:

- Frontend
- Backend
- Administration

The base URL for each group has an important impact on how tokens are issued and validated, on how links are created for actions that require the user to be redirected to Keycloak (for example, when resetting passwords through email links), and, most importantly, how applications will discover these endpoints when fetching the OpenID Connect Discovery document from `/auth/realms/{realm-name}/.well-known/openid-configuration`.

In the next topics, we will be looking into each of these groups, how to define a base URL for each one, and the impact it has on users and applications using Keycloak.

Setting the frontend URL

The **frontend URL** is used to infer the URL used by users and applications to access Keycloak, where the main goal is to logically group all instances of Keycloak in a cluster under a single domain and issuer using a public domain name.

Examples of endpoints in the frontend group include the following:

- An authorization endpoint
- A logout endpoint and others related to session management

By default, Keycloak infers the frontend URL from incoming requests. For example, if you have two Keycloak instances, each one listening on `http://10.0.0.5/auth` and `http://10.0.0.6/auth`, Keycloak is going to issue tokens and create links for actions depending on the URL of the instance that is processing the request.

There are several reasons why this default behavior does not work in a production environment.

The most important one is related to the *issuer* claim in tokens and documents issued by Keycloak. The different instances should be grouped under a single issuer name, otherwise, users and clients will not be able to use them interchangeably because tokens and cookies set by Keycloak will be only valid on the instance where they were created.

Another important aspect is that instances are usually running in a private network. Without setting the frontend URL to match the public domain where Keycloak is exposed, links that redirect users back to Keycloak will be broken, and clients might not be able to make requests based on the endpoints exposed through the OpenID discovery document.

Last but not least, without a frontend URL set, all the benefits you will get from a reverse proxy and clustering are lost.

The expected behavior, however, is that regardless of the node processing the request, the base URL should be the same and aligned with the public domain name where Keycloak is being exposed. By doing that, instances are going to work as if they were one so that users and applications can benefit from all the improvements we will cover later to the general availability, performance, scalability, and failover aspects of Keycloak.

Let's set a frontend URL by running the following CLI script available from the GitHub repository of the book at `Keycloak-Identity-and-Access-Management-for-Modern-Applications/ch9/configure-hostname.cli`:

```
embed-server --server-config=standalone-ha.xml --std-
out=discard
/subsystem=keycloak-server/spi=hostname/provider=default:write-
attribute(name=properties.frontendUrl,value=https://mykeycloak/
auth)
stop-embedded-server
```

To run the script execute the following command:

```
$ cd $KC_HOME
$ bin/jboss-cli.sh --file=./Keycloak-Identity-and-Access-
Management-for-Modern-Applications/ch9/configure-hostname.cli
```

By setting the `frontendUrl` property, as shown previously, you are explicitly saying that any Keycloak instance should advertise its endpoints and issue tokens using the `https://mykeycloak/auth` base URL.

In this section, you learned that setting `frontendUrl` allows you to define the base URL where Keycloak is publicly accessible. You also learned that setting this configuration is crucial to group all instances of Keycloak under a single and logical domain and issuer.

In the next topic, we will be looking at how to configure the URL for backend endpoints.

Setting the backend URL

The backend endpoints are those related to direct communication between Keycloak and applications.

Examples of endpoints in the backend group include the following:

- Token introspection
- User info
- Token endpoint
- JWKS

By default, the backend base URL is also calculated based on the request URL. Usually, you want this URL to be based on a public domain name, so that applications can reach Keycloak from outside its internal network. For that, we configure Keycloak to use the frontend URL as the base URL for backend endpoints.

If you look at the `Keycloak-Identity-and-Access-Management-for-Modern-Applications/ch9/configure-hostname.cli` file, you should see the following configuration:

```
/subsystem=keycloak-server/spi=hostname/provider=default:write-
attribute(name=properties.forceBackendUrlToFrontendUrl,
value=true)
```

When the `forceBackendUrlToFrontendUrl` property is set, Keycloak will advertise backend endpoints using whatever you defined as a frontend URL, thus giving applications an accessible URL and not something else based on the internal hostname used by Keycloak.

In this topic, you learned how to configure the base URL for backend endpoints and how they influence applications when they need to talk directly to Keycloak using the backend endpoints.

In the next topic, you will learn how to set the base URL for the administration endpoints.

Setting the admin URL

You usually do not want to make the Keycloak Administration Console publicly available. For that, you can set the `adminUrl` property to force Keycloak to use a specific, private URL:

```
/subsystem=keycloak-server/spi=hostname/provider=default:write-
attribute(name=properties.adminUrl, value=https://
myprivatekeycloak/auth)
```

By setting the `adminUrl` property, any URL used by the Admin Console will be based on the value you provided. That said, links and static resources used to render the console will only be accessible using the URL you defined.

Although it makes it difficult to access the console from a network that cannot resolve the domain name or reach the server, you still want to enforce specific rules in your reverse proxy so that the `/auth/admin` path is fully protected.

In the next topic, we will be looking at how to enable TLS so that Keycloak is only accessible through a secure channel.

Enabling TLS

Any request to and from Keycloak should be done through a secure channel. For that, you must enable HTTP over TLS, also known as HTTPS. In a nutshell, you should never expose Keycloak endpoints through HTTP.

Keycloak exchanges sensitive data all the time with user agents and applications. Enabling HTTPS is crucial to prevent several forms of attacks, as well as to benefit from different forms of authentication that rely on a TLS session established with the server.

> **Tip**
> The current best practice is to select a key size of at least 2,048 bits. In terms of protocol, Keycloak advertises the most secure protocols, such as TLS v1.2 and TLS v1.3. You should also be able to restrict the list of protocols to only advertise those you want.

The first step to enable HTTPS is to create or reuse a Java KeyStore where the server's private key and certificates are stored. If you are planning to deploy Keycloak in production, you probably have all the key material to enable TLS, as well as your certificates signed by a trusted **Certificate Authority (CA)**.

The next step is to configure the HTTPS listener to use the key material from your Java KeyStore. For that, look at the following script available from the GitHub repository of the book at `Keycloak-Identity-and-Access-Management-for-Modern-Applications/ch9/configure-https.cli`:

```
embed-server --server-config=standalone-ha.xml --std-
out=discard
```

```
/subsystem=elytron/key-store=kcKeyStore:add(path=${jboss.
home.dir}/Keycloak-Identity-and-Access-Management-for-Modern-
Applications/ch9/mykeycloak.keystore,type=JKS,credential-
reference={clear-text=password})
```

```
/subsystem=elytron/key-manager=kcKeyManager:add(key-
store=kcKeyStore,credential-reference={clear-text=password})
```

```
/subsystem=elytron/server-ssl-context=kcSSLContext:add(key-
manager=kcKeyManager)
```

```
batch
```

```
/subsystem=undertow/server=default-server/https-
listener=https:undefine-attribute(name=security-realm)
```

```
/subsystem=undertow/server=default-server/
https-listener=https:write-attribute(name=ssl-
context,value=kcSSLContext)
```

```
run-batch
```

```
stop-embedded-server
```

In this file, we are using a Java KeyStore available from the GitHub repository of the book at `$KC_HOME/Keycloak-Identity-and-Access-Management-for-Modern-Applications/ch9/mykeycloak.keystore`. This KeyStore was built for example purposes using a self-signed certificate and you should not use it in production. Instead, you should replace it with a KeyStore using your own private key and certificate.

Then run the `jboss-cli.sh` tool to apply the configuration:

```
$ cd $KC_HOME
$ bin/jboss-cli.sh --file=./Keycloak-Identity-and-Access-
Management-for-Modern-Applications/ch9/configure-https.cli
```

Now, let's start Keycloak by running the following command:

```
$ cd $KC_HOME
bin/standalone.sh -c standalone-ha.xml
```

If everything is OK, you should be able to access Keycloak at `https://localhost:8443`, and you should be able to see that the certificate being used comes from your Java KeyStore.

In addition to enabling HTTPS, Keycloak also allows you to define TLS constraints on a per-realm basis. Basically, for each realm, you can set whether Keycloak should require HTTPS for incoming requests:

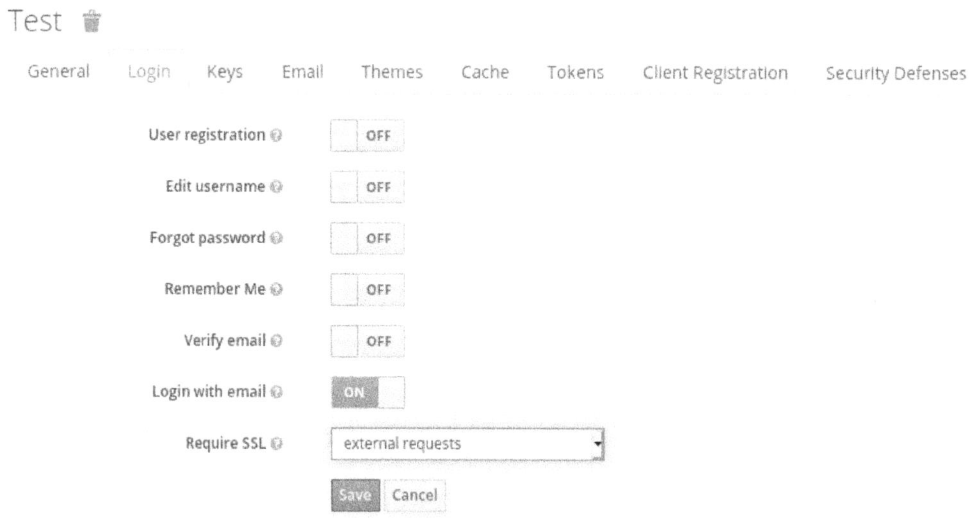

Test 🗑

| General | Login | Keys | Email | Themes | Cache | Tokens | Client Registration | Security Defenses |

User registration ⓘ   OFF

Edit username ⓘ   OFF

Forgot password ⓘ   OFF

Remember Me ⓘ   OFF

Verify email ⓘ   OFF

Login with email ⓘ   ON

Require SSL ⓘ   external requests ▾

Save   Cancel

Figure 9.1 – Enforcing HTTPS on a per-realm basis

By default, Keycloak is going to enforce TLS for any **external requests**. That means clients using the public network can only access Keycloak through HTTPS.

Ideally, you should set the **Require SSL** setting to **all requests,** so that any request to Keycloak is guaranteed to be using a secure protocol.

In this topic, you learned how to enable HTTPS and the importance of doing so. You also learned that Keycloak allows you to define HTTPS constraints on a per-realm basis.

In the next topic, we will be looking at how to configure a production-grade database.

Configuring a database

Keycloak relies on a single database to store all its data. Even when running multiple instances of Keycloak, all of them will be talking to the same database. A database is crucial for the overall performance, availability, scalability, reliability, and integrity of Keycloak. Although Keycloak provides a cache layer to avoid database hits as much as possible, a good database will help to make the system behave better when data needs to be loaded from the database.

By default, Keycloak is configured with a very simple H2 database that should not be used in production, by any means. Instead, you should configure a more robust database such as the following:

- MariaDB 10.1.19
- MariaDB Galera 10.1.19
- MySQL 8.0
- Oracle 19c RAC
- Microsoft SQL Server 2017
- PostgreSQL 11.5

The preceding list is the official list of supported databases and their versions.

> **Note**
> At the time this book was written, the Keycloak version was 13.0.0. The list of supported databases might change in future versions.

In this topic, you are going to configure a PostgreSQL database. The same steps should work for any other database you choose.

To configure a database, a few steps are needed:

- Installing a module on the Keycloak server with the **Java Database Connectivity (JDBC)** driver for the database

- Configuring the JDBC driver so that it can be used by Keycloak

- Configuring Keycloak to connect to the database using a valid URL, username, and password

We are going to perform all the preceding steps using the following script available from the GitHub repository of the book at `Keycloak-Identity-and-Access-Management-for-Modern-Applications/ch9/configure-database.cli`:

```
embed-server --server-config=standalone-ha.xml --std-
out=discard
module add --name=org.postgres --resources=<PATH_TO_JDBC_
DRIVER_JAR> --dependencies=javax.api,javax.transaction.api
/subsystem=datasources/jdbc-driver=postgres:add(driver-
name=postgres, driver-module-name=org.postgres, xa-datasource-
class=org.postgresql.xa.PGXADataSource)
/subsystem=datasources/data-source=KeycloakDS:write-
attribute(name=connection-url,value=<JDBC_URL>)
/subsystem=datasources/data-source=KeycloakDS:write-
attribute(name=driver-name, value=postgres)
/subsystem=datasources/data-source=KeycloakDS:write-
attribute(name=user-name, value=<USERNAME>)
/subsystem=datasources/data-source=KeycloakDS:write-attribute(n
ame=password,value=<PASSWORD>)
stop-embedded-server
```

In this file, you should replace the following references with their real values:

- `PATH_TO_JDBC_DRIVER_JAR` should be replaced with the absolute path where the JDBC driver JAR file is located.

- `JDBC_URL` should be replaced with the URL that should be used to connect to the database. For instance, `jdbc:postgresql://mypostgresql/keycloak`.

- `USERNAME` should be replaced with the username that will be used to connect to the database.

- `PASSWORD` should be replaced with the password of the user connecting to the database.

Then run the `jboss-cli.sh` tool to apply the configuration:

```
$ cd $KC_HOME
$ bin/jboss-cli.sh --file=./Keycloak-Identity-and-Access-
Management-for-Modern-Applications/ch9/configure-database.cli
```

If everything is OK, the next time you start the server you should connect to the database you have configured.

In addition to these basic settings to connect to an external database, there are other settings you should consider before going to production. Probably one of the most important ones, the size of the connection pool should be sized according to the load you expect in your system, and how many concurrent requests should be allowed at a given point in time.

By default, the pool is configured with a max of 20 connections. This value should be enough for most deployments, but if you are facing errors in logs due to connections not available in the pool when under an unexpected load, you may change the pool size by running the following CLI command:

```
/subsystem=datasources/data-source=KeycloakDS:write-
attribute(name=max-pool-size, value=30)
/subsystem=datasources/data-source=KeycloakDS:write-
attribute(name=min-pool-size, value=30)
```

In the preceding example, we are increasing the pool size to a maximum (`max-pool-size`) of 30 connections. We are also defining the minimum size (`min-pool-size`) with the same value. The reason for that is that creating new connections is expensive and keeping a minimum value of 30 connections helps to make sure connections are always available during the server's lifetime.

In this section, you learned about the basic steps to configure a production-grade database in Keycloak. You also learned about the different databases you can use based on the list of supported databases.

In the next section, you will learn about how to configure Keycloak for high availability, starting with the necessary configuration to configure a reverse proxy or load balancer.

Enabling clustering

Most of the time, you will be running a Keycloak cluster when going for production. To respect some key non-functional aspects, as well as the **Service-Level Agreements** (**SLAs**) defined for your services, enabling clustering is crucial.

In terms of availability, clustering allows you to run multiple Keycloak instances, possibly in different availability zones, so that uptime is not impacted if nodes go down.

From a scalability perspective, clustering allows you to scale your nodes up and down according to the load on your system, helping to keep a consistent response time and throughput.

In terms of failover, a cluster helps you to survive failures when nodes are failing, therefore preventing data loss (mainly that kept in caches) as well as avoiding impacts on general availability.

Keycloak is designed for high availability, where, in addition to the persistent data kept in the database, it also uses a cache layer to replicate and keep state in-memory for fast data access. This cache layer is built on top of **Infinispan**, a high-performance key-value in-memory data store.

To enable clustering and full high availability, you should do the following:

- Run the server using a high-availability configuration profile.
- Make sure the reverse proxy is configured to distribute load across the different instances.

Let's start by understanding the different configuration profiles that Keycloak provides. Consider that you run the server as follows:

```
$ cd $KC_HOME
$ bin/standalone.sh
```

Keycloak is going to run using a specific configuration profile defined in the $KC_HOME/standalone/conf/standalone.xml file. The standalone.xml file is a configuration profile that is targeted for running a single Keycloak instance. Useful for testing and development purposes, but not for production.

On the other hand, there is an additional configuration profile defined in the $KC_HOME/standalone/conf/standalone-ha.xml file. This file is targeted for running Keycloak for high availability, where clustering is enabled by default.

To run multiple Keycloak instances and build a cluster, you basically need to run the server as follows:

```
$ cd $KC_HOME
$ bin/standalone.sh -c standalone-ha.xml -Djboss.node.name=kc1
```

> **Note**
>
> Note that we are also setting the `jboss.node.name` system property. This property sets the name of the instance in the cluster and it must be unique across all instances. If not set, the name will be inferred from the host where the instance is running. As we are going to run multiple instances within the same host, we must set this property for each instance.

This command will start the first instance in our cluster. The server will be listening on the default ports and you should be able to access it at `http://localhost:8443`.

Let's now start a second instance by specifying a different port offset using the `jboss.socket.binding.port-offset` system property. This property is going to allow us to run the second instance within the same host without conflicting with the first instance that is listening on the default ports. This is achieved by increasing by 100 the number of each port used by Keycloak so that instead of listening on the default HTTPS `8443` port, the server will be available at `http://localhost:8543/auth`:

```
$ cd $KC_HOME
$ bin/standalone.sh -Djboss.socket.binding.port-offset=100 -c
standalone-ha.xml -Djboss.node.name=kc2
```

Now, perform the same steps to start the third node as follows:

```
$ cd $KC_HOME
$ bin/standalone.sh -Djboss.socket.binding.port-offset=200 -c
standalone-ha.xml -Djboss.node.name=kc3
```

After executing this last command, you should now have three Keycloak instances running on ports `8443`, `8543`, and `8643`, respectively.

> **Note**
>
> In production, you do not need to use the `jboss.socket.binding.port-offset` system property because instances will run either on different hosts or, if using containers, in separate containers.

Keycloak relies on specific caches for failover where state is shared across the different nodes in the cluster. One important configuration you should consider when enabling clustering is to configure how many replicas you need in your cluster and adjust it according to your failover requirements.

By looking at the `$KC_HOME/standalone/configuration/standalone-ha.xml` file, you should see the following cache definitions:

```xml
<distributed-cache name="sessions" owners="1"/>
<distributed-cache name="authenticationSessions" owners="1"/>
<distributed-cache name="clientSessions" owners="1"/>
<distributed-cache name="actionTokens" owners="2">
    <object-memory size="-1"/>
        <expiration interval="300000" max-idle="-1"/>
</distributed-cache>
```

Depending on your availability and failover requirements, you might want to increase the number of owners – the nodes where state is replicated – to at least 2 so that state is replicated to 2 nodes in the cluster. By increasing the number of owners, Keycloak can survive up to 1 node failure without losing any state.

Let's change the number of owners for each of those caches by running the `configure-caches.cli` script available from the GitHub repository of the book at `$KC_HOME/Keycloak-Identity-and-Access-Management-for-Modern-Applications/ch9/configure-caches.cli`:

```
$ cd $KC_HOME
$ bin/jboss-cli.sh --file=./Keycloak-Identity-and-Access-Management-for-Modern-Applications/ch9/configure-caches.cli
```

> **Tip**
>
> The number of owners has a direct impact on the overall performance of Keycloak in terms of network and CPU. As you add more owners, you should expect additional overhead to replicate state across nodes. You should take this into account when defining the number of owners to balance both performance and failover aspects of your deployment.

Another important characteristic of clustering is how Keycloak caches realms data to avoid unnecessary roundtrips to the database, therefore increasing the overall performance of the server. By looking at the `$KC_HOME/standalone/configuration/standalone-ha.xml` file, you should see the following cache definitions:

```xml
<local-cache name="realms">
    <heap-memory size="10000"/>
</local-cache>
<local-cache name="users">
```

```
    <heap-memory size="10000"/>
  </local-cache>
```

Differently than the previous caches, the **realms** and **users** caches are local caches and their entries are not replicated but only kept in-memory on each node in the cluster. The realms cache is responsible for caching any kind of realm data such as clients, groups, roles, identity providers, and authentication flows. On the other hand, the users cache is responsible for caching any kind of user data such as credentials, attributes, and role and group mappings.

By default, Keycloak defines a maximum size of 10,000 entries for both caches. For most deployments, this limit should be enough to completely avoid roundtrips to the database when caches are hot without allocating too much memory. But depending on how much data you have in Keycloak, you might want to adjust this limit accordingly.

For more details about the cache configuration, look the Server Cache Configuration documentation available at `https://www.keycloak.org/docs/latest/server_installation/#cache-configuration`.

In this topic, you learned about the basic steps to enable clustering, where these instances will communicate with each other to share state and work together as if you were running a single instance. You also learned about the importance of clustering in terms of availability and scalability.

In the next topic, you will learn about the main configuration aspects when setting up a reverse proxy in front of a Keycloak cluster so that users can access your cluster through a public domain name.

Configuring a reverse proxy

When running in production, a reverse proxy is a key component to enable high availability. A reverse proxy provides a single and public access point for the different Keycloak instances, distributing the load across them using a set of policies. These instances are usually running in a private network so that they are only reachable through the proxy.

By distributing the load across instances, a reverse proxy helps you to scale your deployment by adding or removing more instances as needed, as well as helping to survive failures when specific nodes are failing to serve requests.

Keycloak can be used with any reverse proxy implementation so you are free to use whatever you are comfortable with. Examples of widely used reverse proxies are Apache HTTP Server, Nginx, F5, and HAProxy.

Regardless of your preference, there is a set of basic requirements that you should be aware of to use your choice with Keycloak:

- TLS termination and re-encryption
- Load balancing
- Session affinity
- Forwarding headers

Some of these requirements are intrinsic to the concept of a reverse proxy and are supported by the different implementations.

Before moving on to the next topics, make sure to update your HAProxy installation with the haproxy.cfg file available from your local copy of the GitHub repository associated with the book at $KC_HOME/Keycloak-Identity-and-Access-Management-for-Modern-Applications/ch9/haproxy.cfg:

```
$ cd $KC_HOME
$ sudo cp Keycloak-Identity-and-Access-Management-for-Modern-Applications/ch9/haproxy.cfg /etc/haproxy/haproxy.cfg
$ sudo cp Keycloak-Identity-and-Access-Management-for-Modern-Applications/ch9/haproxy.crt.pem /etc/haproxy
```

In the next topics, we will be looking at each of the requirements mentioned herein and how to address them using HAProxy.

Distributing the load across nodes

One of the first things you usually do when configuring a reverse proxy is to configure the backend nodes that are going to serve requests from clients. That is one of the main problems solved by reverse proxies. Despite the implementation you choose, you should be able to configure load balancing so that requests are distributed across these nodes using a specific algorithm for optimal throughput, response time, and failover.

Load balancing does not require any specific configuration on the Keycloak side. But here are some things to keep in mind when configuring it:

- The number of backend nodes should respect the expected load, availability, and failover scenarios.

- There are several algorithms that you can choose from to distribute the load across nodes. You should choose what works best for you after running some load tests to make sure you can achieve the desired goals in terms of response time and throughput.

In our HAProxy configuration, the configuration related to load balancing is the following:

```
balance roundrobin
server kc1 127.0.0.1:8443 check ssl verify none cookie kc1
server kc2 127.0.0.1:8543 check ssl verify none cookie kc2
server kc3 127.0.0.1:8643 check ssl verify none cookie kc3
```

In this configuration, we are defining three Keycloak instances as backend nodes as well as using `roundrobin` to distribute the requests across these nodes. We are also using HAProxy to re-encrypt connections to the backend nodes.

> **Note**
>
> You might want to configure your proxy for TLS termination, in this case the communication with Keycloak does not need to be re-encrypted but in plain text using HTTP. While this might be useful to offload the task of performing TLS encryption from Keycloak and save some CPU, or perhaps for real-time analysis of the traffic to Keycloak, depending on your requirements you might need end-to-end encryption as well as have a different certificate for clients accessing the proxy. Keycloak can work with any TLS configuration you set to your proxy.

In this topic, you learned about the importance of load balancing and how it affects your deployment in terms of performance, availability, and failover.

In the next topic, we will be looking at how to configure your proxy to forward information about clients connecting to Keycloak.

Forwarding client information

When running behind a reverse proxy, Keycloak does not talk directly to the client that originated the request, but rather to the reverse proxy itself. This fact has an important consequence for how Keycloak obtains information about the client, such as the IP address.

To overcome this limitation, reverse proxies should be able to forward specific headers to provide Keycloak information about the client where the request originated from. The main headers Keycloak requires from proxies are the following:

- **X-Forward-For**: A header indicating the address of the client where the request originated from

- **X-Forward-Proto**: A header indicating the protocol (for example, HTTPS) that the client is using to communicate with the proxy

- **Host**: A header indicating the host and port number of the proxy

> **Tip**
>
> Special care should be taken when making sure the proxy is setting all these headers properly, and not just forwarding these headers to Keycloak if they are sent by clients.

On Keycloak, the configuration you need to integrate with a proxy is quite simple. Basically, you need to tell Keycloak that it should infer client and request information based on the headers we just discussed. For that, look at the `configure-proxy.cli` file available from your local copy of the GitHub repository associated with the book at `$KC_HOME/Keycloak-Identity-and-Access-Management-for-Modern-Applications/ch9/configure-proxy.cli`:

```
embed-server --server-config=standalone-ha.xml --std-
out=discard
/subsystem=undertow/server=default-server/https-listener=https:
write-attribute(name=proxy-address-forwarding, value=true)
stop-embedded-server
```

Then run the `jboss-cli.sh` tool to apply the configuration:

```
$ cd $KC_HOME
$ bin/jboss-cli.sh --file=./Keycloak-Identity-and-Access-
Management-for-Modern-Applications/ch9/configure-proxy.cli
```

After running the preceding CLI command, Keycloak is ready to respect the information provided by the proxy through the mentioned headers.

On the reverse proxy side, we have the following configuration defined:

```
option forwardfor
http-request add-header X-Forwarded-Proto https
http-request add-header X-Forwarded-Port 443
```

This configuration will make sure that HAProxy sets the mentioned headers so that Keycloak can obtain information about clients making the requests.

In this section, you learned about the importance of configuring your proxy to forward client information to Keycloak through specific HTTP headers. You also learned how to configure Keycloak to respect these headers and use this information when processing requests.

In the next section, we will be looking at the importance of session affinity and its impact on the overall performance of Keycloak.

Keeping session affinity

Another important configuration you should consider is how the proxy is going to respect session affinity. Session affinity is about the proxy using the same backend node to serve requests to a particular client. This capability is especially useful when clients are using flows that require multiple interactions with Keycloak, such as when using the user agent to authenticate users through the authentication code flow.

As you learned in the *Enabling clustering* section, Keycloak tracks state about user and client interactions with the server. This state is kept in in-memory caches and shared across different nodes in the cluster. Session affinity helps to minimize the time taken by Keycloak to look up data on these caches, where clients connecting to these nodes do not need to look up data on other nodes in the cluster.

To configure session affinity, look at the `configure-session-affinity.cli` file available from your local copy of the GitHub repository associated with the book at `$KC_HOME/Keycloak-Identity-and-Access-Management-for-Modern-Applications/ch9/configure-session-affinity.cli`:

```
embed-server --server-config=standalone-ha.xml
--std-out=discard
/subsystem=keycloak-server/spi=stickySessionEncoder:add
/subsystem=keycloak-server/spi=stickySessionEncoder/
provider=infinispan:add(enabled=true,
properties={shouldAttachRoute=false})
stop-embedded-server
```

Then run the `jboss-cli.sh` tool to apply the configuration:

```
$ cd $KC_HOME
$ bin/jboss-cli.sh --file=./Keycloak-Identity-and-Access-
Management-for-Modern-Applications/ch9/configure-session-
affinity.cli
```

By doing that, Keycloak is going to rely on the proxy to keep session affinity between clients and backend nodes.

> **Note**
>
> By default, Keycloak uses a different strategy for session affinity, indicating to the proxy the node to which a client should be tied. We recommend, though, to always rely on the session affinity provided by your proxy and set the `shouldAttachRoute` property to false.

Session affinity has a direct impact on the overall performance. As mentioned before, state is shared across the different nodes in the cluster, so keeping a client connected to a specific backend node is crucial to avoid additional network and CPU overhead.

Now, on the reverse proxy side, we have the following configuration to guarantee that clients are tied to a specific node:

```
cookie KC_ROUTE insert indirect nocache
```

With the preceding configuration, HAProxy is going to set a KC_ROUTE cookie where its value is the first node that the client made the request to. Subsequent requests from the same client will always be served by the same node.

In this topic, you learned about session affinity and the importance of configuring it properly in your proxy as well as in Keycloak.

In the next section, we are going to run some basic tests to make sure the configuration we've done so far is working as expected.

Testing your environment

If you are here, you should have a local environment very close to what will become your production environment.

In the previous topics in this chapter, we have covered the following:

- Setting up Keycloak to use a public domain name for frontend and backend endpoints, as well as logically grouping the different Keycloak instances under a single issuer
- Setting up Keycloak to listen on HTTPS so that all traffic to and from Keycloak is secure
- Setting up Keycloak to use a production-grade database using PostgreSQL
- Setting up clustering so that multiple instances of Keycloak can share the state kept by their caches
- Setting up a reverse proxy, using HAProxy, so that we can finally access all Keycloak instances through a single public domain name

In the following topics, you are going to perform some basic tests on the environment to make sure everything is working as expected.

Before we begin, make sure HAProxy is started by running the following command:

```
$ sudo systemctl restart haproxy
```

Testing load balancing and failover

Firstly, try to access Keycloak at `https://mykeycloak` and log in to the administration console.

Depending on the browser you are using, you should be able to see which backend node is serving your requests. In Firefox, you can open the development tools and look at the cookies sent by your browser when making requests to Keycloak:

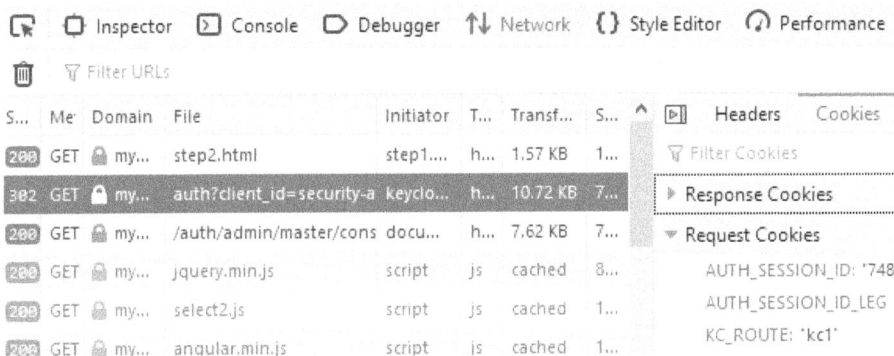

Figure 9.3 – Looking at the cookies sent by the browser

Your browser should be sending a `KC_ROUTE` cookie where its value is the node chosen by the reverse proxy to indicate which Keycloak instance should be serving that request. From the preceding screenshot, requests should be forwarded to `kc1`.

Now, try to shut down the Keycloak instance that was started using the `jboss.node.name` system property set to `kc1`. If you see a different value for the `KC_ROUTE` cookie, you need to shut down the corresponding node.

After shutting down the node, try to refresh the administration console page. If everything is properly configured, you should still be able to access the administration console without having to authenticate again. That is only possible due to teamwork between both the reverse proxy and Keycloak, where Keycloak makes sure data is replicated across instances, and the reverse proxy is able to transparently forward requests to another node.

Testing the frontend and backchannel URLs

Lastly, let's check the OpenID Discovery document and look at how Keycloak is exposing its endpoints. For that, open Keycloak at `https://mykeycloak/auth/realms/master/.well-known/openid-configuration`. As a result, you get a JSON document as follows:

```
  issuer:                                          "https://mykeycloak/auth/realms/master"
▼ authorization_endpoint:                          "https://mykeycloak/auth/realms/master/protocol/openid-connect/auth"
▼ token_endpoint:                                  "https://mykeycloak/auth/realms/master/protocol/openid-connect/token"
▼ introspection_endpoint:                          "https://mykeycloak/auth/realms/master/protocol/openid-connect/token/introspect"
▼ userinfo_endpoint:                               "https://mykeycloak/auth/realms/master/protocol/openid-connect/userinfo"
▼ end_session_endpoint:                            "https://mykeycloak/auth/realms/master/protocol/openid-connect/logout"
▼ jwks_uri:                                        "https://mykeycloak/auth/realms/master/protocol/openid-connect/certs"
▼ check_session_iframe:                            "https://mykeycloak/auth/realms/master/protocol/openid-connect/login-status-iframe.html"
```

Figure 9.4 – The OpenID Discovery document

If everything is set correctly, you should see that, regardless of the node serving the request, Keycloak will advertise all its endpoints using the `https://mykeycloak/auth` base URL.

Summary

In this chapter, we covered the main steps to configure Keycloak for production. With the information provided herein, you should now be aware of the main steps and configuration to successfully deploy Keycloak for high availability. You learned that when deploying Keycloak in production, you should always use a secure channel using HTTPS, as well as the importance of setting up the hostname provider to configure how Keycloak issues tokens and exposes its endpoints through the OpenID Connect Discovery document. You also learned about the importance of using a production-grade database and its impact on the overall performance and availability of Keycloak, as well as on data consistency and integrity. Lastly, you learned how to configure and run a cluster with multiple Keycloak instances and how to use a reverse proxy to distribute load across these instances.

In the next chapter, you will learn how to manage users in Keycloak, as well as integrating Keycloak with different identity stores.

Questions

1. Is the database a single point of failure?
2. Does the default clustering configuration work in whatever platform I choose to deploy Keycloak?
3. What is the best way to deploy Keycloak in Kubernetes or OpenShift?
4. How secure is the communication between nodes in a cluster?
5. Do I need HTTPS when making requests from the reverse proxy?
6. Keycloak nodes have a high CPU usage, is that normal?
7. How much memory does Keycloak need?
8. Is there a tool to perform load tests?

Further reading

For more information on the topics covered in this chapter, refer to the following links:

- Keycloak clustering documentation: `https://www.keycloak.org/docs/latest/server_installation/#_clustering`

- Keycloak proxy configuration: `https://www.keycloak.org/docs/latest/server_installation/#_setting-up-a-load-balancer-or-proxy`

- HAProxy documentation: `https://www.haproxy.org/`

- Keycloak Hostname documentation: `https://www.keycloak.org/docs/latest/server_installation/#_hostname`

- Keycloak Network documentation: `https://www.keycloak.org/docs/latest/server_installation/#_network`

- Keycloak Database documentation: `https://www.keycloak.org/docs/latest/server_installation/#_database`

- Keycloak Operator documentation: `https://www.keycloak.org/docs/latest/server_installation/#_operator`

- WildFly SSL/TLS documentation: `https://docs.wildfly.org/22/WildFly_Elytron_Security.html#configure-ssltls`

10

Managing Users

In the previous chapters, you learned how to deploy, run, and use Keycloak to authenticate and authorize users in your applications. You also learned how to manage users in Keycloak to run some of the examples in this book.

In this chapter, we are going to take a closer look at the capabilities provided by Keycloak that are related to identity management and federation, such as how users are created and managed, how users can manage their own accounts, how to manage credentials, and how to integrate with different identity stores and identity providers to authenticate users and fetch their information through open protocols such as OpenID Connect, **Security Assertion Markup Language** (SAML), and **Lightweight Directory Access Protocol** (LDAP).

In this chapter, we will cover the following topics:

- Managing local users
- Integrating with LDAP and Active Directory
- Integrating with social identity providers
- Integrating with third-party identity providers
- Allowing users to manage their data

By the end of this chapter, you will be able to leverage these capabilities to effectively manage your users, as well as understand how they can be used to solve common problems related to identity management and federation.

Technical requirements

Check out the following link to see the Code in Action video:

```
https://bit.ly/3vIOf4i
```

Managing local users

In the previous chapters, you had to create users in Keycloak to run some of the examples provided in this book. In this section, we are going to deep dive into some key capabilities provided by Keycloak to manage your users once they are stored in Keycloak's internal database. For now on, whenever you read about a local user, you will think about a user stored in a Keycloak database.

As an identity management solution, Keycloak gives you several capabilities to manage user identities. In this section, we will look at the following topics:

- How to create users

- How to manage user credentials

- How to obtain and validate user information

- How to enable user self-registration

- How to extend user information using attributes

In the next section, we are going to start our journey by looking at how to create a local user in Keycloak.

Creating a local user

To create a new user in Keycloak, click on the **Users** link on the left-hand side panel. Once you've done that, you will be presented with a list showing all the users that are available in the realm. At the top right of that list, you have an **Add user** button. By clicking on this button, you will be presented with the user creation page.

When creating a new user, you are only asked for a few pieces of information. In fact, you should be able to create a new user by providing only a **username**. Let's create a user whose username is set to `alice`:

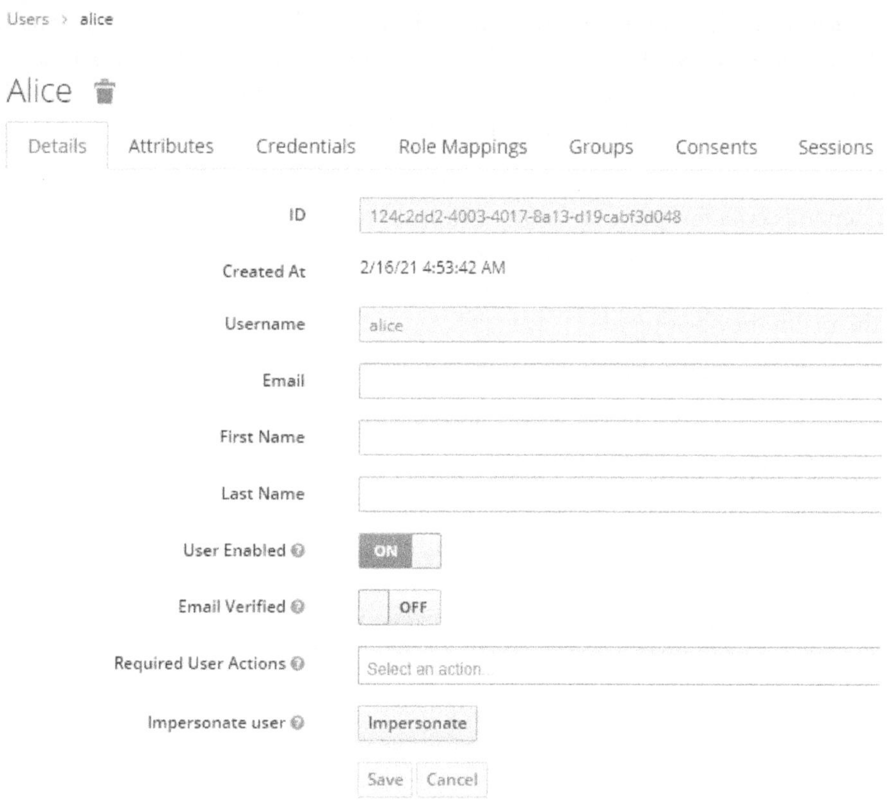

Users > alice

Alice 🗑

| Details | Attributes | Credentials | Role Mappings | Groups | Consents | Sessions |

ID	124c2dd2-4003-4017-8a13-d19cabf3d048
Created At	2/16/21 4:53:42 AM
Username	alice
Email	
First Name	
Last Name	
User Enabled ⍰	ON
Email Verified ⍰	OFF
Required User Actions ⍰	Select an action...
Impersonate user ⍰	Impersonate
	Save Cancel

Figure 10.1 – Creating a new user

Click on **Save** to create the user.

Creating a user is a trivial task. Keycloak depends on a few pieces of basic information about users while still allowing you to decorate them with additional information, as we will see later. This basic set of information is what Keycloak needs to identify a user, to correlate the user with other functionalities, and to issue tokens after authenticating users.

> **Note**
> When you create a new user, that user belongs to the realm you are managing. Users created in a realm can only authenticate through the realm they belong to.

Creating a user using the administration console is useful when the administrator has all the information about a user beforehand. However, depending on the use case, that is not always the case, so you may want to either allow your users to self-register in your realm or ask them for their information as part of the authentication process.

In this section, you learned about how to create a user in Keycloak. You also learned that Keycloak depends on a few pieces of information about users so that they can authenticate in a realm. You also learned that Keycloak allows you to decorate your users with additional information and that once they are created, they can only authenticate through the realm they belong to.

In the next section, we will look at how to manage user credentials.

Managing user credentials

After creating users, they should be able to authenticate in the realm. For that, we need to set up credentials for the user. Keycloak supports different forms of authentication using different types of credentials. As we will see in *Chapter 11, Authenticating Users*, users can authenticate in different ways, such as by using passwords, one-time keys, security devices, X.509 certificates, and so forth.

To manage user credentials, click on the **Credentials** tab after selecting a user from the users list. In this tab, you should be able to see all the credentials associated with a user, as well as perform specific actions such as delete or modify credentials. You will also be provided with shortcuts to easily set a password (the simplest form of authentication, although not the strongest) for a user.

> **Note**
> Keycloak does not expose sensitive data associated with credentials, only the basic and non-sensitive data associated with them. Depending on your security requirements, you may also want to encrypt data at rest in the database.

We are going to look at other types of credentials in the next chapter, but for now, let's create a password for the `alice` user that we just created. For that, fill in the **Password** and **Password Confirmation** fields with any password you want, and turn off the **Temporary** setting. Do not worry about this setting for now as we are going to talk about it in the next chapter. Just keep in mind that by disabling it, we are creating a definitive password for the user. Click on the **Set Password** button to set the user's password:

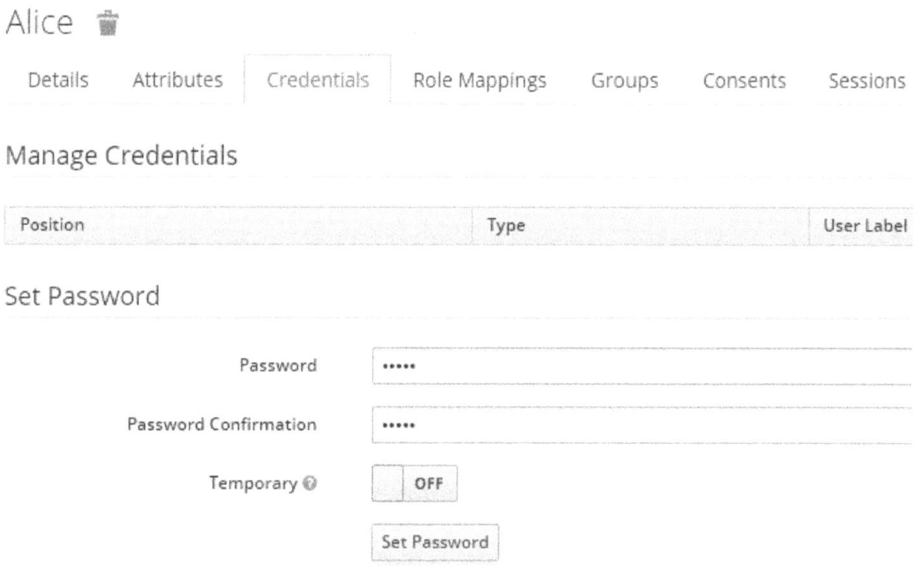

Alice 🗑

| Details | Attributes | Credentials | Role Mappings | Groups | Consents | Sessions |

Manage Credentials

Position	Type	User Label

Set Password

Password	•••••
Password Confirmation	•••••
Temporary ❓	OFF
	Set Password

Figure 10.2 – Setting a new password for a user

After setting the password, you will see that the list of credentials has been updated with the new password we just set for the user. From that list, you can view information about any credential associated with a user – non-sensitive information – as well as delete it.

Now, let's test whether the user can authenticate in our realm. For that, we are going to try to access the account console, an application provided by Keycloak where users can manage their own information. We are going to discuss it in the following sections, but for now, just open your browser at `http://localhost:8080/auth/realms/myrealm/account`. You should be redirected to the `myrealm` login page.

Type in the username and password for the user `alice` and click on the **Login** button. If everything is working properly, you should be able to access the account console as the user `alice`:

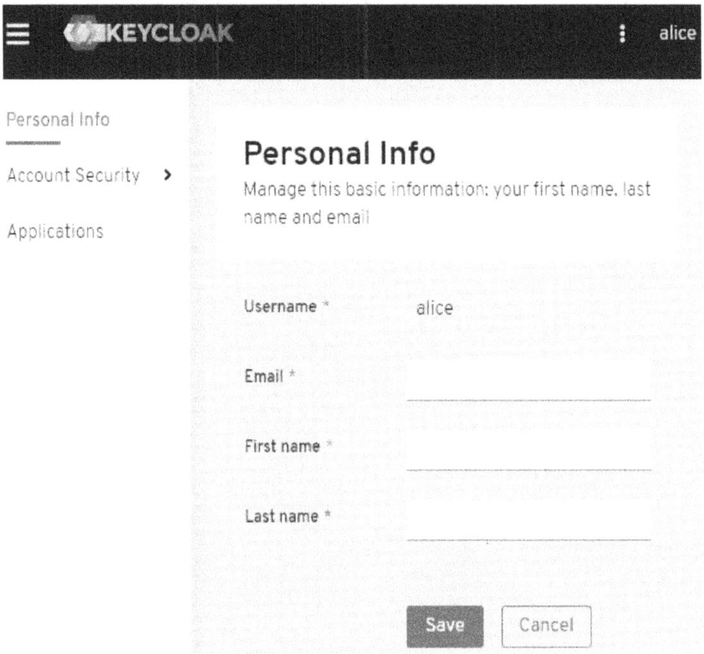

Figure 10.3 – Authenticating as the newly created user

In this section, you learned how to manage user credentials through the administration console. You also learned that Keycloak allows you to manage different types of credentials, with shortcuts for managing the user password. You also learned that, once created, all the credentials associated with a user – not only passwords – can be managed through the **Credentials** tab.

In the next section, we are going to look at how to interact with users during the authentication process to gather more information about them.

Obtaining and validating user information

In the previous sections, we created the user `alice` by providing only a **username**. We also set a password for this user to authenticate in the realm. As you may have noticed, we are missing some important information about `alice`, and we want her to fill in that information to create her account.

Keycloak allows you to interact with users during the authentication process using a functionality called **Required User Actions**. This setting is related to the actions that the user should perform prior to authenticating to a realm. Keycloak provides a good set of common actions covering different scenarios, such as the following:

- **Verify Email**: Send an email to the user – if one was set – to confirm it belongs to that user.

- **Update Password**: Ask the user to update their password.

- **Update Profile**: Ask the user to update their profile by providing their first name, last name, and email.

There are other options, but the preceding actions should give you an idea of how powerful this setting is and how you can interact with your users when they are authenticating.

Let's configure the **Update Profile** action for `alice` and obtain the information we are missing about her account. For that, select `alice` from the users list and select **Update Profile** from the list of available actions in the **Required User Actions** field. Then, click on the **Save** button:

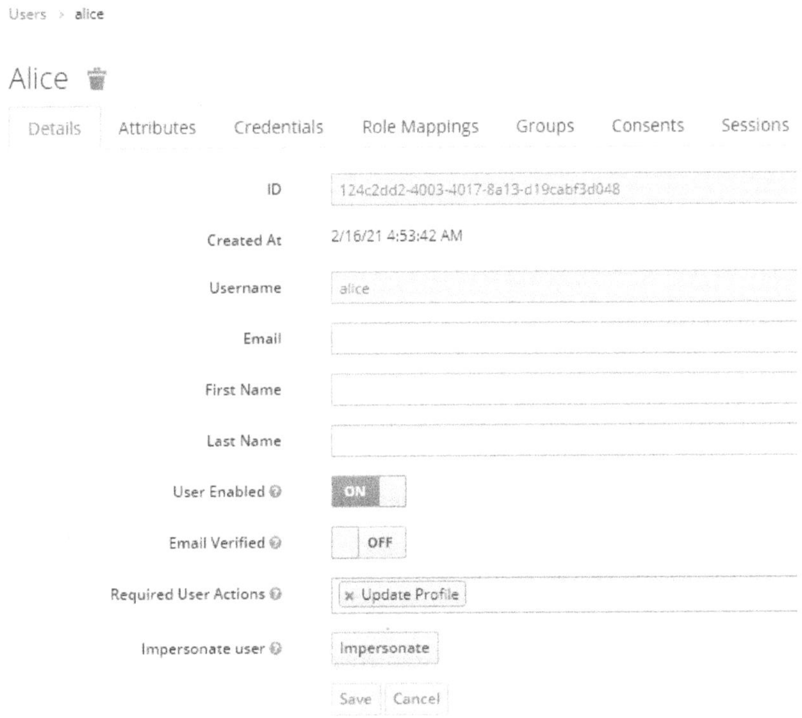

Figure 10.4 – Forcing users to update their profile while logging in to update missing account information

Now, let's try to access the account console as `alice`. For that, open your browser at `http://localhost:8080/auth/realms/myrealm/account`. You should now be redirected to the `myrealm` login page.

Type in the username and password for `alice` and click on the **Login** button. If everything is working properly, you should be redirected to a page asking for the information we are missing from that user. Fill in all the fields and click on the **Submit** button:

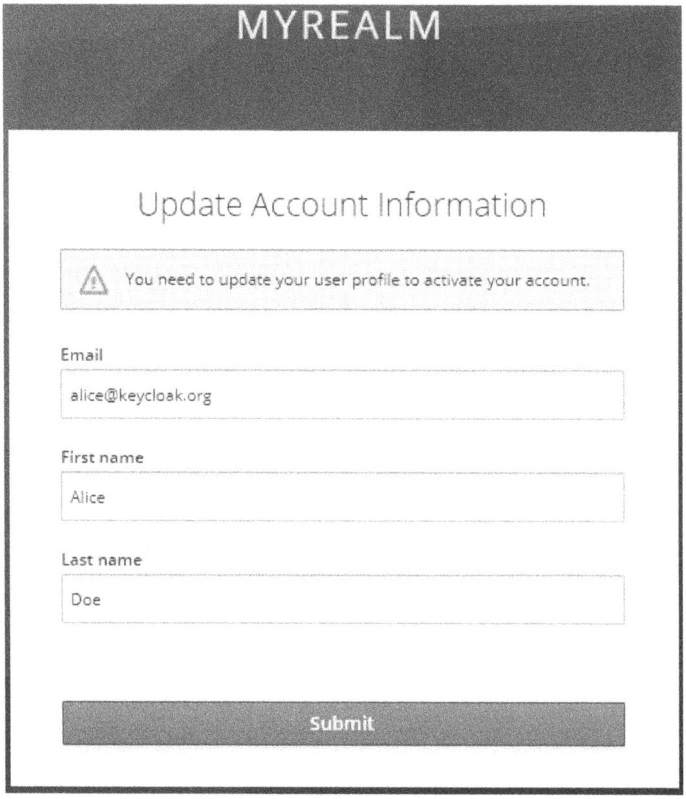

Figure 10.5 – Asking a user to update their account information

Once you submit the information, Keycloak is going to update the user with the information provided. The updated information should now be available when you access the account console.

The same idea applies to any other required action you set for a user, where each is related to specific steps that the user is required to complete before authenticating to a realm. For instance, if you set the **Update Password** action, the user is going to be asked to reset their password, whereas the **Verify Email** action is going to make sure the email associated with the user is valid through an email verification process.

In this section, you learned how Keycloak allows you, as an administrator, to interact with your users to obtain and validate information about their accounts.

In the next section, we are going to look at how to allow users to self-register their accounts.

Enabling self-registration

Depending on your requirements, you might want to allow users to self-register in a realm and delegate them the responsibility of filling in their information. Compared to manually creating a user, Keycloak is going to provide a link on the login page for user self-registration.

For that, click on **Realm Settings** in the left-hand side menu and then click on the **Login** tab. In this tab, enable the **User registration** option.

Now, let's create a new user by going through the self-registration process. Open your browser at `http://localhost:8080/auth/realms/myrealm/account`. At the login page, click on the **Register** link:

Figure 10.6 – Allowing users to sign up to a realm

Once you've done that, you should be presented with a registration page, asking you to provide the same information that you did when you created users through the administration console. Fill in the fields with any information you want and click on the **Register** button to create the new user.

Now, go back to the Keycloak administration console and check whether the user you just created is shown in the users list. If everything is correct, you should be able to see the user you just created in that list.

Self-registration is a powerful feature and a must-have for certain use cases where users should be allowed to sign up to a realm. It also provides the necessary level of flexibility so that you can customize the registration page to obtain additional information about users, such as their mobile number or address, according to your needs. We are going to talk about customization in *Chapter 13, Extending Keycloak.*

In this section, you learned how to enable self-registration for a realm so that users can create their own account in a realm without any intervention from an administrator.

In the next section, we will look at how to manage additional information about users.

Managing user attributes

Keycloak allows you to manage additional metadata about users using attributes. As you learned in the previous sections, Keycloak relies on a basic set of information to identify and authenticate users. This information is also made available when you're introspecting tokens or accessing a user's profile. To manage the attributes of a user, select the respective user from the users list and click on the **Attributes** tab. Each attribute has a key – the name of the attribute – and a text value.

User attributes can solve different types of problems, from passing additional information about users to applications, to enabling different forms of authorization, such as **Attribute-Based Access Control (ABAC)**.

When using attributes, you are probably going to need to create protocol mappers so that they can be mapped to tokens to make them available to applications, or even when querying the `introspection` token and `userinfo` endpoints.

When extending Keycloak, as we are going to see in *Chapter 13, Extending Keycloak,* you should also be able to extend the account console to populate user accounts with additional information using attributes. The same goes for customizing the update profile page, which is shown to users during the authentication process, as we learned in the previous sections. Here, you can store custom information that was gathered during this step using attributes.

In this section, you learned how to extend Keycloak's user model by using user attributes. You also learned that by leveraging user attributes, you can extend different parts of Keycloak to obtain additional information from users and store it as user attributes. You also learned that user attributes are commonly used to pass additional information about users to applications using protocol mappers.

In the upcoming sections, we are going to look at how to integrate with third-party identity providers and identity stores to manage users from sources other than a Keycloak database. We will start by learning how to fetch user information from LDAP directories.

Integrating with LDAP and Active Directory

Many organizations still use an LDAP directory as their single source of truth for digital identities. Keycloak allows you to integrate with different LDAP server implementations so that you can leverage your existing security infrastructure and use all the authentication and authorization capabilities provided by Keycloak.

Keycloak can integrate using LDAP in different ways; it can act as a stateful broker where data from your LDAP directory is imported into the Keycloak database, as well as kept in sync with your LDAP directory, or it can act as a stateless broker delegating credential verification to your LDAP directory. You should also be able to set up multiple LDAP directories within a single realm and configure a priority order that Keycloak should respect when authenticating users.

In Keycloak, the term "user federation" refers to the capability of integrating with external identity stores. LDAP is a form of user federation and, as such, can be configured by clicking on the **User Federation** link on the left-hand side menu of the administration console.

To configure a new LDAP server, select **ldap** from the list of available providers:

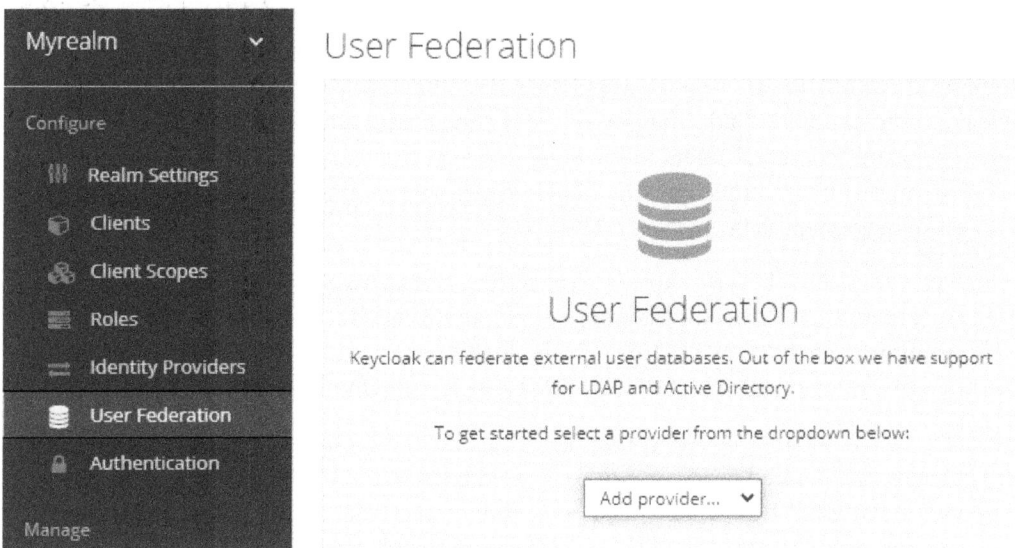

Figure 10.7 – Creating a new LDAP user federation provider

After selecting the provider, you will be presented with a page containing all the settings you'll need to integrate with an LDAP directory. Keycloak supports the most common LDAP vendors, including Active Directory. The **Vendor** field allows you to choose one of these vendors and Keycloak does its best to find the best default setting for the vendor you choose.

If you are interested in integrating Keycloak using LDAP, you should become familiar with most of the settings on this page, mainly those related to connection settings and the structure of the LDAP directory. Here, we will focus on the additional settings provided by Keycloak to customize the integration, starting with the **Import Users** setting.

The **Import Users** setting allows you to define whether Keycloak should import data from your LDAP server into the database. By default, this setting is enabled so that whenever users authenticate through an LDAP provider, the information about that user is persisted into the database. One of the main reasons this setting is enabled by default is that if it wasn't, you wouldn't be able to leverage all of Keycloak's capabilities – you would only be able to use it as a broker to authenticate your users using the LDAP directory.

Basically, when a user tries to authenticate, Keycloak will check whether the user is available from its database. If no user is found, Keycloak will try to look up the user in your LDAP directory. If the user trying to authenticate is there, Keycloak will authenticate the user using the LDAP protocol and, if successful, import the user into the database. Once imported, the user is considered a federated user and a link is created between the user and the LDAP provider.

This link between the user and the LDAP provider is a key aspect of user federation. By looking at the link the user has to a specific user federation provider, such as LDAP, Keycloak is able to differentiate whether a user is a **local user** or a **federated user**. In this context, the term "federated" refers to the trust that's created between Keycloak and an external identity store – in this case, the LDAP directory – so that both can share identity and access management data.

Keycloak provides some key synchronization settings for managing how data is read and written back to an LDAP directory. Before you do anything else, you should decide which synchronization strategy you want through the **Edit Mode** setting. You can choose from three different strategies: **READ_ONLY**, **WRITABLE**, and **UNSYNCED**.

The **READ_ONLY** strategy allows you to use your LDAP directory in read-only mode, where changes to federated users are not replicated back to the LDAP directory. On the other hand, the **WRITABLE** strategy is a powerful strategy that allows you to replicate any change that's made to federated users back to the LDAP directory.

Whether you should use a read-only or writable strategy depends on your use case. Under some circumstances, LDAP is the single source of truth for identities in the organization that you do not have much control over. If you are using Keycloak to modernize your security infrastructure while still centralizing identity management in your LDAP directory, then the READ_ONLY strategy makes sense.

However, if you have plans to migrate from LDAP and want to centralize identity management through Keycloak, then the writable strategy should help you during that journey. It should also allow you to keep your LDAP active and in sync with the changes that are made through Keycloak.

Once you've decided which strategy works best for you, you can look at additional settings provided by Keycloak to control how synchronization should happen. Keycloak allows you to synchronize user information by manually triggering the synchronization process through the administration console, or by scheduling a time when synchronization should happen automatically.

To trigger a manual synchronization for user information, you should click on the **Synchronize All Users** button, which becomes available once you've created your LDAP provider. In fact, it is a good practice to run a full synchronization right after creating your provider. The reason for this is that this step is going to help you avoid importing users when they authenticate for the very first time. You are also provided other actions to perform, including synchronizing local users that have changed after the last synchronization, removing users that have been imported from the LDAP provider, and removing the link between users and an LDAP provider, effectively changing the user to a regular local user.

Once your users have been imported, you can schedule periodic synchronization according to your needs. Synchronization can be scheduled for a full or partial sync.

A full sync means that Keycloak is going to check the LDAP tree for changes that need to be replicated to the database, so that new users that are created in LDAP, as well as updated information about those users, are kept in sync.

A partial sync means that Keycloak is going to look up new users and make changes to existing users after the last synchronization happened, hence helping keep Keycloak updated using a more efficient strategy.

In this section, you learned about user federation and how Keycloak can integrate with existing LDAP servers to authenticate users and synchronize information.

In the next section, you will learn about LDAP mappers and their importance in terms of fetching additional information from an LDAP directory, as well as the behavior of the integration.

Understanding LDAP mappers

Just like users, Keycloak can also fetch other types of information from LDAP. Different to how you fetch users from LDAP – which is part of the core functionality of an LDAP provider – this information is fetched using mappers.

An LDAP mapper is a special, and powerful, functionality in Keycloak for mapping information from LDAP into Keycloak and vice versa. It provides another extension point to LDAP's integration and fine-grained control over how to read and write LDAP data for users, groups, roles, certificates, or even information that is only available when you're using a specific LDAP vendor, such as Active Directory. Whenever you need to map a specific set of data from LDAP, you should go through the list of supported mappers and find one that suits your needs.

When creating a new provider, Keycloak automatically configures a set of mappers, depending on the configuration of the provider. For instance, depending on the import mode or the edit mode, a different set of mappers is created. That is why deciding on these two settings is important prior to creating the provider. Otherwise, you would need to change mappers accordingly when changing these settings once a provider has been created.

To manage the mappers associated with an LDAP provider, click on the **Mappers** tab of the provider you are managing. On this tab, you are presented with a list of all the mappers that are currently active for the provider. From this page, you can also associate new mappers with your provider. You can do this by clicking on the **Create** button in the top-right corner of the list.

There are several types of mappers that you can use, with each being specific to a particular task. In the next few sections, we are going to look at how to create mappers to manage group and role data from LDAP.

Synchronizing groups

To manage group data from LDAP, click on the **Create** button in the top-right corner of the mappers list.

Type in a name for the new mapper and select `group-ldap-mapper` from the **Mapper Type** field.

Some of the settings on this page are specific to how groups are organized in the LDAP tree. For instance, you must provide the **Distinguished Name** (**DN**) of where your groups are located, the attribute that will be used to fetch the group name, as well as how membership information is defined in your LDAP tree so that Keycloak can automatically discover the groups that users belong to.

The `group-ldap-mapper` type gives you several settings to configure how groups should be fetched from LDAP and how data synchronization should work. Some of the settings are specific to how groups are organized in the LDAP tree.

The first step when creating this mapper is to set the location of the groups in your LDAP tree. For that, you should fill in the **LDAP Groups DN** field with the base DN where all your groups are located. You should also be able to provide an additional filter if you have a more complex LDAP tree, where groups should be fetched based on some criteria. For that, you can set a filter using the **LDAP Filter** field.

Keycloak is going to look up group entries from the base DN based on the object classes you've defined for group entries. You can set the object classes using the **Group Object Classes** field.

The next step is to configure how Keycloak should map information from group entries to Keycloak.

The name of a group can be mapped from these entries using the **Group Name LDAP Attribute** field. You can change this field to whatever LDAP attribute you are using to store the group's name. Usually, the **Common Name** (**CN**) attribute is used for this purpose.

Now that you understand how to look up groups from LDAP and map their information to Keycloak, it is time to understand how to map group hierarchy and user membership.

In LDAP, groups are usually organized in a hierarchy to represent your organizational tree. Keycloak allows you to map and preserve the group hierarchy by automatically creating it when you're fetching groups from LDAP. The first step is to set the attribute that was used to infer the relationship between the groups in the hierarchy using the **Membership LDAP Attribute** field. Keycloak is going to look up the children of a group by looking at the value of this attribute. Its format is usually the **Fully Qualified Name** (**FQN**) of another group entry.

> **Tip**
> You should still be able to set a different format for the membership attribute if you are still relying on `memberUid` to reference another group in the LDAP tree. For that, choose UID in the **Membership Attribute Type** field.

Keycloak also allows you to map user membership from LDAP so that when you're importing users, they are automatically assigned to the groups they belong to. For that, you can set different strategies for how this relationship is obtained from LDAP. The **User Groups Retrieve Strategy** field allows you to choose whether user membership should be fetched based on the `member` attribute of groups – similar to when fetching the group hierarchy – or whether membership should be fetched based on the presence of another attribute within the user entry in LDAP – usually, this is the `memberOf` attribute.

Regarding synchronization, the mapper allows you to have fine-grained control over how group information is kept in sync with your LDAP directory, as well as how groups should be imported into Keycloak.

If you are using a writable LDAP provider, the mapper defaults to writing back any changes you make to groups that have been imported from LDAP, including user membership. This behavior is managed through the **Mode** field, which provides different strategies on how group information should be imported and synced back to LDAP.

By default, groups that have been imported from LDAP are created as top-level groups in Keycloak. Sometimes, it might be useful to import groups into a specific group in Keycloak to differentiate them from local groups. For that, you can set the `Groups Path` field to any existing group you have in Keycloak.

In this section, you learned how to map group information using the `group-ldap-mapper` mapper. You also learned that Keycloak is very flexible regarding how this data is fetched and kept in sync with LDAP.

In the next section, we will be looking at how to map roles from LDAP.

Synchronizing roles

Like groups, roles are also mapped from LDAP using a specific mapper. To import role data, click on the **Create** button in the top-right corner of the mappers list.

Type in a name for the new mapper and select `role-ldap-mapper` from the **Mapper Type** field.

As you can see, the core settings for role mapping are pretty much the same ones that you learned about in the previous section. Mainly, they are related to configuring how Keycloak is going to look up entries in your LDAP tree.

In this section, we are going to focus on the behavior and the specific properties related to how Keycloak maps role information from LDAP.

Roles are automatically imported from Keycloak whenever the user authenticates in Keycloak. Keycloak also allows you to manually trigger a synchronization once you've created the mapper.

When importing roles, Keycloak defaults to creating these roles as realm roles, where users are automatically granted their roles in LDAP. This behavior is controlled by the **Use Realm Roles Mapping** field, which can also be disabled so that imported roles are created as client roles for a specific client in Keycloak.

In this section, you learned how to integrate Keycloak with LDAP and how users, groups, and role information can be obtained from it. You also learned that Keycloak is very flexible regarding mapping different types of information from LDAP through a functionality called LDAP mappers. Lastly, you learned that Keycloak gives you fine-grained control over how data is imported, as well as how data is replicated back to LDAP whenever you make changes to the information that's imported from LDAP.

In the next section, we are going to look at how to integrate with third-party identity providers by leveraging Keycloak as an identity broker to authenticate and replicate their users.

Integrating with third-party identity providers

Keycloak can integrate with third-party identity providers using a set of open standard protocols.

In the previous section, you learned about user federation and how to easily integrate with LDAP. Identity providers leverage user federation to create cross-domain trust between Keycloak and an identity provider, where the identity data about users is shared and used by Keycloak to create, authenticate, and authorize users.

Integration with third-party identity providers is possible by using Keycloak as an identity broker, where Keycloak acts as an intermediary service for authenticating and replicating users from a targeted identity provider.

Identity brokering can solve different types of problems. As we will see in the next section, it can be used to integrate with social providers, as an integration point to a legacy identity and access management system, or to share identity data between a business partner and your organization.

In Keycloak, you can integrate with two main types of identity providers, depending on the security protocol they support:

- SAML v2
- OpenID Connect v1.0

Through identity brokering, you can provide a much better experience for users, where they can leverage an existing account to authenticate and sign up in your realm. Once these users have been created and their information has been imported from the third-party provider, they become users of your realm and can enjoy all the features provided by Keycloak and respect the security constraints imposed by your realm.

In this section, we are going to look at how to create an OpenID Connect v1.0 identity provider. For simplicity, we are going to use another realm in the same Keycloak server to represent the third-party identity provider we are trying to integrate with. However, the same concepts and steps you are about to learn should be valid for any other OpenID Connect-compliant identity provider.

Creating a OpenID Connect identity provider

Firstly, create a realm in Keycloak called `third-party-provider`. In this realm, create a client with the following settings:

- **Client ID**: `broker-app`
- **Root URL**: `http://localhost:8080/auth/realms/myrealm/broker/oidc/endpoint`

After creating the `broker-app` client in Keycloak, change the **Access Type** settings on the client details page to **Confidential**.

Make sure to keep a note of the client secret that's generated as we are going to use it later when we configure the identity provider.

Now, create a user called `third-party-user` in the `third-party-provider` realm and make sure to set a password for them.

Now, let's create a new identity provider in the `myrealm` realm. For that, click on the **Identity Providers** link in the left-hand side menu:

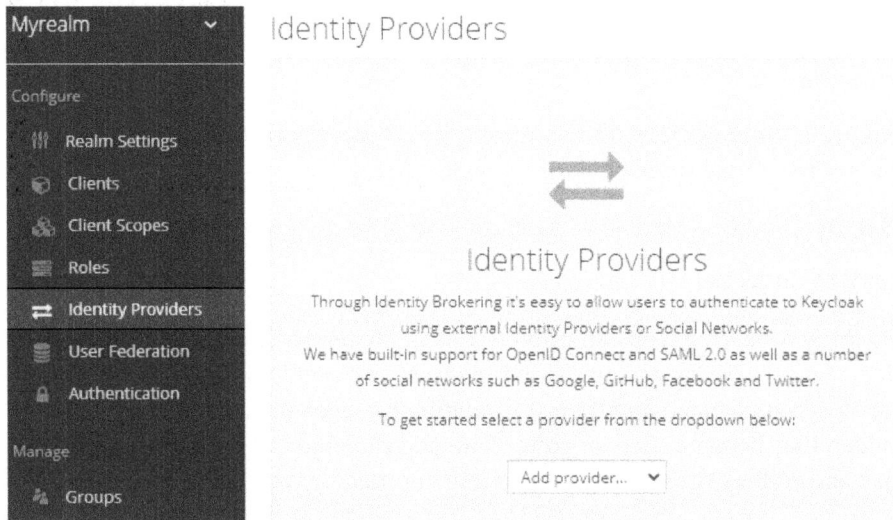

Figure 10.8 – Creating a new identity provider

The **Identity Providers** page allows you to either create a new provider or list all the providers that have been configured for a realm. If the realm does not have a provider yet, you will be prompted to select the type of the provider to create a new one.

Let's select **OpenID Connect v1.0** from the list of providers. After that, you should be redirected to the provider settings page.

> **Note**
>
> On this page, you have a read-only **Redirect URI** field, whose value is the URL we set for the `broker-app` client as a **root URL**. This URL is the location where users are going to be redirected to once they've authenticated through the identity provider. In our case, users are going to be redirected back to the `myrealm` realm after successfully authenticating through the identity provider.

As you learned in *Chapter 4, Authenticating Users with OpenID Connect*, an **OpenID Connect Provider** (**OP**) advertises the endpoints that can be used to interact with them through a document available from a specific endpoint. By using this endpoint, we can quickly configure our identity provider, since most of the settings on the **Provider settings** page are going to be filled in automatically with the information from the OP you are integrating with.

At the bottom of the **Provider settings** page, there is an **Import from URL** field that you should set with the location where the OP is exposing its discovery document. In our case, this document is located at `http://localhost:8080/auth/realms/third-party-provider/.well-known/openid-configuration`.

After setting the URL, click on the **Import** button. Once you've done that, you should see that some of the other fields on this page were automatically populated with the information from the discovery document.

Now, let's fill in some additional information to finish configuring the provider. For that, fill in the following fields:

- **Display Name**: `My Third-Party Provider`
- **Client Authentication**: `Client secret sent as post`
- **Client ID**: `broker-app`
- **Client Secret**: `<CLIENT_SECRET>`

Finally, click on **Save** to create the identity provider.

> **Note**
>
> Note that both the **Client ID** and **Client Secret** fields refer to the `broker-app` client in the `third-party-provider` realm. This is the client used by the identity provider to authenticate users in that realm.

Now, let's test whether new users can authenticate and sign up to our realm using the newly created provider. For that, open your browser at `http://localhost:8080/auth/realms/myrealm/account` to access the account console:

Figure 10.9 – Login page with an option to authenticate using an identity provider

Note that you will be presented with the option to authenticate with `My Third-Party Provider`, which is the provider we just created.

Click on the **My Third-Party Provider** button; you should be redirected to the `third-party-provider` realm to authenticate. At the login page, provide the username and password for the `third-party-user` user to log in.

If everything is working properly, you should be redirected to a page asking for additional information about the user. Fill in all the fields and click on the **Submit** button.

Once the user has been authenticated to the third-party provider, a set of tokens will be issued to Keycloak. These represent the user's identity and the permissions that have been granted to the user when authenticating to the `third-party-provider` realm. By looking at these tokens, Keycloak is capable of fetching user information and creating or updating the user in your realm.

Now, if you list the users that are available in the `myrealm` realm, you should see that the `third-party-user` user is among them. This means you can manage them just like any other user in your realm.

There are several settings you can choose from when configuring a provider. For instance, Keycloak can be used to store tokens that have been issued by an identity provider, a useful capability if you need to use these tokens to access APIs protected by the provider. Once stored, Keycloak allows you to obtain these tokens through another functionality called **token exchange**.

Keycloak also allows you to define a specific authentication flow when the user is authenticating for the first time using an identity provider. This is a powerful feature that allows you to gather additional information about your users or even force them to set up credentials.

Depending on your requirements, you can also configure your realm to only allow users to authenticate and link their accounts with an identity provider through the account console. This is achieved by turning on the **Account Linking Only** field. This ensures that users can't select the identity provider on the login page, only when they're in the account console.

There are many other settings you can choose from, and you can find them in the Keycloak documentation at `https://www.keycloak.org/docs/latest/server_admin/#_identity_broker`.

In this section, you learned how Keycloak can be used to integrate with third-party identity providers using open standard protocols. You also learned that Keycloak allows you to quickly integrate with any identity provider using either the OpenID Connect or SAML2 protocols. You also learned that this integration is possible since you can use Keycloak as an identity broker, where users are authenticated and created based on the information that's returned by these providers.

In the next section, you will learn about how to extend the concepts presented in this chapter to integrate your realm with different social providers.

Integrating with social identity providers

A common requirement for applications that use Keycloak is the possibility to authenticate users using different social providers, such as Google, GitHub, Instagram, and Twitter.

Integration with social providers follows the same principles that you learned about in the previous section, where Keycloak acts as a broker to authenticate and exchange identity data about users using a well-known and open standard security protocol.

To integrate with a social provider, click on the **Identity Providers** link in the left-hand side menu.

Keycloak allows you to select from different social providers. To integrate with them, you only need to fill in some information that you usually obtain from the social provider you are integrating with.

Let's configure GitHub as a social provider to allow users to authenticate using their GitHub account. Firstly, make sure you have a valid GitHub account. If not, you can create one at `https://github.com`.

Now, let's create a GitHub social provider in our realm by selecting GitHub from the list of available providers. Once you've selected GitHub, you should be presented with a page containing a few settings that you need to fill in to create the provider.

To use GitHub, we need to create an OAuth app at `https://github.com/settings/developers`. When creating the application, you will be asked to provide an authorization callback URL or redirect URL. This URL is the endpoint in Keycloak that is going to receive the response from GitHub once the user is successfully authenticated – or when an error occurs. When creating a social provider in Keycloak, you are given a **redirect URI**, which you should use to configure the application in GitHub. This URL is available from the **Redirect URI** field. Copy and paste the value of this field and use it to create the app in GitHub.

Depending on the social provider you are integrating with, you are going to be asked for additional information to make the integration possible. For GitHub, we need a client ID and client secret, both of which are provided by GitHub once you've created your app. Fill in both the **Client ID** and **Client Secret** fields with the values you got from GitHub.

Now, click on the **Save** button to create the provider.

Now, let's test whether the users in our realm can authenticate and sign up to our realm using the newly created provider. For that, open your browser at `http://localhost:8080/auth/realms/myrealm/account` to access the account console.

You should now be at the login page of Keycloak. Note that you will be presented with the option to authenticate with GitHub, the provider we just created. Click on the **GitHub** button to be redirected to GitHub to authenticate.

After authenticating with GitHub, you might be presented with a consent page, asking you to grant permissions to your realm for accessing information about the user. After approving the consent, Keycloak is going to create a user based on the information that was obtained from GitHub. You should be automatically authenticated and redirected to the account console.

In this section, you learned how Keycloak makes it easier to integrate with different social providers. By integrating with GitHub, you learned about the basic steps and concepts around integrating with any other social provider that supports the OpenID Connect or OAuth2 protocols.

In the next section, we are going to learn about how users can manage their data using the Keycloak Account Console.

Allowing users to manage their data

In the previous sections, you learned how to manage users through the admin console as an administrator. You also learned that users can self-register in a realm. However, one of the main capabilities of Keycloak is to also allow users to manage their own accounts through a service called Keycloak Account Console.

The Keycloak Account Console is a regular application provided by Keycloak and is where users can manage their own accounts. They can also do the following:

- Update their user profile
- Update their password
- Enable second-factor authentication
- View applications, including what applications they have authenticated to
- View open sessions, including remotely signing out of other sessions

To access the account console, open `http://localhost:8080/auth/realms/myrealm/account/` in a browser. You will be redirected to a welcome page, as follows:

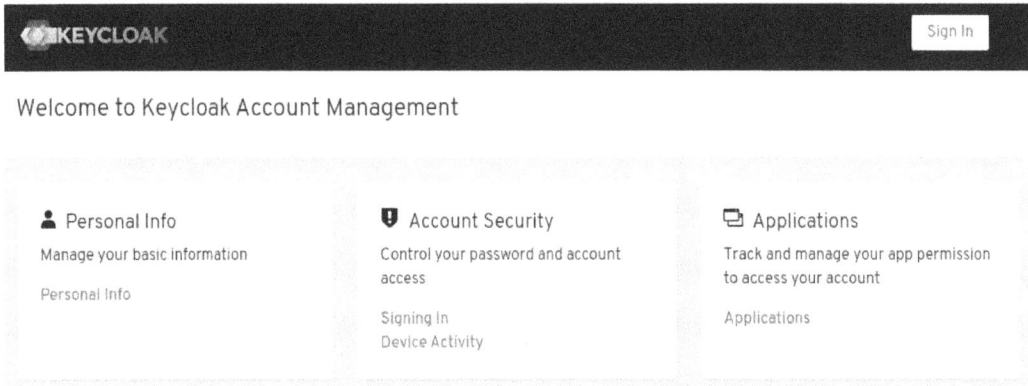

Figure 10.10 – The Keycloak Account Console

To log into the account console, you should either click on any of the links on that page or click on the **Sign In** button in the top-right corner of the page. By doing any of these things, you should be redirected to the login page and, after providing the user credentials, you should be redirected back to the account console:

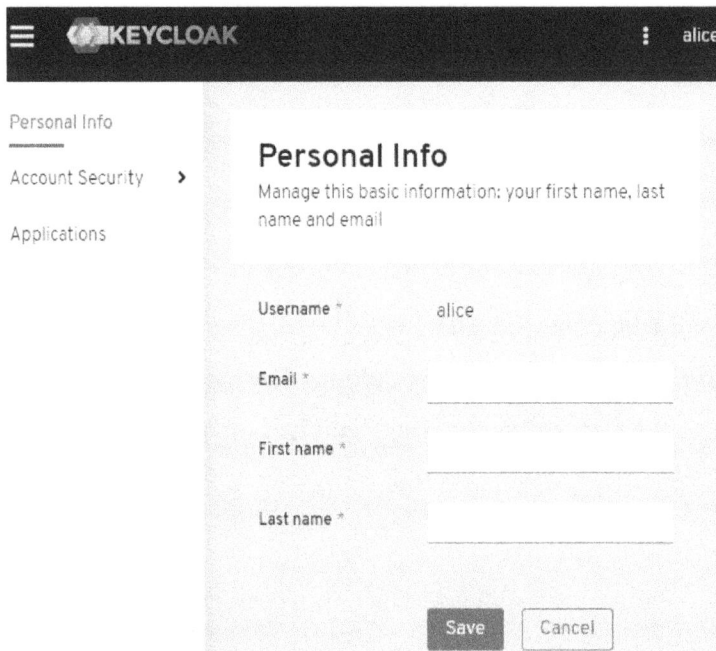

Figure 10.11 – Authenticating to the account console

Once authenticated, users can view and manage different information about their accounts:

- **Personal Info**: Allows users to manage profile information such as email, first name, and last name.

- **Account Security**: Allows users to manage their credentials, as well as set up two-factor and multi-factor authentication using OTP and security devices, respectively. In this area, users should also be able to track their account activity.

- **Applications**: Allows users to manage the applications they have logged in and logged out from, as well as the permissions that have been granted to applications.

As a regular application, Keycloak automatically creates an `account` client in your realm to allow users to authenticate and access their account data. When users are created in a realm, they are automatically granted a `manage-account` client role. This role belongs to the `account` client and controls whether a user should have access to the `account` console. To disable access to the `account` console for a user, change the role mappings for the user to remove this role.

> **Tip**
> You can also find the URL of the account console through the Keycloak admin console. In the admin console, click on **Clients**. From there, you will find the URL of the account console next to the `account` client.

As we will see in the following chapters, Keycloak allows you to customize the look and feel of the account console, as well as how information is presented and managed through it, allowing you to obtain and store additional information from users.

In this section, you learned how users can manage their accounts through the account console. You also learned that Keycloak allows you to control what users can view and manage in their accounts, by either relying on your realm settings or by managing the roles that have been granted to the user.

Summary

In this chapter, you were presented with the main aspects of user management in Keycloak. You learned that users can be created directly in Keycloak or by integrating with different third-party identity providers and external identity stores. You also learned that Keycloak enables these integrations by leveraging open standard protocols such as OpenID Connect, SAML, and LDAP. You also learned that users are provided with capabilities to sign up for a realm, either by enabling self-registration to a realm or by integrating with a third-party provider. Finally, you learned that users can also manage their accounts through the Keycloak Account Console.

In the next chapter, we are going to look at how users can authenticate using different credentials, as well as how Keycloak is the perfect fit for strong authentication.

Questions

1. Can I integrate my own user database with Keycloak?

2. Does Keycloak query the LDAP directory every time the user authenticates?

3. How do I differentiate users that have been created using a third-party or social identity provider?

Further reading

For more information on the topics that were covered in this chapter, you can refer to the following links:

- Keycloak user management: `https://www.keycloak.org/docs/latest/server_admin/#user-management`

- Keycloak user federation: `https://www.keycloak.org/docs/latest/server_admin/#_user-storage-federation`

- Keycloak identity brokering: `https://www.keycloak.org/docs/latest/server_admin/#_identity_broker`

- Keycloak Account Console: `https://www.keycloak.org/docs/latest/server_admin/#_account-service`

11
Authenticating Users

In the previous chapters, you learned how to manage users. You also walked through examples that involved users authenticating in Keycloak.

By now, you should be aware of how easy it is to set up Keycloak to promptly authenticate your users, but there is much more to authentication than just using a login page and asking users for passwords.

In this chapter, we are going to take a closer look at how authentication works, as well as the different authentication methods you can use to authenticate users. You will also be presented with more details about how password-based authentication works and how Keycloak can be used as a strong authentication system by leveraging **two-factor authentication (2FA)** and **multi-factor authentication (MFA)**. For that, you will learn about the different types of credentials you can choose from to authenticate users and how they work together to increase the overall security of your system.

In this chapter, we will cover the following topics:

- Understanding authentication flows
- Using passwords
- Using OTPs
- Using Web Authentication (WebAuthn)
- Using strong authentication

Technical requirements

Before we begin, create a `myrealm` realm and a user called `alice` in this realm.

In the next few sections, we will be using the Keycloak account console to authenticate `alice` using the different authentication strategies.

Check out the following link to see the Code in Action video: `https://bit.ly/3h58eGh`

Understanding authentication flows

In Keycloak, authentication is driven by a set of sequential steps or executions that are grouped together to define how the identity should be verified, depending on the authentication flow. Depending on the flow, the authentication requirements, as well as the steps to verify the identity of the actor trying to authenticate into a realm, changes.

Keycloak has a set of well-defined flows representing how end users and clients – the actors – can authenticate into a realm. For end users, the authentication flow usually involves using the browser as an intermediary. The steps for the clients are based on backchannel requests to the token endpoint.

Keycloak is very flexible in terms of how you can define these flows. By default, realms are created with built-in definitions that cover the most common requirements to authenticate end users and clients, which you can change or extend any time to address your own authentication requirements.

To understand this better, let's look at the available authentication flow definitions for the `myrealm` realm. For that, open the administration console and click on the **Authentication** link in the left-hand side menu:

Authentication

| Flows | Bindings | Required Actions | Password Policy | OTP Policy | WebAuthn Policy ❷ | WebAuthn Passwordless Policy ❷ |

| Browser ⌄ ❶ | | | | | | | New | Copy |

Auth Type			Requirement				
Cookie			○ REQUIRED	◉ ALTERNATIVE	○ DISABLED		
Kerberos			○ REQUIRED	○ ALTERNATIVE	◉ DISABLED		
Identity Provider Redirector			○ REQUIRED	◉ ALTERNATIVE	○ DISABLED		Actions ⌄
Forms ❷			○ REQUIRED	◉ ALTERNATIVE	○ DISABLED	○ CONDITIONAL	
	Username Password Form		◉ REQUIRED				
	Browser - Conditional OTP ❷		○ REQUIRED	◉ ALTERNATIVE	○ DISABLED	○ CONDITIONAL	
		Condition - User Configured	◉ REQUIRED	○ DISABLED			
		OTP Form	◉ REQUIRED	○ ALTERNATIVE	○ DISABLED		

Figure 11.1 – Authentication flow definitions

From this page, you can select and see the definition for a given authentication flow, as well as a list of all the definitions available in the realm. Don't worry about understanding this page right now – we are going to go over it in the next section.

In the second tab, called **Bindings**, you have the relationships between the definitions from the first tab and the authentication flow that they are related to. This is the place where you choose the definition to be used when you're executing a determined flow to authenticate end users and clients:

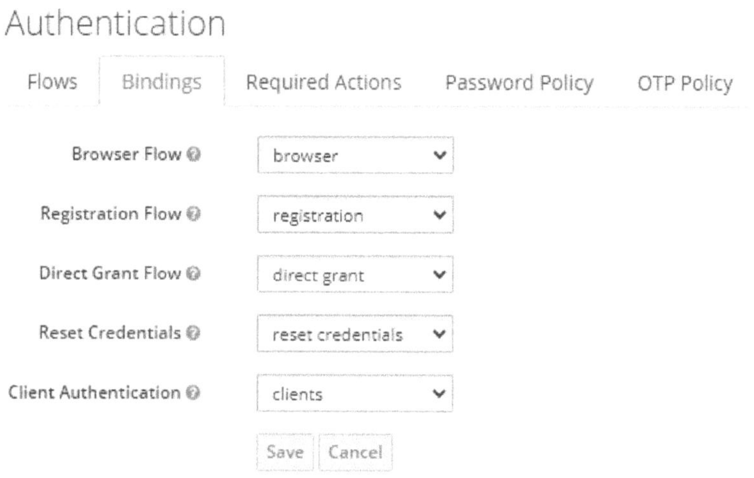

Authentication

| Flows | Bindings | Required Actions | Password Policy | OTP Policy |

Browser Flow   `browser`

Registration Flow   `registration`

Direct Grant Flow   `direct grant`

Reset Credentials   `reset credentials`

Client Authentication   `clients`

Save   Cancel

Figure 11.2 – The bindings between authentication flow definitions and the flow

In the context of authentication, you can configure the following flows:

- Browser Flow
- Direct Grant Flow
- Client Authentication

Browser Flow is related to how end users authenticate using a browser. Every time the end user authenticates in Keycloak, the steps from the definition associated with this flow are executed. As shown in the preceding screenshot, all the steps from the **browser** authentication flow definition are going to be executed when you're authenticating users through the browser.

The same goes for **Direct Grant Flow** and **Client Authentication**. However, these two flows are related to how clients authenticate in a realm – **Client Authentication** – or when clients are authenticating users – **Direct Grant Flow** – using backchannel requests to obtain tokens using the token endpoint.

> **Note**
>
> In the **Bindings** tab, you will also find the configuration for the user registration – **Registration Flow** – and password reset – **Reset Credentials** – flows. These two flows also have definitions associated with them so that you can configure the steps for user self-registration, as well as the steps for when users need to reset their passwords, respectively.

Configuring an authentication flow

Keycloak allows you to customize any of the authentication flows from the **Bindings** tab. To do this, you can change the settings of the authentication flow definition associated with them or create your own using an existing one as a template.

The easiest – and recommended – way to create a flow is to use an existing definition as a template by selecting a definition from the **Flows** tab and clicking on the **Copy** button. The reason for this is that you can easily roll back your changes and switch to the definition you used as a template, in case the flow is broken by your changes.

Let's have a quick look at how to customize **Browser Flow** and see how it affects end users authenticating in a realm using a browser. For that, select **Browser Flow** from the select box of the **Flows** tab. Then, click on the **Copy** button to create a new flow based on it. You should be prompted to choose a name for the new flow. Let's name it My Browser and click on the **OK** button to create a new flow.

An authentication flow is a hierarchical tree containing different authentication executions – the authentication steps – as well as other authentication flows – also known as subflows.

Authentication executions are the actual steps that perform some action when you're authenticating an actor. These actions can be related to obtaining some input from the actor – such as asking end users for only their username when using the browser – or to authenticate the actor using a specific authentication mechanism, such as when you're authenticating clients using different types of credentials.

The elements in an authentication flow are executed sequentially, from top to bottom. The decision regarding whether the next step in the flow should be executed depends on the outcome of the current step and its settings. When a step is marked as **REQUIRED**, it must complete successfully prior to moving to the next one. If a required step completes successfully, the flow stops if there are no other required steps in the flow. On the other hand, when a step is marked as **ALTERNATIVE**, the flow can continue, even though the step was not completed successfully, so that other steps have a chance to successfully perform their actions.

For authentication flows and subflows, the **REQUIRED** and **ALTERNATIVE** settings are related to whether all the required executions or any of the executions within the flow completed successfully, respectively.

Taking the **My Browser** flow definition as an example, authentication is defined as follows:

1. First, the **Cookie** execution tries to seamlessly reauthenticate the user if there is a cookie in the request that maps to a valid user session. In other words, do not try to authenticate users if they previously authenticated to the realm. This step is marked as **ALTERNATIVE**, indicating that if the user could not be authenticated at this step, the flow will continue.

2. If **Kerberos** execution is enabled, try to authenticate the user using any Kerberos credentials. Note that by default, this execution is disabled.

3. **Identity Provider Redirector** checks whether the realm has been configured to automatically redirect the user to a predefined identity provider. It is also marked as **ALTERNATIVE**; not completing this step will continue the flow.

4. **My Browser Forms** is a subflow that groups specific steps to authenticate the user using password-based authentication and possibly 2FA using a **One-Time Password (OTP)**. Note that this step is marked as **ALTERNATIVE**, so if any of the previous steps completed successfully, it will not be executed. Otherwise, users would be forced to provide their credentials again, even though they have already been authenticated.

5. The first step in the subflow is to authenticate the user using a username and password in a single step using the **Username Password Form** execution. This is the login page you saw when you authenticated into a realm. Note that this step must complete successfully as it is marked as **REQUIRED**.

6. If the previous step was successful – the user was authenticated initially – then there is another subflow you can use called **My Browser Browser – Conditional OTP** to check whether 2FA using an OTP should be performed. In this subflow, **Condition – User Configured** checks whether the user has an OTP credential set and, if so, performs the **OTP Form** step to authenticate the user using OTP.

Now, let's change how users authenticate in the realm by gathering both the username and password in different steps and from different pages, instead of asking for the credentials using a single login page. For that, click on the **Actions** menu on the right-hand side of the **Username Password Form** execution and click on the **Delete** option. At the moment, your flow should look as follows:

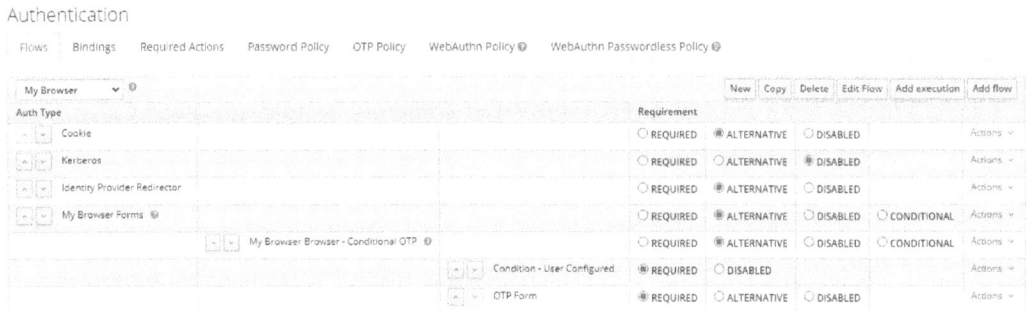

Figure 11.3 – Removing the Username Password Form execution from the flow

Now, let's add two steps to this flow to ask the user for the username and then ask for the password. For that, click on the **Actions** menu on the right-hand side of the **My Browser Forms** subflow and click on the **Add execution** button.

Once you've done that, you should be redirected to a page where you can choose the authentication execution to include as a step of the subflow:

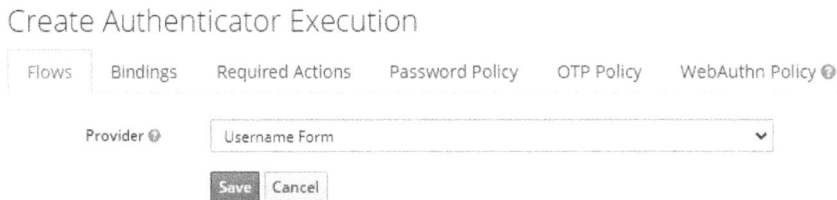

Figure 11.4 – Choosing an authentication execution

On this page, you should be able to select from a vast list of authentication executions. In our case, we are going to select **Username Form** from the **Provider** select box and click on the **Save** button to add the execution to the subflow.

Once the execution has been added to the flow, you should see it within the subflow. By default, executions are added to the bottom of the flow, but in our case, we want this execution at the top of the subflow so that we can obtain the username first. For that, click on the up arrow on the left-hand side of **Username Form** until it becomes the first execution in the subflow.

Perform the same steps you did previously to add the **Password Form** authentication execution to the subflow to obtain the password and authenticate the user. Make sure **Password Form** is the second execution in the subflow.

Let's make sure that both the **Username Form** and **Password Form** executions are marked as **REQUIRED**. For that, click on the **REQUIRED** setting for each authentication execution. This is an important step as it forces our end users to provide both pieces of information when they're logging into the realm.

Now, the **My Browser** authentication flow should look like this:

Authentication

| Flows | Bindings | Required Actions | Password Policy | OTP Policy | WebAuthn Policy ❷ | WebAuthn Passwordless Policy ❷ |

| My Browser ∨ ❷ | | | | | New | Copy | Delete | Edit Flow | Add execution | Add flow |

Auth Type			Requirement				
∧ ∨ Cookie			○ REQUIRED	⦿ ALTERNATIVE	○ DISABLED		Actions ∨
∧ ∨ Kerberos			○ REQUIRED	○ ALTERNATIVE	⦿ DISABLED		Actions ∨
∧ ∨ Identity Provider Redirector			○ REQUIRED	⦿ ALTERNATIVE	○ DISABLED		Actions ∨
∧ ∨ My Browser Forms ❷			○ REQUIRED	⦿ ALTERNATIVE	○ DISABLED	○ CONDITIONAL	Actions ∨
	∧ ∨ Username Form		⦿ REQUIRED				Actions ∨
	∧ ∨ Password Form		⦿ REQUIRED	○ ALTERNATIVE	○ DISABLED		Actions ∨
	∧ ∨ My Browser Browser - Conditional OTP ❷		○ REQUIRED	⦿ ALTERNATIVE	○ DISABLED	○ CONDITIONAL	Actions ∨
		∧ ∨ Condition - User Configured	⦿ REQUIRED	○ DISABLED			Actions ∨
		∧ ∨ OTP Form	⦿ REQUIRED	○ ALTERNATIVE	○ DISABLED		Actions ∨

Figure 11.5 – The final configuration for the My Browser authentication flow

Finally, click on the **Bindings** tab and change **Browser Flow** to associate it with the **My Browser** authentication flow definition we just created. At this point, the configuration in the **Bindings** tab should look as follows:

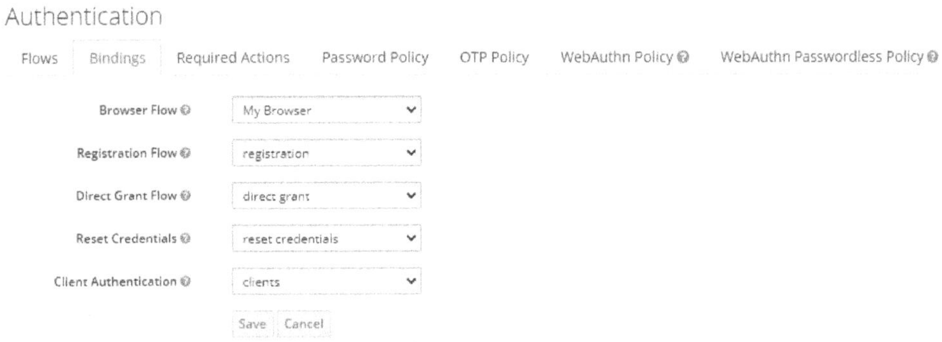

Authentication

| Flows | Bindings | Required Actions | Password Policy | OTP Policy | WebAuthn Policy ❷ | WebAuthn Passwordless Policy ❷ |

Browser Flow ❷	My Browser ∨
Registration Flow ❷	registration ∨
Direct Grant Flow ❷	direct grant ∨
Reset Credentials ❷	reset credentials ∨
Client Authentication ❷	clients ∨

Save   Cancel

Figure 11.6 – Binding the My Browser authentication flow definition to Browser Flow

Now, let's try to log into the Keycloak account console as `alice`. For that, open your browser at `http://localhost:8080/auth/realms/myrealm/account` and log in using your user credentials. When authenticating to the realm, you should notice that the username and password of the user are obtained and validated in multiple steps.

In this section, you learned about the main aspects of authentication flows. You learned that Keycloak allows you to customize how users and clients authenticate by creating or changing authentication flow definitions. You also learned that by leveraging authentication flows, you can adapt Keycloak so that it fits into your authentication requirements.

In the next few sections, we will look at the different authentication methods supported by Keycloak.

Using passwords

In the previous chapters, you were basically using passwords to authenticate users. You were also quickly introduced to how to set up passwords when managing users. In this section, we are going to look closer at how password-based authentication works and how passwords are managed.

> **Note**
>
> We are not going to cover how users authenticate using passwords here because you are already familiar with that, but we will be covering additional details around this form of authentication.

Password-based authentication is probably one of the most popular methods for authenticating users. It is easy to implement and is what most end users are used to when they need to authenticate into a system. However, the simplicity of this credential type has some disadvantages and weaknesses, all of which we will cover later in this section.

To help us overcome some of the disadvantages of password-based authentication, Keycloak relies on common best practices to make sure passwords are secure in transit and at rest. It also allows you to define policies so that you can govern some key aspects of password management, such as expiry, password format, and reusing previous passwords.

Passwords are the simplest type of credential that you can set for your users and are used by Keycloak to authenticate users by default. Passwords are managed on a per-user basis, as you learned in the previous chapter. On the **User details** page, there is a **Credentials** tab, which provides everything you need to reset and delete the user's password:

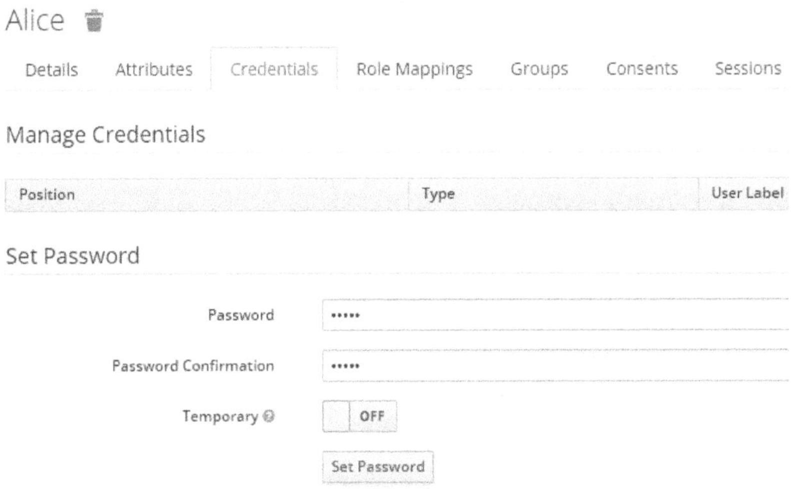

Alice 🗑

| Details | Attributes | Credentials | Role Mappings | Groups | Consents | Sessions |

Manage Credentials

Position	Type	User Label

Set Password

Password	•••••
Password Confirmation	•••••
Temporary ❓	OFF
	Set Password

Figure 11.7 – Managing user passwords

Keycloak uses a strong password **hashing algorithm** to prevent brute-force attacks, as well as to securely store passwords. The default hashing algorithm used by Keycloak is **PBKDF2**, a well-known and widely used algorithm to keep passwords secure at rest.

Whenever you set a password for a user, its value is going to be combined with a secure random number, also known as a **salt**, and later hashed multiple times – the number of **iterations** – to create a derived key that is hard to crack. When stored, the password is never in plain text. Instead, the derived key is stored together with the necessary metadata to validate the password afterward.

Keycloak is preconfigured for hashing passwords using **HMAC-SHA-256** and has an iteration count of **27,500**. You should be able to use a stronger hashing algorithm such as **HMAC-SHA-512** or change the number of iterations when you're configuring password policies, as we are going to see later.

> **Tip**
> The PBKDF2 algorithm is costly in terms of CPU. Depending on the CPU you have available for Keycloak, it might impact its performance. The default of 27,500 iterations is what we recommend for most deployments, but you should be able to either lower or increase this number, depending on your requirements, to have a balance between performance and security.

Password-based authentication is not the most secure method of authenticating users, since there is a long list of weaknesses associated with it. To name a few, passwords are usually stolen or leaked, they are susceptible to phishing attacks, and some users just do not care about how strong their passwords are, making your system as secure as how your users define, keep, and use their passwords. The fact that users usually use the same password across different systems also makes your system as secure as the weakest system in this chain. In terms of usability, when using policies to force users to use strong passwords, they become larger and complicated, which makes them hard to remember or even type when they're authenticating to a system.

Keycloak helps you improve the overall security of password-based authentication, but it does not solve all such problems. Passwords, when used alone, are just a single factor for authenticating users, so you should consider using additional factors to improve the overall security of your system. As we are going to see in the upcoming sections, password-based authentication is not the only option you have to authenticate users in Keycloak, allowing you to employ strong authentication to your system by combining other forms of authentication or even by removing passwords completely.

In this section, you learned about the key aspects of how passwords are managed in Keycloak. You also learned that Keycloak relies on common best practices to keep passwords secure, and that you can also use policies to control different aspects of password management.

In the next section, you will learn how Keycloak allows you to configure password policies to employ stronger passwords.

Changing password policies

Keycloak allows you to define different types of policies for passwords. These policies can be created by clicking on the **Authentication** link on the left-hand side menu, and then clicking on the **Password Policy** tab:

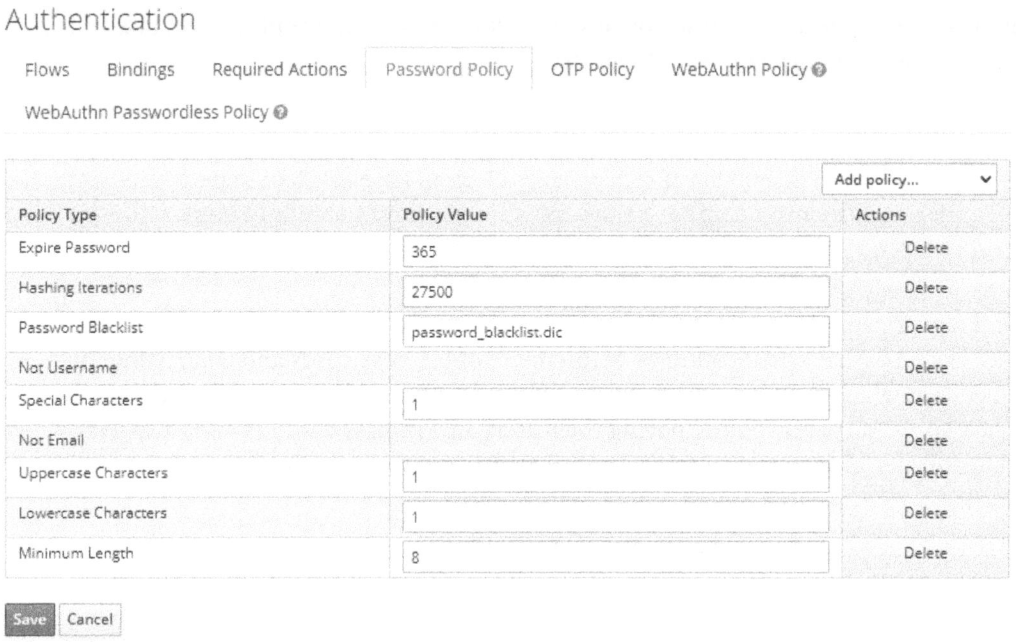

Authentication

Flows   Bindings   Required Actions   Password Policy   OTP Policy   WebAuthn Policy ❷

WebAuthn Passwordless Policy ❷

		Add policy... ⌄
Policy Type	Policy Value	Actions
Expire Password	365	Delete
Hashing Iterations	27500	Delete
Password Blacklist	password_blacklist.dic	Delete
Not Username		Delete
Special Characters	1	Delete
Not Email		Delete
Uppercase Characters	1	Delete
Lowercase Characters	1	Delete
Minimum Length	8	Delete

Save   Cancel

Figure 11.8 – Password policies settings

In this tab, you can choose from different policies and manage specific aspects of password management, such as the following:

- Enforce the number of special characters, digits, and lowercase or uppercase characters in passwords.

- Define a minimum length.

- Define an expiration time.

- Avoid having the user's username in passwords.

- Define a blacklist dictionary.

- Avoid reusing previous passwords.

You can easily create any of these policies by clicking on the **Add policy** select box and then selecting the policy you want to create.

> Tip
>
> For a detailed description of each policy available in Keycloak, look at the documentation at `https://www.keycloak.org/docs/latest/server_admin/#_password-policies`.

By leveraging password policies, you should be able to overcome some of the weaknesses of password-based authentication by enforcing stronger passwords and controlling the frequency at which they should be updated. You should be able to easily define rules for passwords, such as avoiding having their username in passwords, forcing a specific number of special, lowercase, and uppercase characters, forcing a minimum length, and so forth.

In this section, you learned that Keycloak allows you to control different aspects of password management by using different types of policies.

In the next section, we will look at the different options we can use to reset user passwords.

Resetting user passwords

Keycloak allows you to reset users password using different strategies. As an administrator, you can use the administration console to choose a password for a user or force the user to update their password when they log in. Users should also be able to reset their passwords when they're on the login page or when they're managing their account through the Keycloak account console.

When you change the password of a user through the administration console, Keycloak defaults to marking the new password as temporary. A temporary password means that the next time the user tries to log into a realm, they must provide a new password.

You can control whether a password that's been set by an administrator is temporary by turning on the **Temporary** switch when you're on the **Credentials** tab of the **User details** page. If you turn off this setting, the user will not be asked to change their password when they log in.

A temporary password is nothing but a shortcut for setting a required action for a user to force them to update their password. The **Update Password** required action can be set at any time by an administrator to force a specific user to update their password:

Users > alice

Alice 🗑

| Details | Attributes | Credentials | Role Mappings | Groups | Consents | Sessions |

ID	3a9e0dc1-d929-4956-8fa9-ed9d156a0f86
Created At	2/23/21 3:09:32 PM
Username	alice
Email	
First Name	
Last Name	
User Enabled ⊘	ON
Email Verified ⊘	OFF
Required User Actions ⊘	✕ Update Password
Impersonate user ⊘	Impersonate
	Save Cancel

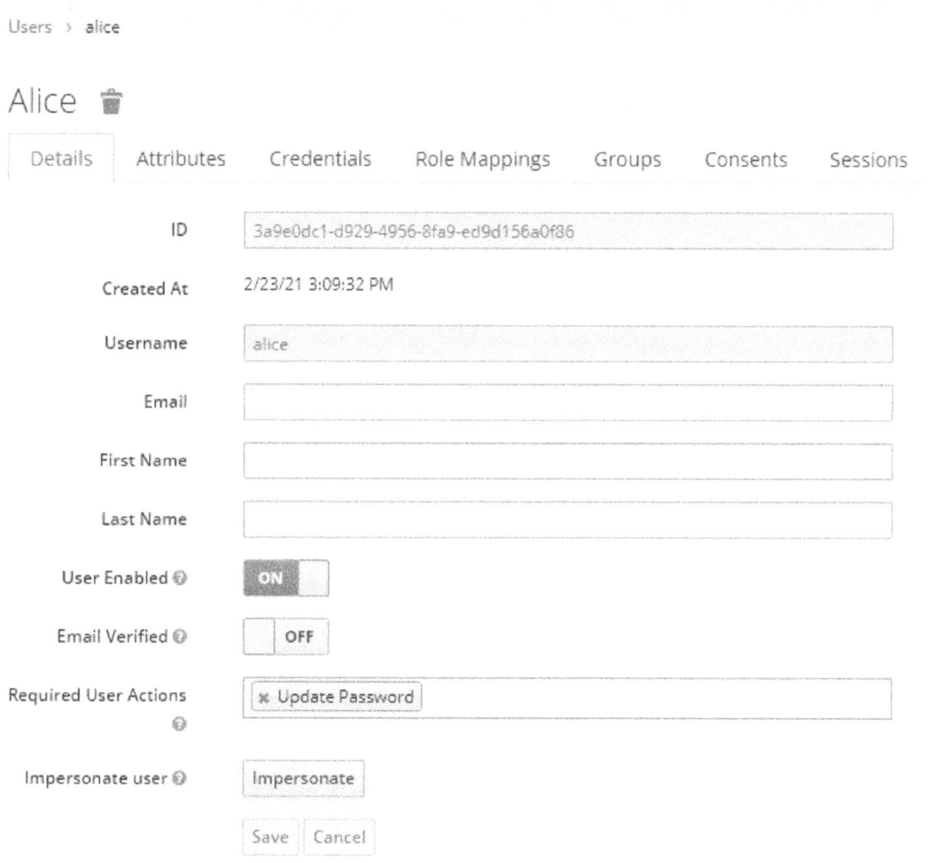

Figure 11.9 – Using the Update Password required action to force users to update their password

From a user's perspective, passwords can be updated either by going to the Keycloak Account Console or by starting a specific flow on the login page.

From the account console, users can change their passwords by clicking on the **Update** button when they're on the **Signing In** page:

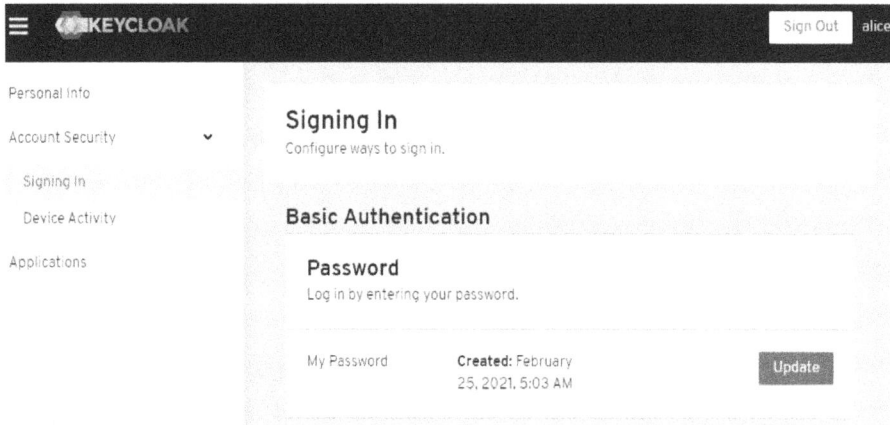

Figure 11.10 – Updating the password using the Account Console

If the user has forgotten or lost their password, they can start a specific flow to reset their password on the login page. This flow is disabled by default. To enable it, you click on the **Realm Settings** link on the left-hand side menu of the administration console and click on the **Login** tab. On this tab, turn on the **Forgot password** setting. A link will appear on the login page that users can click on to reset their passwords:

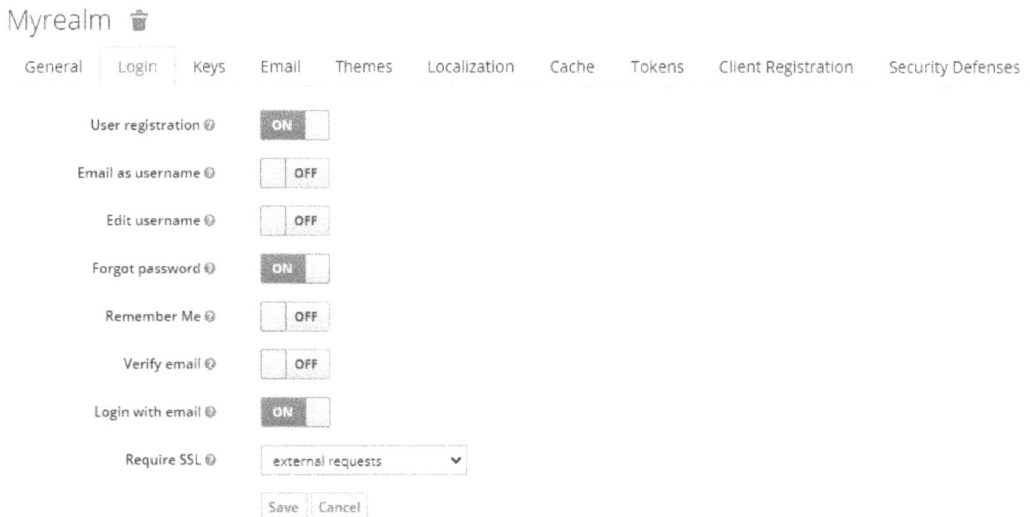

Figure 11.11 – Changing the realm settings to allow users to reset their passwords

When this setting is enabled, users should be presented with a **Forgot Password?** link on the login page:

Figure 11.12 – The Forgot Password? link on the login page

By clicking on the **Forgot Password?** link, the users will be asked to provide their username or email so that they can receive a link by email to reset their password.

> **Note**
>
> Note that this flow is based on email verification, where users should have a valid email address associated with their accounts. Your realm should also be configured to send emails using your preferred SMTP server. For more details on how to set up an SMTP server, look at the documentation at `https://www.keycloak.org/docs/latest/server_admin/#_email`.

In this section, we covered the different ways we can manage passwords. You learned that passwords can be set by an administrator, and that users can be forced to update their password when they're authenticating to a realm. You also learned that users can change or reset passwords through the account console or the login page, respectively.

You were also presented with more details on how password-based authentication works in Keycloak. You learned how Keycloak keeps passwords secure at rest, as well as how Keycloak helps you employ strong passwords and control the different aspects of password management by leveraging password policies. Finally, you learned that password-based authentication is only one, and not the most secure, of the available options you can use to authenticate users.

In the next section, we are going to look at how to authenticate users more securely by combining passwords and **OTPs** to enable **2FA**.

Using OTPs

As an additional layer of security, Keycloak allows you to use a second factor – or evidence – when authenticating users. In addition to providing a password – something users know – users are obligated to provide secondary evidence about their identity – something they have – which can be a code or a security key in their possession.

OTP is probably one of the most common ways to enable 2FA for user accounts. They are relatively easy to use and add an additional layer of security when you're authenticating users.

Although it's a useful method for 2FA, OTP has some disadvantages. It relies on a shared key between the server and users and does not provide the best usability for end users, while still open to common attacks such as phishing or scams. As we are going to see later, Keycloak helps you overcome these limitations by using a security device as a second factor using WebAuthn.

> **Note**
> As we will see in the following sections, 2FA is an important part of **MFA**.

Keycloak makes it easy to configure and authenticate users using OTP, where realms are automatically configured to support 2FA using OTP. Users are also allowed to easily set up 2FA for their accounts by registering their devices to generate OTP codes.

In the next few sections, we will look at how to configure and authenticate using OTP.

Changing OTP policies

Keycloak allows you to define different policies for OTPs. These policies can be changed by clicking on the **Authentication** link on the left-hand side menu and then clicking on the **OTP Policy** tab:

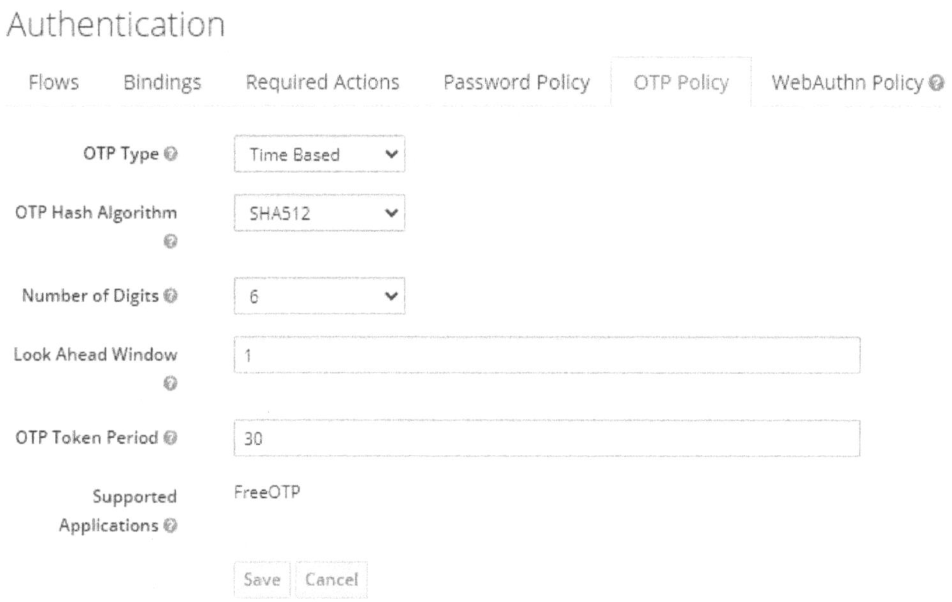

Authentication

| Flows | Bindings | Required Actions | Password Policy | OTP Policy | WebAuthn Policy ❷ |

OTP Type ❷   [Time Based ▾]

OTP Hash Algorithm   [SHA512 ▾]
❷

Number of Digits ❷   [6 ▾]

Look Ahead Window   [1]
❷

OTP Token Period ❷   [30]

Supported   FreeOTP
Applications ❷

[Save] [Cancel]

Figure 11.13 – OTP Policy tab

An OTP is a code based on a secret key – hashed using a specific algorithm – and a moving factor that can be either the current time or a counter, where this code can only be used once to authenticate a user. Keycloak can authenticate and allow users to generate codes using two main algorithms:

- **Time-Based One-Time Password (TOTP)**

- **HMAC-Based One-Time Password (HOTP)**

By default, realms created in Keycloak are configured to use TOTP. They are also configured with only six digits and have a validity window of 30 seconds. You can change these settings any time, based on your requirements.

> **Tip**
> When you change the details in this tab – mainly the OTP type and the hash algorithm – make sure the apps that are being used by your users to generate codes support the configuration.

The difference between the two algorithms is the moving factor that's used to generate the code and how they are validated. As the name implies, a TOTP is based on time, so the code is only valid for a certain period – usually 30 seconds. On the other hand, HOTP is based on a counter. The validity of the code is infinite until the code is validated and the counter is increased.

The decision of which algorithm to use is use case-specific. However, TOTP provides better security than HOTP because if the code is lost or leaked, its validity window is reduced, hence reducing the attack surface when it comes to using OTPs.

> **Note**
>
> Due to TOTP being based on time, you should be aware that the host where Keycloak is deployed should have the clock in sync with the devices being used by your users to generate codes. If the clock is not in sync, users might be unable to authenticate using TOTP. You should be able to define a clock skew compensation to reduce the difference between clocks. For that, set **Look Ahead Window** with the number of seconds to compensate for the time difference.

From a user's perspective, Keycloak allows users to obtain OTP codes from their own personal devices – such as their smartphones or tablets – using two main mobile applications available from the Android and iOS app stores:

- **FreeOTP**
- **Google Authenticator**

As you will learn in the next few sections, by using either of these apps, your users can easily enable 2FA for their accounts and authenticate in a realm using OTP.

In this section, your learned about OTP and how to change its settings. You also learned that users can use their preferred devices to generate codes using the FreeOTP and Google Authenticator apps.

Now, let's look at the different strategies we can use to authenticate users using OTPs.

Allowing users to choose whether they want to use OTP

Once your users have been successfully authenticated using their passwords, Keycloak is going to check whether they have any OTP credentials associated with their account. If no OTP credentials have been set, Keycloak authenticates the user and redirects the user back to the application. That is the behavior you have seen so far when a user has been authenticating to a realm.

However, if the user has an OTP credential set, Keycloak is going to perform an additional step during the authentication flow to obtain the OTP from the user and validate it, prior to authenticating the user.

Let's see how this works by logging into the account console using the user `alice`. For that, open your browser at `http://localhost:8080/auth/realms/myrealm/account` and log in using the appropriate user credentials. Note that at the moment, `alice` is only using her password to authenticate.

In the account console, users can set up 2FA using OTP by clicking on the **Set up Authenticator Application** button when they're on the **Signing In** page:

Figure 11.14 – Configuring 2FA using OTP

After choosing to set up a new authenticator, your users will be presented with a QR code representing the shared key that will be used to generate the codes. By using your smartphone, you should be able to scan this QR code using either the FreeOTP or Google Authenticator mobile applications:

Figure 11.15 – Configuring a new OTP

After scanning the QR code using any of these applications, they are going to start generating the codes that we will be using to complete the OTP credential registration process, as well as to authenticate the user later, once we've finish this step. Note that codes are generated every 30 seconds since we are using TOTP.

To complete the OTP credential registration process, set the **One-time code** field with any code from the mobile application you are using and click on the **Submit** button. Optionally, users can also define an alias for the OTP credential they are creating.

Now, let's try to authenticate again as `alice`. To do that, click on the **Sign Out** link at the top-left corner of the page to log out from the account console, and then authenticate again using the username and password of that user:

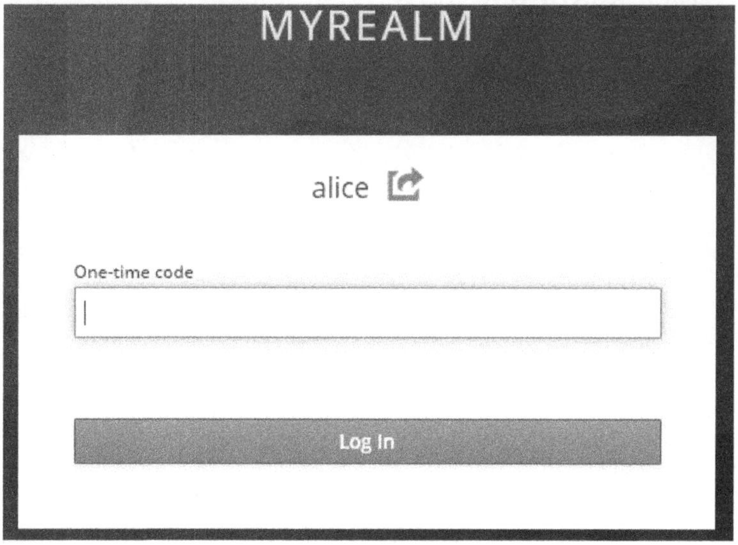

Figure 11.16 – User is prompted to provide the code when logging in

Compared to what happened previously, now, you will be presented with a page asking you to provide a code. Use your smartphone to obtain a code and fill in the **One-time code** field. By clicking the **Log In** button, you should be able to access the account console if Keycloak was able to successfully validate the code you provided.

In this section, you learned that Keycloak defaults to requiring 2FA, but only if the user is associated with an OTP credential. You also learned that by leveraging the account console, users can easily set up 2FA for their accounts.

In the next section, you are going to learn how to force 2FA for all users in a realm.

Forcing users to authenticate using OTP

For some use cases, the decision of whether to authenticate using OTP is not up to users but based on the security constraints that have been defined for a realm. Keycloak allows you to change the default behavior of OTP authentication to force users to either set up an OTP credential prior to authenticating, or to use an existing one to successfully authenticate to a realm.

To enable this behavior, click on the **Authentication** link on the left-hand side menu and then select **Browser** from the list of available flows.

On this page, you are going to change the requirements for the **Browser - Conditional OTP** step and mark it as **REQUIRED**:

Authentication

| Flows | Bindings | Required Actions | Password Policy | OTP Policy | WebAuthn Policy 🕐 | WebAuthn Passwordless Policy 🕐 |

| Browser ▾ 🕐 | | | | | | New Copy |

Auth Type			Requirement			
Cookie			○ REQUIRED	⦿ ALTERNATIVE	○ DISABLED	
Kerberos			○ REQUIRED	○ ALTERNATIVE	⦿ DISABLED	
Identity Provider Redirector			○ REQUIRED	⦿ ALTERNATIVE	○ DISABLED	Actions ▾
Forms 🕐			○ REQUIRED	⦿ ALTERNATIVE	○ DISABLED	○ CONDITIONAL
	Username Password Form		⦿ REQUIRED			
	Browser - Conditional OTP 🕐		⦿ REQUIRED	○ ALTERNATIVE	○ DISABLED	○ CONDITIONAL
		Condition - User Configured	⦿ REQUIRED	○ DISABLED		
		OTP Form	⦿ REQUIRED	○ ALTERNATIVE	○ DISABLED	

Figure 11.17 – Enforcing 2FA for a realm

Now, go to the user settings for `alice` and remove the OTP credential associated with the account.

> **Note**
>
> Note that similar to passwords, administrators can set a required action to force users to configure OTP when they are logging in. For OTP, the name of the required action is **Configure OTP**.

Now, let's log into the account console using `alice`. For that, open your browser at `http://localhost:8080/auth/realms/myrealm/account` and log in using the user's credentials.

Compared to what happened previously, the user is now forced to set up an OTP credential. The steps to do so are the same as when using the account console, as you learned in the previous section. The main difference here is that users are obligated to set up an OTP credential if they do not have one. Only after that can they authenticate in a realm.

In this section, you learned how to use OTP to enable 2FA to a realm. You learned that 2FA provides a stronger authentication than only using passwords to authenticate users. You also learned that users can easily enable 2FA to their accounts by using the FreeOTP or Google Authenticator app.

We are going to extend the concepts we've presented in this chapter to set up a stronger authentication using WebAuthn for two-factor and multiple-factor authentication.

Using Web Authentication (WebAuthn)

The WebAuthn protocol aims to improve the security and usability of authenticating users over the internet. For that, it provides additional capabilities for server and security devices to communicate with each other – using the browser as an intermediary – to authenticate users using a cryptography protocol.

WebAuthn is based on asymmetric keys – a private-public key pair – to securely register users' devices and authenticate them in a system. There is no shared key between devices and the server, only a public key. By acting as an intermediary between security devices and the server, WebAuthn makes it possible to use these devices for 2FA, MFA using biometrics, or to seamlessly authenticate users without any explicit credentials other than their security devices: a concept also known as username-less and password-less authentication.

When used for 2FA, WebAuthn is a more secure method than OTP because there is no shared key between Keycloak and the third-party applications used to generate codes. Instead, users are granted a security device that relies on strong cryptography to communicate the second factor without exposing any sensitive data.

For users, WebAuthn improves their experience when they're authenticating into a system by completely eliminating the need to deal with passwords or OTP codes. Instead, they can use their devices to seamlessly authenticate themselves.

A security device – or authenticator – can be anything as long as it complies with a set of requirements from FIDO2. It can be a smartphone with support for fingerprints, a security key that's attached through a USB, or a **Near-Field Communication** (**NFC**) device.

WebAuthn gives you fine-grained control over the different aspects of how users register and authenticate through these devices. It allows you to control the requirements of how to verify the identity of the user in possession of a device or whether credentials should be stored in the device, hence eliminating the need for storing credentials on the server.

In Keycloak, you can use WebAuthn to solve different use cases:

- Allow users to register devices either during authentication or using the account console.

- Use security devices for 2FA as a more secure alternative to OTP.

- Use security devices for MFA using any form of biometric authorization supported by these devices.

- Use security devices for username-less or password-less authentication.

You should also be able to allow your users to choose from multiple authentication methods when they're on the login page. For instance, you can allow users to choose whether they want to use password-less authentication using WebAuthn or password-based authentication with OTP as a second factor.

> **Tip**
>
> For more details about how to use WebAuthn in Keycloak, look at the documentation available at `https://www.keycloak.org/docs/latest/server_admin/#_webauthn`.

In this section, you learned about some of the key concepts surrounding WebAuthn and how it helps to employ strong authentication. You also learned that WebAuthn improves user experience when security devices are used as a second factor or by removing the need to type in any credentials.

In the next section, we are going to learn how to define an authentication flow to authenticate users using WebAuthn.

Enabling WebAuthn for an authentication flow

To allow users to authenticate using their devices, we are going to need to create an authentication flow definition that supports WebAuthn.

Based on what you learned in the *Understanding authentication flows* section, create a new flow by performing the following steps:

1. Create a new flow by using the **My Browser** flow – you created it in the first section – as a template. Name the new flow My WebAuthn.

2. Delete the **OTP Form** execution from the **My WebAuthn My Browser Browser – Conditional OTP** subflow.

3. Add a new execution to the **My WebAuthn My Browser Browser – Conditional OTP** subflow by selecting the **WebAuthn Authenticator** execution.

4. Mark **My WebAuthn My Browser Browser – Conditional OTP** as a **CONDITIONAL** flow.

At this point, you should have a flow definition that looks as follows:

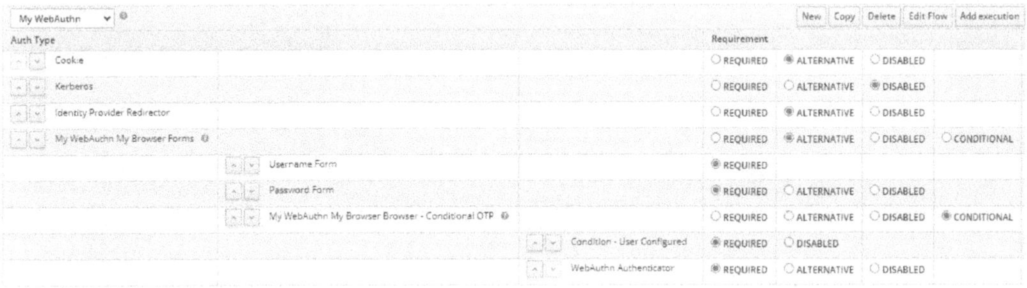

My WebAuthn ▾ ⊕				New	Copy	Delete	Edit Flow	Add execution
Auth Type			Requirement					
⌄ ⌄ Cookie			○ REQUIRED	⦿ ALTERNATIVE	○ DISABLED			
⌄ ⌄ Kerberos			○ REQUIRED	○ ALTERNATIVE	⦿ DISABLED			
⌄ ⌄ Identity Provider Redirector			○ REQUIRED	⦿ ALTERNATIVE	○ DISABLED			
⌄ ⌄ My WebAuthn My Browser Forms ⊕			○ REQUIRED	⦿ ALTERNATIVE	○ DISABLED	○ CONDITIONAL		
	⌄ ⌄ Username Form		⦿ REQUIRED					
	⌄ ⌄ Password Form		⦿ REQUIRED	○ ALTERNATIVE	○ DISABLED			
	⌄ ⌄ My WebAuthn My Browser Browser - Conditional OTP ⊕		○ REQUIRED	○ ALTERNATIVE	○ DISABLED	⦿ CONDITIONAL		
		⌄ ⌄ Condition - User Configured	⦿ REQUIRED	○ DISABLED				
		⌄ ⌄ WebAuthn Authenticator	⦿ REQUIRED	○ ALTERNATIVE	○ DISABLED			

Figure 11.18 – Creating an authentication flow definition to authenticate using a security device

Finally, associate this authentication flow definition with **Browser Flow** on the **Bindings** tab.

As you may have noticed, we are basically replacing OTP with WebAuthn for 2FA. You did not have to do much except replace the **OTP Form** execution with the **WebAuthn Authenticator** execution.

If you try to log in, you will still only be able to log in using the password because the user hasn't been configured with a security device yet.

In the next section, you will learn how users can register security devices using the account console.

Registering a security device and authenticating

The first step of enabling WebAuthn to a realm is to allow users to register their devices. Like for passwords and OTP, the registration of a security device relies on a specific required action.

For that, click on the **Authentication** link on the left-hand side menu and then click on the **Required Actions** tab. In this tab, we'll register a new required action by clicking on the **Register** button on the top-right corner of the list and selecting the **Webauthn Register** required action from the list of options. Click on the **OK** button to finish this step:

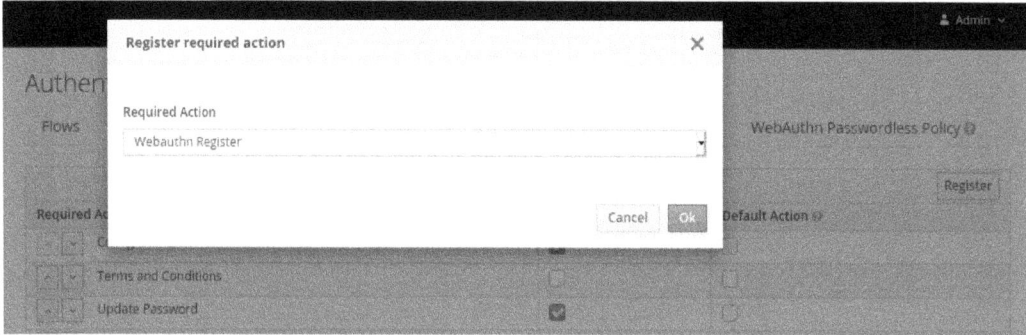

Figure 11.19 – Registering the Webauthn Register required action

After registering the **Webauthn Register** required action, you should be able to use the account console to register your security device. For that, open your browser at `http://localhost:8080/auth/realms/myrealm/account` and log in using the required user credentials. In the account console, click on the **Signing In** link on the left-hand side menu:

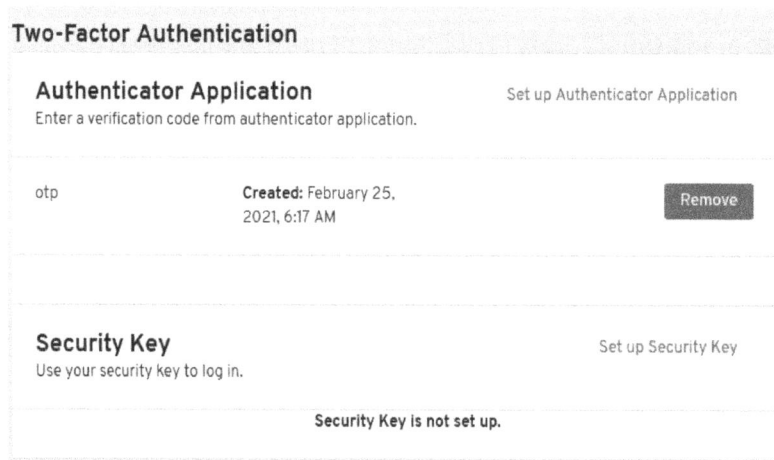

Figure 11.20 – List of available devices

On this page, look at the **Security Key** section and click on **Set up Security Key** to register a security device:

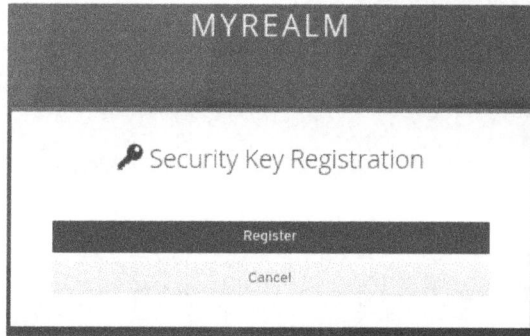

Figure 11.21 – Registering the device

To register the new device, click on the **Register** button. The browser should ask you to use your security device to complete the registration – such as by touching it – and ask what you want to name the device. You can use any name you want.

After successfully registering the device, it should be listed among the available options for 2FA:

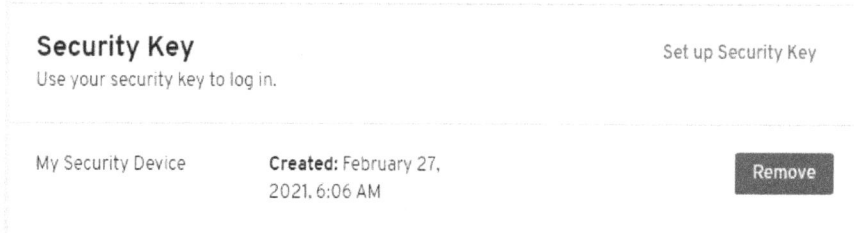

Figure 11.22 – Security device successfully registered

Now, let's try to authenticate again as `alice`. For that, click on the **Sign Out** link at the top-left corner of the page to log out from the account console, and authenticate again using the username and password of the user:

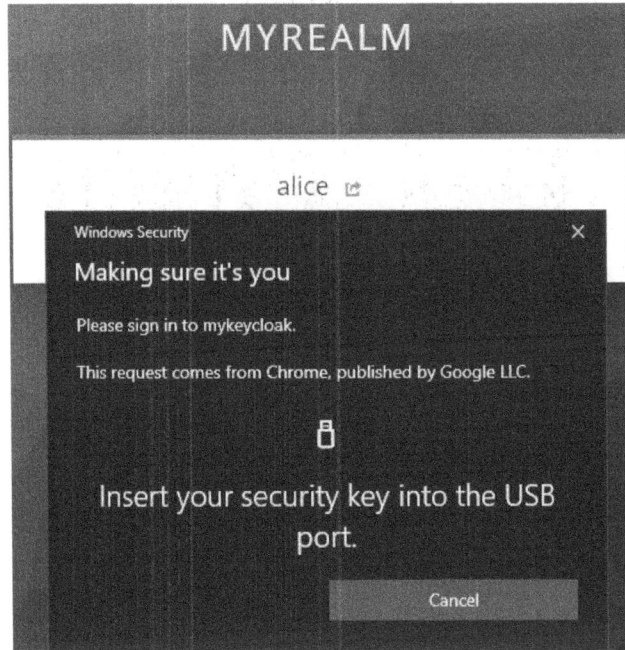

Figure 11.23 – User is requested to interact with the security device to complete the authentication process

When authenticating as `alice`, you should be prompted to interact with the security device to complete the authentication. Note that this behavior is quite similar to using OTP as a second factor, but the user does not need to type in any code, nor are they sent over the wire.

In this section, you learned how to register security devices using the account console. You also learned how easy it is to use WebAuthn and security devices for 2FA. You then learned that Keycloak allows you to use WebAuthn for multi-factor authentication by relying on any biometrics authorization provided by a security device.

In the next section, you will be presented with some key concepts around strong authentication.

Using strong authentication

Strong authentication is a term that's widely used nowadays. What it means depends on the context where it is used. In general, strong authentication is about employing either two-factor or multiple-factor authentication to authenticate users.

As you learned in the previous sections, Keycloak provides the necessary capabilities to enable either 2FA or MFA for a realm. If your requirements for strong authentication only require the use of 2FA, you are good to go with either OTP or a security device when you're using WebAuthn.

However, MFA is probably the strongest form of authentication you can get, where biometric authorization is a key aspect of securely identifying and authenticating the user. In this case, you should consider using WebAuthn and setting up security devices to verify the identity of the user – using fingerprint scanning, for instance – to make sure the user using the device is indeed the user trying to authenticate.

Strong authentication can also involve leveraging 2FA or MFA to enable other authentication factors, such as the history of IP addresses and devices that users are using to authenticate. In this case, you might want to select the best factor to authenticate a user, depending on a risk score or based on the user's behavior. Alternatively, you may just wish to force the user to reauthenticate when they're accessing sensitive data or performing a critical action on your system.

At the time of writing this book, Keycloak does not provide built-in support for some common authentication paradigms such as adaptive authentication, risk-based authentication, or step-up authentication.

However, as you learned in this chapter, Keycloak is very flexible in terms of how you can configure as well as implement new forms of authentication for a realm. As you will see in *Chapter 13, Extending Keycloak*, Keycloak provides a set of **Service Provider Interfaces** (**SPIs**) that developers can use to extend its core capabilities.

In this section, you had a quick overview of strong authentication and how Keycloak can help you to achieve it. Now, let's take a look at this chapter's summary.

Summary

In this chapter, you were provided with more details on how to authenticate users in Keycloak. First, you were introduced to authentication flows and how they play an important role in defining how users – as well as clients – authenticate in a realm. You were presented with the main authentication methods supported by Keycloak and how to configure them to promptly authenticate users, as well as how to combine them to support 2FA and MFA. Finally, you were briefly introduced to strong authentication and how Keycloak can help you employ secure authentication methods for a realm.

By leveraging the information in this chapter, you should now be able to customize Keycloak to authenticate users according to your needs and using different authentication methods.

In the next chapter, you are going to look at session management and how it correlates with authentication.

Questions

1. How do I change the look and feel of the pages shown in this chapter?

   Keycloak allows you to customize its look and feel entirely, not just for the pages that were presented in this chapter. As we are going to see in *Chapter 13, Extending Keycloak*, you should be able to change the look and feel of pages by changing the different themes provided by Keycloak. You can find more details in the documentation at `https://www.keycloak.org/docs/latest/server_development/#_themes`.

2. I cannot follow the WebAuthn examples and register a security device. What am I missing?

   WebAuthn requires you to use a FIDO - or FIDO2-compliant security device. You should also consider accessing Keycloak using HTTPS and using a valid domain name. WebAuthn is strict about domain names and secure connections if the server is accessed from a different domain than the client. You should also make sure the browser you are using has support for the WebAuthn API. You should also consider looking at the demo on the WebAuthn site to check how your security device works there.

Further reading

- Keycloak authentication documentation: `https://www.keycloak.org/docs/latest/server_admin/#authenticationKeycloak`

- Keycloak required actions: `https://www.keycloak.org/docs/latest/server_admin/#required-actions`

- Keycloak login page settings: `https://www.keycloak.org/docs/latest/server_admin/#login-page-settings`

- Keycloak Account Console: `https://www.keycloak.org/docs/latest/server_admin/#_account-service`

- WebAuthn: `https://webauthn.io/`

12
Managing Tokens and Sessions

In addition to acting as a centralized authentication and authorization service, Keycloak is, at its core, a session and token management system.

As part of the authentication process, Keycloak may create server-side sessions and correlate them with tokens. By relying on these sessions, Keycloak is able to keep the state of the authentication context where sessions originated, track users' and clients' activity, check the validity of tokens, and decide when users and clients should re-authenticate.

In this chapter, we are going to look at how Keycloak allows you to manage tokens and their underlying sessions, as well as understanding the different aspects that you should be aware of when doing so. For that, we are going to cover the following topics:

- Managing sessions
- Managing tokens

Technical requirements

During this chapter, you are going to use the Keycloak administration console to follow some of the examples herein provided, therefore make sure you have Keycloak up and running as per what you learned from *Chapter 1*, *Getting Started with Keycloak*.

Managing sessions

Session management has a direct impact on some key aspects such as user experience, security, and performance.

From a user experience perspective, Keycloak relies on sessions to determine whether users and clients are authenticated, for how long they should be authenticated, and when it is time to re-authenticate them. This characteristic of sessions is basically what gives users the single sign-on experience when authenticating to different clients within the same realm, and what makes a unified authentication experience possible.

From a security perspective, sessions provide a security layer for tracking and controlling user activity and for making sure that tokens issued to clients are still valid passports to act on behalf of users. They are also important to limit and control the time users can stay connected to a realm and its clients, helping to reduce the attack surface when sessions or tokens are leaked or stolen. As we are going to see later in this topic, sessions can be invalidated prematurely by administrators, users, and clients as a reaction to or prevention of unauthorized access from malicious actors.

From a performance perspective, sessions are kept in memory and they have a direct impact on the overall performance of Keycloak. As you learned from *Chapter 9*, *Configuring Keycloak for Production*, Keycloak stores sessions in shared caches where the number of active sessions and for how long they are kept alive are key factors that need to be balanced to optimize memory and CPU resources.

With all that in mind, Keycloak provides you with a flexible session and token management to balance all three aspects mentioned herein. Administrators should be able to track the active sessions for users and clients, check which clients users are authenticated to, force a single or global logout for invalidating sessions, revoke tokens, and control the different aspects of sessions' and tokens' lifetimes.

In the next topic, we are going to start looking at how to manage sessions' lifetimes.

Managing session lifetimes

One of the first questions you need to answer before going to production with Keycloak is how often users and clients should re-authenticate. To help you with this question, you should be aware of how Keycloak creates sessions and how to define their lifetimes.

The session lifetime determines when sessions should expire and be destroyed. Once expired, the users and clients associated with these sessions are no longer authenticated and are forced to re-authenticate to establish a new session.

> **Note**
>
> Keycloak expires sessions using a background task that runs from time to time, checking for expired sessions. By default, the task runs every 15 minutes. You are free to change this value if you really need to. The default setting should be enough for most deployments.

Keycloak creates sessions at different levels when authenticating users. Firstly, a user session is created to track the user activity regardless of the client. This first level is what is called the **Single Sign-on (SSO)** session, also referred to as a user session. At the second level, Keycloak creates a client session to track the user activity for each client the user is authenticated to in the user session. Client sessions are strictly related to the validity of tokens and how they are used by applications.

As a top-level session, the SSO session lifetime is a global setting used to control how often users and clients need to re-authenticate. Keycloak allows you to configure the maximum time that SSO sessions should be kept alive and the idle period after which to expire sessions prematurely. When an SSO session expires, all client sessions associated with it also expire.

> **Note**
>
> The SSO session is like an HTTP session. Both are used to track and keep state across multiple requests from the same agent.

To configure these settings, you should click on **Realm Settings** on the left-side panel and then click on the **Tokens** tab:

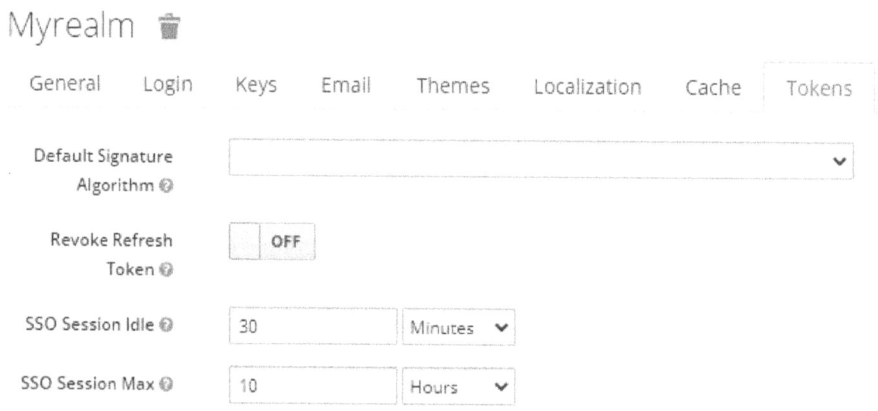

Myrealm 🗑

General	Login	Keys	Email	Themes	Localization	Cache	Tokens

Default Signature
Algorithm ❔   [⌄]

Revoke Refresh
Token ❔   [OFF   ]

SSO Session Idle ❔   [30   ]   [Minutes ⌄]

SSO Session Max ❔   [10   ]   [Hours   ⌄]

Figure 12.1 – Configuring SSO session lifetime

From this tab, you can set both maximum and idle times for SSO sessions by setting the **SSO Session Max** and **SSO Session Idle** settings, respectively. These two settings together effectively tell Keycloak that sessions should be kept alive for a certain amount of time and no longer than that, and that in the meantime Keycloak should check user activity within a certain period – the idle period – to decide whether sessions should expire prematurely.

Let's understand these two settings by example. By default, Keycloak defines a 10-hour lifetime for SSO sessions. This time effectively means that sessions can live up to 10 hours and no longer than that.

However, the idle timeout is set as 30 minutes by default, and that effectively means that if Keycloak does not see any user activity within a 30-minute period, sessions are going to be destroyed, regardless of the maximum time set. The idle timeout is bumped every time users interact with Keycloak, either directly through the authorization endpoint – when using a browser – or indirectly when tokens are refreshed by clients.

If a user authenticates and moves away from the keyboard and the client does not refresh its tokens during this period, the user session will be destroyed in 30 minutes. However, if the user is constantly interacting with Keycloak using the browser, or the client is constantly refreshing its tokens, the user session can last up to 10 hours.

Like SSO sessions, administrators can set the **Client Session Idle** and the **Client Session Max** settings to set the idle and maximum time for client sessions, respectively:

| Client Session Idle ❷ | 0 | Minutes ⌄ |
| Client Session Max ❷ | 0 | Minutes ⌄ |

Figure 12.2 – Configuring client session lifetime

These two settings provide administrators with more fine-grained control over the session lifetime of clients, making it possible to define hard limits for how long tokens are valid and force clients to re-authenticate whenever they try to refresh tokens. In other words, tokens issued to any client in a realm are only valid up to the maximum time you set, with the possibility to prematurely expire client sessions and invalidate tokens if the client is not refreshing its tokens within the idle period.

However, and differently than SSO sessions, when a client session is invalidated, users are not necessarily forced to re-authenticate if their SSO sessions did not expire, but it will force clients to re-authenticate to obtain a new set of tokens. Note that when a client session expires, users might be redirected to Keycloak as a consequence of forcing the client to re-authenticate, potentially causing some impact on the user experience when users are using a browser.

By default, Keycloak defines the same configuration set for SSO sessions to control the client session lifetime. By changing the value of the **Client Session Idle** and the **Client Session Max** settings to any other value than 0, you should be able to define a different lifetime for client sessions.

> **Note**
>
> As you will learn from the next topic, *Managing tokens*, Keycloak also allows administrators to override both **Client Session Max** and **Client Session Idle** settings on a per-client basis.

As a rule of thumb, the session lifetime should be as short as possible considering the security, performance, and user experience aspects. By using a short lifetime, you can reduce the impact of session hijack attacks or when tokens are leaked or stolen. It also avoids overloading the server with sessions that do not show any user activity and therefore helps to save server resources such as memory and CPU. However, a short session lifetime has a direct impact on user experience and how often users need to re-authenticate. In a user-first approach, you will probably start with what is the best for your users and then adjust the session lifetime accordingly to your security requirements and the constraints you have on resources such as memory and CPU.

In this topic, you learned about how to manage session lifetime and its impact on user experience, security, and performance. You also learned that during the authentication and token issuance processes, Keycloak may create an SSO session on a per-user basis and client sessions for each client the user is authenticated to.

In the next topic, you are going to learn how to track and manage user and client sessions.

Managing active sessions

Keycloak gives administrators great traceability and visibility of sessions at different levels:

- Per realm
- Per client
- Per user

At the realm level, administrators can look at statistics of the number of active sessions on a per-client basis. For that, click on the **Sessions** link on the left-side panel:

Sessions

| Realm Sessions | Revocation |

		Logout all
Client	Active Sessions	Offline Sessions
security-admin-console	1	0
account	1	0

Figure 12.3 – Managing active sessions in a realm

From this page, you can click on any client to get more details about its active sessions:

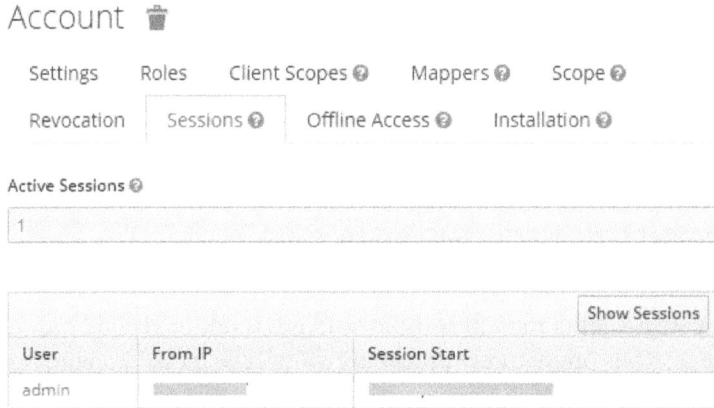

Figure 12.4 – Managing active sessions in a client

By selecting a client, you should be redirected to the **Sessions** tab on the client details page. From this page, you can click on the **Show Sessions** button to get the active sessions in the client on a per-user basis. On this page, you should have access to a few more details about sessions, such as the IP address of the user and when the session started.

By clicking on any user on this page, you are redirected to the user details page, the third and the last level of visibility for active sessions:

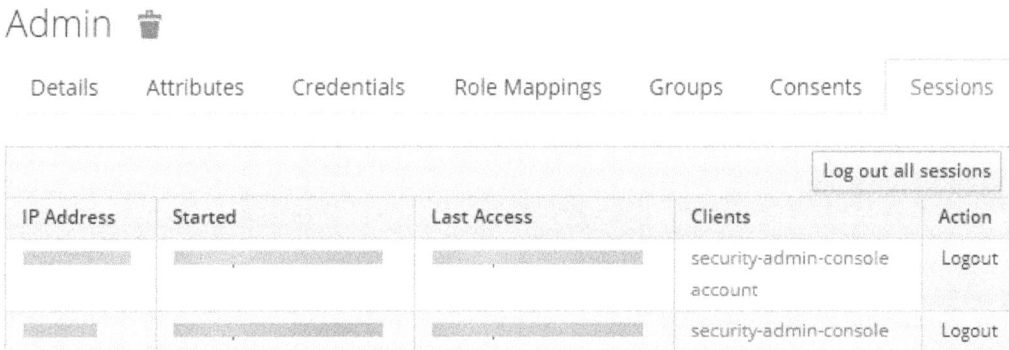

Figure 12.5 – Managing sessions for a user

On the user details page, you should click on the **Sessions** tab to look at all active sessions for the user. On this tab, you are given more details about sessions, such as when the session started, the last time Keycloak recorded activity from the user, and all clients – and client sessions – associated with a user session.

Under normal circumstances, you should expect users with a single session and many clients. This is especially true in a typical SSO scenario when users are using a browser to authenticate, and the same session is reused to authenticate to different clients. However, it might happen that users close their browser, clear their cookies, or just use different devices to authenticate. Under these circumstances, you might have multiple user sessions for a single user.

In this section, you learned how to get more visibility on the sessions active in a realm. You also learned that Keycloak gives you different levels of visibility on a per-realm, per-client, and per-user basis. Finally, you learned that at each level you are given additional information about sessions.

In the next topic, you are going to look at these different levels of visibility in more detail and how to expire sessions prematurely by forcing a single or global logout.

Expiring user sessions prematurely

In addition to providing statistics on sessions, Keycloak also provides mechanisms for expiring sessions prematurely when at the different levels that you learned about in the previous topic.

When looking at the active sessions at the realm level, you can expire all active sessions in a realm by clicking on the **Logout all** button:

Sessions

Realm Sessions	Revocation

		Logout all
Client	Active Sessions	Offline Sessions
security-admin-console	1	0
account	1	0

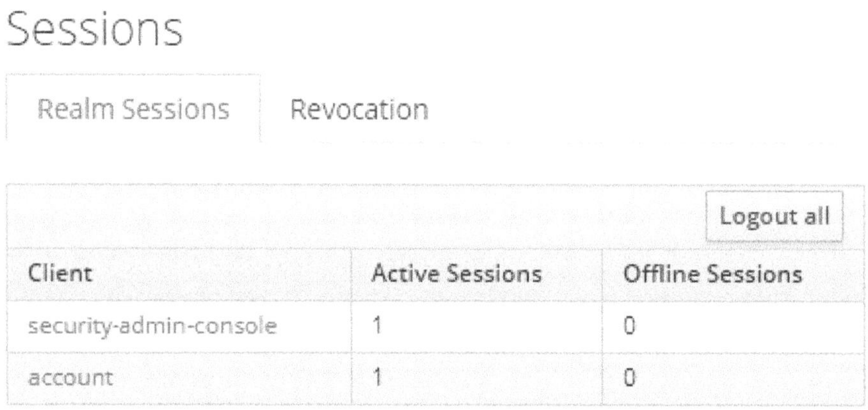

Figure 12.6 – Forcing session expiration at the realm level

When clicking on the **Logout all** button, Keycloak is going to promptly expire all sessions by iterating over all of them and removing their references. On this page, you should also be able to reactively revoke tokens on the **Revocation** tab, as you will learn in the next section.

When at the user level, you can expire individual sessions by clicking on the **Logout** button or simply expire all sessions by clicking on the **Log out all sessions** button:

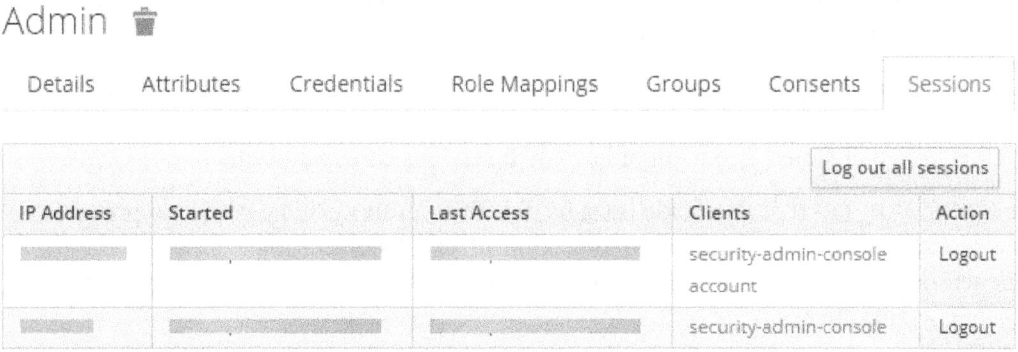

Admin 🗑

Details	Attributes	Credentials	Role Mappings	Groups	Consents	Sessions

				Log out all sessions

IP Address	Started	Last Access	Clients	Action
			security-admin-console account	Logout
			security-admin-console	Logout

Figure 12.7 – Expiring user sessions

Tip

When expiring sessions using any of the options presented here, Keycloak might send notifications to applications so that they can also invalidate their local sessions. However, this is a capability only available for applications using Keycloak adapters. For more details, look at the documentation at `https://www.keycloak.org/docs/latest/server_admin/#oidc-clients` on how to use the **Admin URL** to receive events from Keycloak.

Note that when using any of the preceding methods to log out all sessions either at the realm or user level, Keycloak iterates over sessions and expires them one by one. At the user level, you should not expect many active user sessions but probably many client sessions depending on the number of clients that users are authenticated to. However, expiring sessions at the realm level for every user authenticated in a realm might be an expensive operation.

In this topic, you learned how to prematurely expire user sessions using the Keycloak administration console. You were also presented with some considerations on how to expire sessions using the different options herein presented.

In the next section, you are going to look at how Keycloak uses cookies to track user and client sessions.

Understanding cookies and their relation to sessions

As you know, HTTP is a stateless protocol where cookies are often used to share state between browsers and servers. Keycloak heavily relies on HTTP cookies to track user sessions when users are interacting with it using a browser.

After successfully authenticating a user, Keycloak sets a `KEYCLOAK_IDENTITY` cookie to correlate a browser session with the corresponding user session on the server. If this cookie is leaked or stolen, users might have their sessions compromised.

The `KEYCLOAK_IDENTITY` cookie is set by default as an `HttpOnly` cookie to prevent **cross-site scripting** (**XSS**) and session hijacking attacks. Its expiration is based on the value set to the maximum time set to user sessions and its value has enough entropy to prevent guessing attacks.

> **Note**
>
> If you enabled the remember ne setting in a realm and users marked the remember me option when logging in, the `KEYCLOAK_IDENTITY` cookie is set with a 1-year expiration. In this case, the maximum time set for user sessions is not considered.

You can add more security barriers to this cookie, and the main one is to make sure Keycloak is only accessed through a secure channel using HTTP over TLS (HTTPS). When using HTTPS, the `secure` attribute is set to the cookie to prevent it from being transmitted in cleartext, as well as the `SameSite=none` attribute to make sure the cookie is only sent in cross-site requests through a secure connection. For more details on how to enable TLS, check *Chapter 9, Configuring Keycloak for Production*.

Regarding session expiration, the `KEYCLOAK_IDENTITY` cookie does not automatically expire when using any of the methods presented in the previous topic. Therefore, browsers may still send this cookie, but they are no longer referencing an active session. Upon receiving an invalid cookie, Keycloak is going to invalidate it and force the user to re-authenticate.

In this topic, you had a brief introduction to how Keycloak tracks user sessions using cookies. You also learned that protecting cookies is crucial to keep user sessions secure and how Keycloak helps to enforce strict policies on them.

In this section, you learned about some key aspects of session management in Keycloak. You learned that Keycloak is constantly creating server-side sessions to track authenticated users and the clients they are authenticated to. You also learned about the importance of properly configuring a session's lifetime and its impact on the user experience, security, and performance of applications and Keycloak. Lastly, you were presented with different options to expire sessions through the administration console and how Keycloak leverages cookies to track sessions when users are using a browser.

In the next section, you are going to look at how to manage tokens and their correlation with sessions.

Managing tokens

As you learned from the previous section, tokens are usually bound to sessions. Therefore, the token validity – not necessarily their lifetimes – depends on sessions.

Tokens have their own lifetime and how long they are considered valid depends on how they are validated. By leveraging **JSON Web Token (JWT)** as a format for tokens, Keycloak enables applications to validate and introspect tokens locally without any additional roundtrip to the server. However, this capability has a consequence where tokens, although within their lifetime, might not be valid anymore if their sessions have expired.

Without taking this into account, you might end up in a situation where tokens are no longer valid but are still accepted by applications because they are within their lifetime, therefore increasing the attack surface if tokens are leaked. As you are going to learn from this chapter, you should always consider a clear strategy for token expiration and revocation.

When applications obtain tokens from Keycloak, they are given a set of tokens:

- ID token
- Access token
- Refresh token

As you learned from previous chapters, depending on the authorization grant the client is using, Keycloak might issue all those tokens or only a subset of them. Each token has its own lifetime.

Except for refresh tokens, as we are going to see in a moment, the ID token and access token share the same lifetime. Both tokens are short-lived and commonly used by public clients (for example, single-page applications) where token storage is not the most secure. In the case of an access token, it is frequently sent over the wire and susceptible to interception. Their lifetime and validity are key factors to reduce the impact when they leak or are revoked.

On the other hand, refresh tokens have a longer lifetime, and their validity depends on the lifetime set for user and client sessions. This characteristic is what makes it possible to have short lifetimes for ID tokens and access tokens and what makes it possible to refresh these tokens when they expire. By living longer, refresh tokens are the perfect target for attackers, and they also need a clear strategy for expiration and revocation.

> **Note**
>
> As you will see in *Chapter 14, Securing Keycloak and Applications,* you can use additional layers of security for protecting tokens from being misused when they leak, such as key rotation. Yet, token lifetime is crucial to determine the overall security of your clients and their behavior.

In this section, you were briefly introduced to some basic concepts regarding tokens, such as their lifetime and validity and how they might impact the overall security of applications.

In the next topic, you are going to look at how to manage tokens' lifetimes.

Managing ID tokens' and access tokens' lifetimes

Keycloak allows you to set tokens' lifetimes similarly to sessions. For that, click on the **Tokens** tab when on the **Realm Settings** page. On the **Tokens** tab, you should be able to limit the lifetime for all three tokens mentioned in the previous topic, with the possibility to define specific settings for refresh tokens.

For ID tokens and access tokens, their lifetime can be set by changing the **Access Token Lifespan** setting to any value you want. By default, Keycloak sets the lifespan for these tokens to only **5** minutes:

Access Token Lifespan ❷   5   Minutes ∨

Figure 12.8 – Setting the ID token and access token lifespan

> **Note**
> The name is confusing, but behind the scenes, Keycloak uses the **Access Token Lifespan** setting to also calculate the lifetime for ID tokens.

Keycloak also allows you to override **Access Token Lifespan** on a per-client basis. For that, navigate to the details page of a client and, on the **Settings** tab, click on the **Advanced Settings** section:

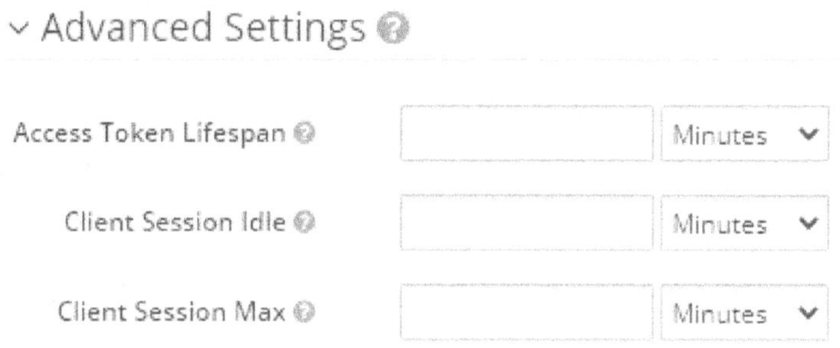

∨ Advanced Settings ⊚

Access Token Lifespan ⊚   [   ]   Minutes ∨

Client Session Idle ⊚   [   ]   Minutes ∨

Client Session Max ⊚   [   ]   Minutes ∨

Figure 12.9 – Overriding the ID token and access token lifetime on a per-client basis

In the **Advanced Settings** set the **Access Token Lifespan** to override the lifetime for ID tokens and access tokens for a particular client.

The value you set should be as short as possible to reduce the impact when tokens leak, therefore forcing clients to refresh their tokens. However, a too-short value might also impact the performance of your application and Keycloak itself as you will have more frequent refresh token requests. The default value should be enough for most use cases, but you can adjust the value according to your needs.

This setting is especially important for access tokens as they are frequently transmitted over the wire as a bearer token to access applications, as per *RFC 6750 – Bearer Token Usage*. As mentioned before, tokens issued by Keycloak are based on the JWT format, enabling applications to validate tokens without an additional round trip to introspect the token using the token introspection endpoint of Keycloak, but validating the token signature and some standard claims related to lifetime. Therefore, and depending on your security requirements, you might not tolerate a situation where the token is within its lifetime, but the refresh tokens are no longer backed by an active session in Keycloak. Under this circumstance, you might want the additional overhead of using the token introspection endpoint in favor of security.

Here, the lifetime also has a direct impact on the user experience and on the complexity of clients. Short-lived tokens are usually used together with long-lived refresh tokens to avoid users re-authenticating whenever tokens expire. Clients using refresh tokens are more complex to implement though due to the additional logic to deal with refresh tokens. On the other hand, long-lived tokens help to make clients simpler by removing the need for frequent refreshes with additional risks in case tokens happen to leak. It is up to you to find the right balance that fits your needs.

In this topic, you learned about how to set the lifetime for ID and access tokens. You learned that as a best practice, the lifetime should be as short as possible and what the correlation between short-lived tokens, refresh tokens, client complexity, security, and performance is. Finally, you learned that the validity of tokens can be out of sync with the state of their sessions and how you can avoid that by using the token introspection endpoint instead of performing local validations of tokens.

In the next topic, you will learn how to manage the lifetime of refresh tokens.

Managing refresh tokens' lifetimes

The lifetime of refresh tokens is defined by the same **SSO Session Max** and **Client Session Max** settings that you learned about in the previous section to set the lifetimes of user sessions and client sessions, respectively.

Firstly, refresh tokens' lifetimes are calculated based on the time set for client sessions, either by setting the **Client Session Max** setting at the realm level or overriding the same setting on a per-client basis. If a lifetime is not explicitly set for client sessions, then Keycloak will fall back to the value you set for user sessions, through the **SSO Session Max** setting.

To override the refresh token lifetime on a per-client basis, navigate to the details page of a client and on the **Settings** tab, click on the **Advanced Settings** section:

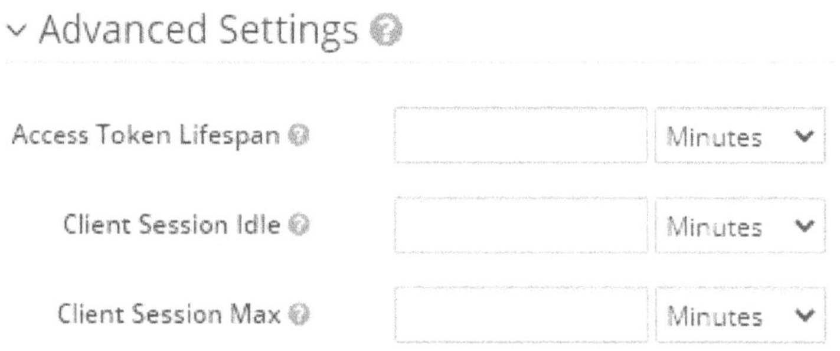

Figure 12.10 – Overriding the refresh token lifetime on a per-client basis

In the **Advanced Settings**, you can override the refresh token lifetime by setting the **Client Session Max** and **Client Session Idle** settings. Note that by default Keycloak does not define an explicit value for these settings at the client level so that they are implicitly set with the values set at the realm-level, as you learned in the previous section.

With regards to refresh tokens, you should consider the following:

- Refresh tokens are always bound to a client session after authenticating users in Keycloak using specific authorization grants such as the authorization code, resource owner password, or device flow.

- Refresh tokens are considered valid if the user and client sessions they are bound with have not expired.

- Clients should be able to use refresh tokens to obtain new tokens only if their respective client sessions are still active.

By taking these three considerations into account you should be able to realize how refresh tokens are crucial to getting short-lived ID tokens and access tokens, as well as how much they are critical to the overall security of your applications by allowing you to define more strict policies in regard to token lifetime on a per-client basis.

Refreshing token lifetime can be adjusted depending on how much clients can keep their tokens secure. For instance, a confidential client could have refresh tokens that live longer, whereas for public clients you might want a smaller window. Note however that as soon as a refresh token expires, users will be forced to re-authenticate to the client, therefore impacting the user experience, if using a browser.

One of the worst things that might happen is when a refresh token is leaked. It would enable attackers to obtain tokens from Keycloak and gain access to applications by impersonating the client to which the tokens were issued. There are different barriers that you can impose to avoid or reduce the impact when that happens. One of them is refreshing token rotation.

In this topic, you learned about how to manage refreshing tokens' lifetimes and its importance for enabling short-lived tokens and the overall security of applications.

In the next section, we are going to look at how to enable refreshing token rotation to prevent attackers from reusing refresh tokens.

Enabling refreshing token rotation

As a protection measure for when refresh tokens are leaked, Keycloak allows you to enable refreshing token rotation.

Refreshing token rotation is a strategy to reduce the impact when a refresh token is leaked by invalidating it prior to issuing a new one when a legitimate client is making refresh token requests. When enabled, rotation helps to quickly identify when the refresh token leaked and force either the attacker or the legitimate client to re-authenticate to obtain a fresh set of tokens, including a new and valid refresh token. Considering that only the legitimate client is capable of authenticating to the token endpoint, only it will be able to successfully obtain a new refresh token.

To enable refresh token rotation, navigate to the **Tokens** tab on the **Realm Settings** page and enable the **Revoke Refresh Token** setting:

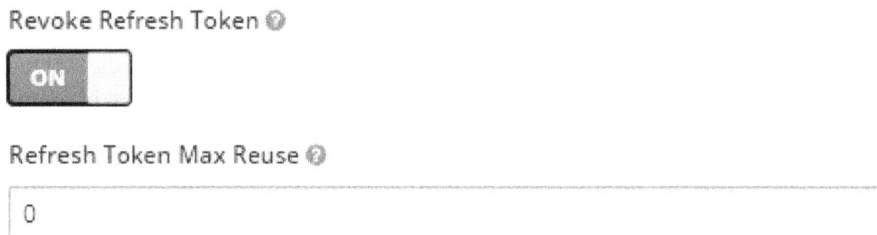

Revoke Refresh Token @

| ON |

Refresh Token Max Reuse @

| 0 |

Figure 12.11 – Enabling refresh token rotation

By enabling that setting, you are presented with an additional **Refresh Token Max Reuse** setting to define how many times a refresh token can be used by a client until a new one is issued, thus, invalidating the previous refresh token.

By default, the **Refresh Token Max Reuse** setting is set to 0 and that effectively means that a refresh token can only be used once. If a client tries to reuse the same refresh token, Keycloak is going to deny the request and force the client to re-authenticate the user. If you increase the value by 1, for instance, it will allow clients to use the same refresh token only twice.

In practice, refreshing token rotation is usually a good practice for reducing the attack surface when refresh tokens are leaked. It is also useful to quickly identify when that happens and react to possible exploits. However, it is not the only security measure you should consider, especially when dealing with public clients.

Public clients are inherently insecure as they do not need to provide any credentials to authenticate to the token endpoint. As such, you should consider using Mutual TLS Client Authentication to enforce the usage of sender-constrained tokens where the client certificate is used to bind the tokens to the client they were issued for, therefore preventing an attacker from using potentially leaked refresh tokens when presenting them to the token endpoint. For more details, check *Chapter 14, Securing Keycloak and Applications.*

In the next topic, you will learn about how to revoke tokens to either simply expire tokens when they are no longer necessary or as a reaction to possible exploits.

Revoking tokens

Keycloak allows you to revoke tokens using different methods. As you learned from the previous section, *Managing sessions,* tokens are bound with sessions and when sessions expire tokens are no longer considered valid by Keycloak.

One of the easiest ways to globally invalidate tokens, regardless of the user and client, is to use a not-before-revocation policy to force tokens to expire based on a time.

As you also learned from the previous section, Keycloak allows you to manage the active sessions in a realm by clicking on the **Sessions** item in the left-side pane. When on the **Sessions** page, you can click on the **Revocation** tab to revoke tokens created before a given time:

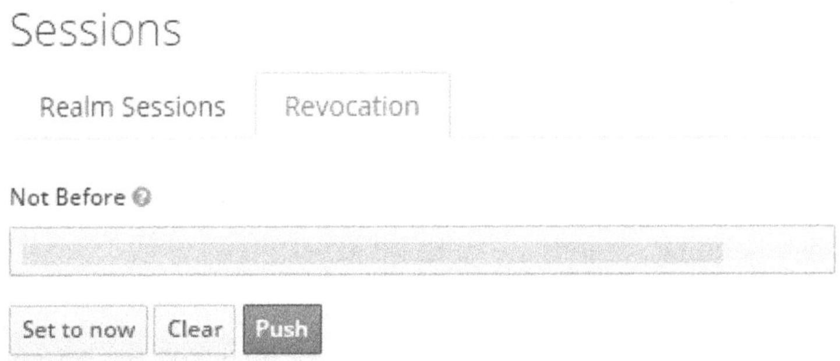

Figure 12.12 – Expiring sessions using a time-based revocation policy

By clicking on the **Set to now** button, Keycloak will automatically fill the **Not Before** field with the current time and update the realm settings to fail token validation whenever a token was created before the time set.

> **Note**
>
> Note that when revoking tokens using a not-before policy, applications are not immediately communicated about the revocation status. For that, you can click on the **Push** button to send a notification to clients. However, this is a capability only available for applications using Keycloak adapters. For more details, look at the documentation at `https://www.keycloak.org/docs/latest/server_admin/#oidc-clients` on how to use the **Admin URL** to receive events from Keycloak.

Keycloak also allows you to revoke tokens by either expiring their underlying sessions – user or client sessions – or by using a revocation endpoint as defined per RFC 7009.

By revoking tokens using session expiration, administrators should be able to leverage what you learned in the previous section, *Managing sessions*, to automatically invalidate any token associated with a session.

On the other hand, Keycloak also allows clients to revoke their tokens using a specific endpoint, the token revocation endpoint, based on RFC 7009. By using this approach, clients can help Keycloak to track unused tokens, reduce the time tokens are susceptible to leaking, and clean up any data associated with them to save memory and CPU resources. For more details on how to revoke tokens using the token revocation endpoint, look at the documentation at `https://www.keycloak.org/docs/latest/server_admin/#_oidc-endpoints`.

All the methods mentioned herein help to react to the leakage of tokens or to revoke them as soon as they are no longer used.

Except for a not-before-revocation policy, all other methods imply expiring the user and client sessions by either expiring all active sessions in a realm or only client sessions when using the token revocation endpoint. The not-before policy only impacts how tokens are validated; their corresponding sessions are still kept alive.

In this section, you learned about some key aspects of token management and how tokens correlate with session management. Firstly, you were presented with the key concepts and considerations around token lifetime, as well as about the different settings to configure it. Then you learned how refresh tokens enable short-lived access tokens and their importance to the overall security and performance of applications. Lastly, you learned about how refresh token rotation can help to reduce the attack surface when refresh tokens are leaked, as well as about the different methods for revoking tokens.

Summary

In this chapter, you were provided with some key aspects around token and session management. By leveraging what you learned from this chapter, you should be able to define clear policies for the session expiration and token revocation considering their impact on security, user experience, and the performance of applications and Keycloak.

In the next chapter, you are going to look at one of the main aspects of Keycloak – extensibility – and how to extend it to adapt and fill unmet needs.

Questions

1. Does Keycloak store sessions in the database?

2. What is an offline session?

3. How can you prevent Keycloak from losing session state during restarts?

4. In what circumstances are sessions not created?

Further reading

Refer to the following links for more information on topics covered in this chapter:

- Keycloak User and Session Management: `https://www.keycloak.org/docs/latest/server_admin/#user-session-management`

- Mutual-TLS Client Authentication: `https://www.keycloak.org/docs/latest/server_admin/#advanced-settings`

- Token Revocation Endpoint: `https://tools.ietf.org/html/rfc7009`

- Keycloak Threat Model Mitigation `https://www.keycloak.org/docs/latest/server_admin/#compromised-access-and-refresh-tokens`

- OAuth 2.0 Threat Model and Security Considerations: `https://tools.ietf.org/html/rfc6819`

- OAuth 2.0 Security Best Current Practice: `https://tools.ietf.org/html/draft-ietf-oauth-security-topicshttps://www.keycloak.org/docs/latest/server_admin/#_account-service`

13
Extending Keycloak

At this point, you should have a good idea in terms of what Keycloak has to offer as an **Identity and Access Management (IAM)** solution. You may also be trying to correlate what you have learned so far with the use cases you need to solve and how to leverage Keycloak capabilities to fit into your requirements.

Although Keycloak offers a rich configuration model that allows you to easily adapt its capabilities according to your needs, it is expected that the configuration is not enough to sort out all of them.

Among other questions, you are probably asking yourself how to change Keycloak pages to comply with your own **User Interface (UI)** and **User Experience (UX)** patterns. Or perhaps how Keycloak can leverage and integrate to a legacy database identity store for fetching identity-related data for existing users. Or maybe – and I promise this is my last attempt – you want to send audit events to a fraud detection system and integrate with it for risk-based authentication.

In this chapter, you will learn how to go beyond any limitation in configuration by extending Keycloak to either customize existing capabilities or to add new ones. For that, you are going to have an overview of the design of Keycloak and why it is the perfect choice to not only quickly deploy IAM to your ecosystem, but also to easily adapt IAM to fit into your needs.

For that, we are going to cover the following topics in this chapter:

- Understanding Service Provider Interfaces
- Changing the look and feel
- Customizing authentication flows
- Looking at other customization points

By the end of this chapter, you should be aware of how to leverage customization hooks to change the look and feel of Keycloak according to your UI and UX requirements, understand the concept of a **Service Provider Interface** (**SPI**) and the role they play when it comes to customization, and finally look at some references and code examples regarding how customizations are implemented and installed.

> **Help Keycloak**
>
> As a widely used open source project, Keycloak was designed with extensibility in mind, where contributions are made daily to extend or add new capabilities. With the basic learning from this chapter, it is also expected that you can help us to constantly improve and enrich the set of functionalities of Keycloak.

Technical requirements

During this chapter, you are going to need a development environment with the **Java Development Kit** (**JDK**) 11 specifications.

You also need to have a local copy of the GitHub repository associated with the book. If you have Git installed, you can clone the repository by running this command in a terminal:

```
$ git clone https://github.com/PacktPublishing/Keycloak-
Identity-and-Access-Management-for-Modern-Applications.git
```

Alternatively, you can download a ZIP of the repository from https://github.com/ PacktPublishing/Keycloak-Identity-and-Access-Management-for-Modern-Applications/archive/master.zip.

The examples you are going to follow along with in this chapter are available from the following directory within the repository:

```
$ cd Keycloak-Identity-and-Access-Management-for-Modern-
Applications/ch13
```

For this chapter, you also need to create a `myrealm` realm to follow some examples. You will also need to create an `alice` user to authenticate to the account console when running examples.

Let's start our journey by first looking at what an SPI is and why it is a key concept when looking forward to extending Keycloak.

Check out the following link to see the Code in Action video: `https://bit.ly/3vLWzjL`

Understanding Service Provider Interfaces

If you are already familiar with the Java language, you probably know what an SPI is. If not, think about it as a pluggable mechanism for adding or changing behavior to an extensible Java application without changing its code base.

Keycloak is built with extensibility in mind where features are implemented using a set of well-defined interfaces. Features such as the ability to authenticate users using different authentication mechanisms, auditing, integration with legacy systems for fetching identity data, map claims into tokens, register new users and update their profiles, and to integrate with third-party identity providers are all backed by a set of service interfaces and a corresponding SPI. The same is also true for core features, such as caching, storage, or the different security protocols supported by Keycloak, although for those, you would hardly have a need to customize:

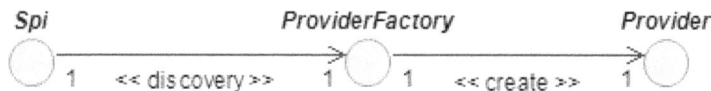

Figure 13.1 – Keycloak Service Provider Interface (SPI)

In Keycloak, a feature is defined based on three main interfaces:

- **Spi**
- **ProviderFactory**
- **Provider**

> **Note**
>
> For simplicity purposes, we are now going to use the term *provider*
> whenever referring to a combination of a **ProviderFactory** and **Provider**
> implementation, where a *custom provider* refers to customizations for an
> existing SPI or feature.

The SPI – according to Java terminology – is a top-level interface for loading and
describing the different implementations of a feature.

The **ProviderFactory** is a service factory interface and, as the name suggests, defines
a contract for managing the life cycle of a particular implementation and for creating
Provider instances. A factory is also responsible for defining a unique identifier for itself
in the scope of the SPI to not clash with other provider implementations.

Provider is the actual service interface that you implement to realize a feature. The
following is the main interface you are going to implement to customize existing features
or to add new ones:

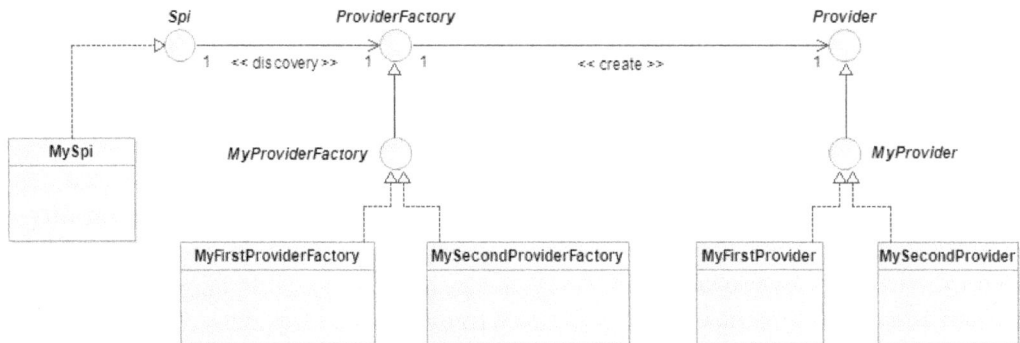

Figure 13.2 – Realization of the three main interfaces

By allowing multiple implementations of a feature or **Spi**, Keycloak allows you to create
your own implementations and enrich it by either adding new features or changing its
behavior. Let's understand how this translates into practice by looking at the list of SPIs
and their respective providers. Open the administration console and click on the user icon
in the top-right corner of the page. Once you click the icon, you are going to be presented
with a sub-menu with an option called **Server Info**:

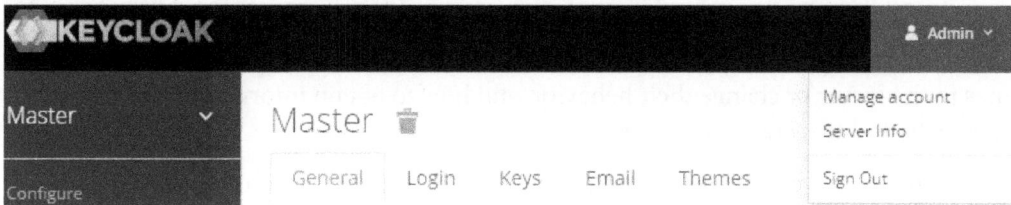

Figure 13.3 – Accessing server runtime information

After clicking on the **Server Info** option, you are presented with a page with information about the server runtime and a second tab called **Providers**. Click on the **Providers** tab to list all the providers installed on the server.

By looking at the list of providers, you can clearly see the realization of the diagrams presented earlier. As an example, type `social` in the input box at the top of the list to filter the results to only those related to integrating with social identity providers:

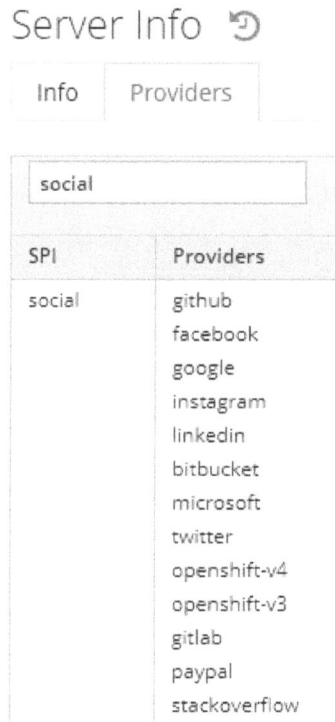

Figure 13.4 – List of the different implementations of social identity providers

As you can see from that list, the `social` SPI has different providers for each social identity provider that you learned from *Chapter 10, Managing Users*. The same applies for any other SPI, such as `required-action`, `protocol-mapper`, and so forth.

In this topic, you had a quick overview of Keycloak design, with a focus on extensibility. You learned that Keycloak relies on a set of well-defined interfaces to plug additional features to the server or change their behavior, and how to obtain information about the available SPIs and their respective providers.

In the next topic, you will be looking at how to package and deploy your custom providers to the server.

Packaging a custom provider

Keycloak expects custom providers packaged in a **Java ARchive** (**JAR**). In addition to their classes – the **ProviderFactory** and **Provider** implementations – you should also include a service descriptor file to allow Keycloak to discover and initialize your custom provider at runtime.

The service descriptor is a regular file placed in the META-INF/services directory within the JAR file, and its name is the fully qualified name of the **ProviderFactory** type you are implementing.

Taking as an example the fictitious com.acme.MyProviderFactory factory – yes, we added a package to make clear the point around using a fully qualified name – used in the diagram in the previous topic, the JAR file should look like this:

```
: mycustomprovider.jar
META-INF/services/com.acme.MyProviderFactory
MyFirstProviderFactory.class
MyFirstProvider.class
```

Here, the META-INF/services/com.acme.MyProviderFactory file should contain a reference to your implementation of com.acme.MyProviderFactory:

```
MyFirstProviderFactory
```

In this topic, you learned how providers are packaged into a JAR and how Keycloak leverages existing mechanisms from the Java language to discover provider implementations.

Now that you are aware of the structure of the JAR expected by Keycloak, we can start looking at the different approaches for installing custom providers.

Installing a custom provider

The final step when implementing a custom provider is to install it on Keycloak. For that, you can choose from a number of different approaches:

- Deploying as a JAR
- Creating a WildFly module
- Deploying as a **Java Enterprise Edition (JEE) Enterprise JavaBeans (EJB)** JAR

Deploying the JAR file directly to the server is probably the most common and simpler approach for installing custom providers. It is just a matter of copying the JAR file to the `$KC_HOME/standalone/deployments` directory.

When using this approach, Keycloak automatically configures the runtime dependencies that are necessary to properly deploy your provider.

> **Tip**
> You should also be able to deploy the JAR into **Enterprise application ARchive (EAR)** or **Web application ARchive (WAR)** packages. However, Keycloak is not meant to be used for deploying full applications even though they might be related to your custom provider capabilities. As much as possible, try using plain Java classes when writing your providers.

Custom providers can also be deployed by adding a module to the server. If you are not familiar with the concept of modules, Keycloak is based on the WildFly application server, which relies on JBoss modules to define and load runtime dependencies. These modules are located in the `$KC_HOME/modules` directory.

We are not going to cover this approach in detail. For that, you can look at the Keycloak documentation at `https://www.keycloak.org/docs/latest/server_development/#register-a-provider-using-modules`. However, here are some considerations in terms of when this approach is applicable:

- It is very handy when you need to deploy multiple providers sharing a common set of dependencies. In this case, you might want to create modules for each dependency and just reference them from other modules.
- In production, and potentially for security reasons, you might want to disable the deployment scanner to prevent unexpected changes at runtime.
- It provides more isolation and control over the provider class loader and its dependencies.

Finally, Keycloak allows you to install providers as an EJB. By using this approach, you can leverage some key capabilities provided by WildFly and JEE. Usually, you will not need this approach for implementing or deploying providers because, most of the time, they are implemented as plain Java types, relying solely on Keycloak APIs and SPIs. However, depending on the circumstances, you might want to use the **Java Persistence API (JPA)** to leverage an existing database or use **Java Message Service (JMS)** in your providers, and that is one of the main reasons why you have this option available from Keycloak. For more details regarding this approach for deploying providers, review the documentation at `https://www.keycloak.org/docs/latest/server_development/#leveraging-java-ee`.

Understanding the KeycloakSessionFactory and KeycloakSession components

Keycloak relies on two main components to manage providers: `KeycloakSessionFactory` and `KeycloakSession`.

> **Note**
> We are not going to dive into detail on this topic about their purposes and how they are used, but provide you with an introductory topic before understanding the life cycle of providers and then move to the code examples available in this chapter.

At its core is `KeycloakSessionFactory`, which serves as a registry for all providers installed on the server and responsible for managing their life cycle. When Keycloak is starting, a `KeycloakSessionFactory` is created to initialize and register any provider factory installed on the server. The other way around is also true, where, when Keycloak is gracefully shutting down, `KeycloakSessionFactory` gives a last chance to factories to close any resource created during the initialization phase.

On the other hand, when Keycloak is up and running and processing requests, a `KeycloakSession` is created and bound to each request. `KeycloakSession` is created from `KeycloakSessionFactory` and it serves as an entry point for managing realms, users, clients, sessions, accessing contextual information about the current realm and the request, and for obtaining provider instances. The provider instances obtained from a session are created only once and cached during the lifetime of `KeycloakSession`. `KeycloakSession` is the component that you, as a provider developer, are going to use most when implementing providers.

By understanding these two components and what they are, even superficially, you should now be able to follow the next topics and sections whenever we mention these components. Do not worry about trying to understand these components in more detail right now because that will come naturally when you start implementing your own providers as well as when looking at how other providers are implemented in Keycloak.

In the next step, you are going to look at the life cycle of providers.

Understanding the life cycle of a provider

Providers have a well-defined life cycle for initialization and deinitialization.

During the installation of providers, Keycloak calls specific methods on the **ProviderFactory** implementations for initialization purposes. The same applies when the server is gracefully shutting down, where method calls are made to release resources created during the initialization phase.

That said, the life cycle of a **ProviderFactory** is bound to the server lifetime, where initialization and deinitialization are performed only once, when `KeycloakSessionFactory` is being initialized or closed:

> **Note**
>
> The only exception to this is when you are redeploying providers at runtime. In this case, initialization and deinitialization might happen multiple times.

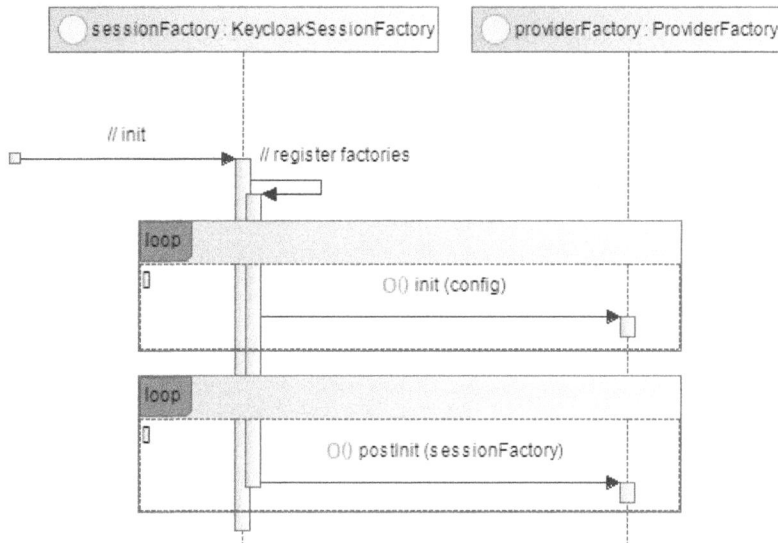

Figure 13.5 – Initialization of factories during server startup

The following steps occur during the initialization phase of providers:

1. Keycloak loads all the available factories for each SPI.

2. For each factory, the `init` method is called with the provider configuration.

3. Once all factories have been initialized and registered, the `postInit` method is called on each factory to perform additional initialization steps based on `KeycloakSessionFactory`.

> **Note**
>
> Regarding deinitialization, the steps are similar, but during this phase, only the **close** method is invoked for each factory.

The `init` method is called early when factories are still being registered to initialize them based on any configuration set to a particular provider in the `$KC_HOME/standalone/configuration/standalone.xml` file. If the factory neither depends on other factories nor on `KeycloakSession` to initialize itself, this step should be enough to initialize a factory.

However, the `postInit` method is only called once all the factories have been registered, thereby enabling factories to perform additional steps during initialization using other providers and `KeycloakSession` itself.

On the other hand, the life cycle of a provider is bound to a request. As mentioned earlier, a provider is created from its corresponding **ProviderFactory**, and that happens only once during the request life cycle. Regarding deinitialization, the `close` method on a provider is called at the end of the request:

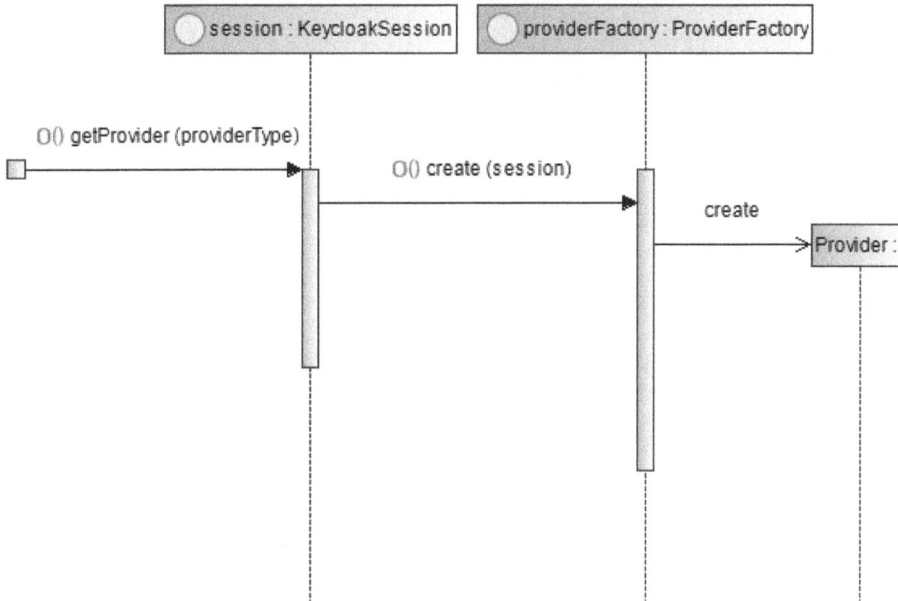

Figure 13.6 – Creating a provider

In this topic, you learned about the life cycle of providers and how they are initialized either at server boot time or when deploying a provider. You also learned that at runtime, provider instances are created at runtime in the scope of a request and bound to a `KeycloakSession`.

In the next topic, you are going to look at how to configure a provider using the server configuration file.

Configuring providers

Providers are usually configured by changing the `$KC_HOME/standalone/configuration/standalone.xml` file. Any configuration set to a provider will be available during the initialization phase.

The configuration is defined within the `keycloak-server` subsystem as follows:

```
<subsystem xmlns=''urn:jboss:domain:keycloak-server:1.1''>
    <spi name=''hostname''>
        <default-provider>default</default-provider>
            <provider name=''default'' enabled=''true''>
                <properties>
```

```
                    <property name=''frontendUrl''
value=''https://mykeycloak/auth''/>
                </properties>
            </provider>
    </spi>

    ...

</subsystem>
```

> **Note**
>
> The preceding snippet from the configuration is one of the settings you did in
> *Chapter 9, Configuring Keycloak for Production*.

As you may have noticed, the configuration follows the same principles that you learned at the beginning of this section. For each SPI, you can define the configuration properties for its provider implementations. In the preceding snippet, a configuration is being set for a `default` provider within the `hostname` SPI. In this case, the `frontendUrl` property is being set and will be available to the factory during the initialization phase.

In addition to setting configuration properties for providers, you should also be able to define a default provider in case the SPI has multiple provider implementations. This is achieved by the `<default-provider>` element in the configuration, whose value is the identifier of the provider you want to set as the default. If an SPI has a single provider implementation, this setting is not necessary.

In this topic, you had a quick overview of how to configure providers by setting their configuration using the server configuration files.

In the next sections, you are going to walk through the steps for choosing a capability to extend, implementing a provider using an SPI, and installing the provider to the server. The examples you are about to see are related to the most common types of customizations that you might need when changing Keycloak to fit into your use cases and requirements.

Changing the look and feel

One of the main customization hooks – and probably what people use most – is changing Keycloak built-in themes to fit into your branding and to respect your UI and UX requirements.

Keycloak provides an amazingly simple experience for changing themes and allows you to change most – if not all – of its UI, from the end user-facing pages to the administration console itself.

In this topic, you will learn about the basics of theming by going through examples of how to change the look and feel of the login page. By understanding these basics, you should then be able to apply the same concepts to any other UI you want to customize.

> **Note**
> This is probably one of the most documented features of Keycloak. Consider looking at the documentation available at `https://www.keycloak.org/docs/latest/server_development/#_themes`.

Understanding themes

Just like any other feature in Keycloak, themes are backed by their own SPI. However, instead of having to implement Java code to change themes, Keycloak offers a simple and elegant way of doing so solely based on plain CSS classes, JavaScript, and any other HTML construct. In fact, depending on your needs, changing themes should be just a matter of defining a new CSS stylesheet.

Another important aspect of themes is internationalization. As a worldwide project, Keycloak has contributions to support different languages and it is most likely that users from your country would already benefit from messages in their native language, without any additional effort from your side.

In Keycloak, the built-in themes are included as part of the distribution in the `themes` directory:

```
$ cd $KC_HOME\themes
$ ls
├── base
├── keycloak
├── keycloak-preview
├── keycloak.v2
```

Each directory in the `themes` directory is a built-in theme with all the necessary configuration and resources to render the pages you have seen so far.

The `keycloak` theme, for instance, is the default theme if no theme is set to a realm. This is the theme you have been using in this book when running examples.

> **Note**
>
> The base theme is not really a theme, but a skeleton used by other themes where page templates, message bundles for internationalization, and common resources are located. Other themes, such as the keycloak theme, extend the base theme to define the layout by using specific CSS stylesheets, JavaScript, images, and so on.

Within each theme directory, you have sub-directories for the different sets of UIs in Keycloak that are open for customization. Each of these sub-directories represents a *theme type*:

```
$ cd keycloak
$ ls
.
├── account
├── admin
├── common
├── email
├── login
└── welcome
```

By looking at the different theme types and their names, you should have an idea of what you can change in a theme. Let's understand what they are:

- account: UI definitions for the account console
- admin: UI definitions for the administration console
- common: Common resources used across theme types
- email: UI definitions for emails
- login: UI definitions for login-related pages, including pages for updating profiles, resetting passwords, and so on
- welcome: UI definitions for the welcome page

Within each theme type, you have a mandatory file called theme.properties in which you define the configuration for a given theme type, for instance:

- Inherit the configuration from another theme
- Import resources from another theme
- CSS styles

- JavaScript resources
- Map your CSS styles to those used by Keycloak components, such as input boxes and buttons

One important aspect of the configuration is that you are not forced to create a configuration from scratch when customizing a theme type, but leverage the configuration from another theme and change only what you need to. This is very handy if you just want to make punctual changes to an existing theme.

Now that you know what themes are, where they are located, and how they are structured, let's understand how you set a theme for a realm and a client.

Let's look first at how to define a theme to a realm. For that, open the administration console and click on the **Realm Settings** item on the left-side panel. Once at this page, click on the **Themes** tab:

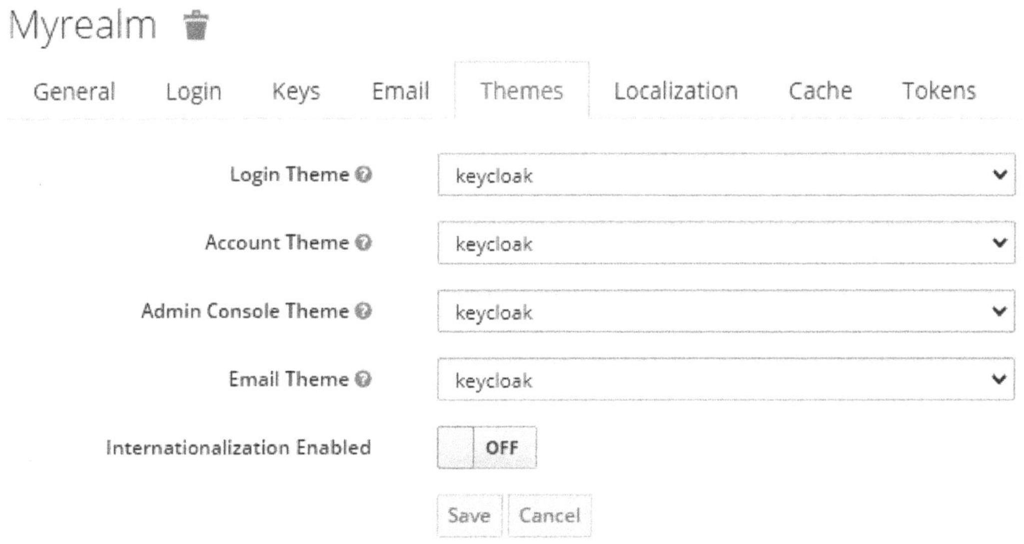

Myrealm 🗑

| General | Login | Keys | Email | Themes | Localization | Cache | Tokens |

Login Theme ❔   keycloak   ⌄

Account Theme ❔   keycloak   ⌄

Admin Console Theme ❔   keycloak   ⌄

Email Theme ❔   keycloak   ⌄

Internationalization Enabled   OFF

Save   Cancel

Figure 13.7 – Defining themes for a realm

From the **Themes** page, you can set a theme for any of the available theme types. The select box for each theme type is built based on the directory structure of the themes directory, plus any other theme deployed to the server. Only the themes that define a particular theme type are available from their corresponding select box.

> **Note**
>
> The only exception is the `welcome` theme type, which is defined differently because it is neither specific to a realm nor a client. For more details, look at the documentation at `https://www.keycloak.org/docs/latest/server_development/#configure-theme`.

At this page, you also have additional options for managing internationalization. By enabling the **Internationalization Enabled** setting, you are presented with additional options to define which localizations or languages you want to support, as well as a default localization if none can be inferred from the request or based on the authenticated user preferences.

> **Tip**
>
> Localization support is feature-rich; you can even define localized messages via the administration console. By default, they are loaded from properties files within the `messages` directory for each theme type. For more details, look at the `base` theme directory as well as the documentation at `https://www.keycloak.org/docs/latest/server_admin/#_themes`.

Keycloak also allows you to define a theme on a per-client basis, but only for the login-related pages. By allowing that, you should be able to provide a customized end user experience depending on the client they arc authenticating to. To define a `login` theme for a client, select a client and, on the client details page, choose a theme from the **Login Theme** setting:

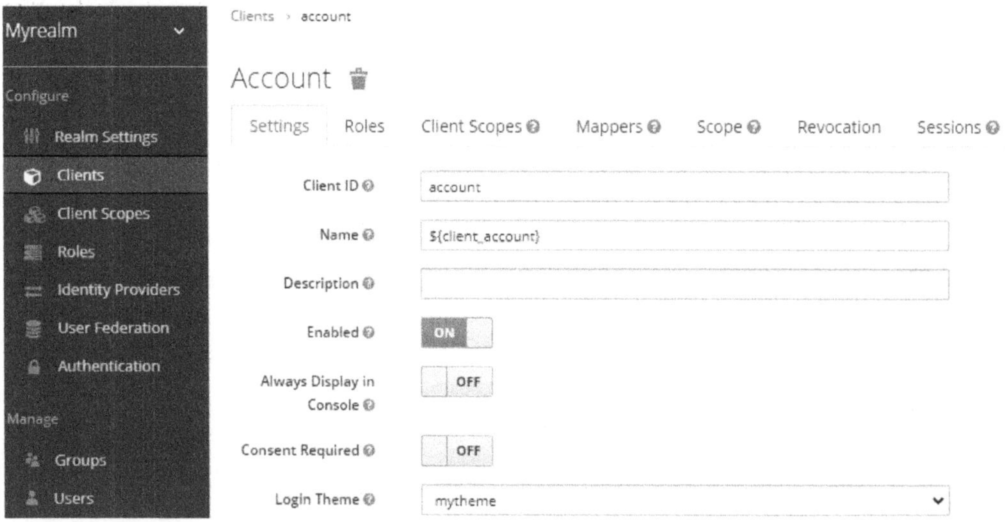

Figure 13.8 – Defining a login theme to a client

In terms of look and feel, Keycloak gives you several options to adapt it accordingly to your needs. In this topic, you had an overview about themes, how they are configured, and how to set a theme for the different theme types so as to change their look and feel.

In the next topic, we are going to create a theme from scratch so that you can quickly start creating your own themes according to your needs.

Creating and deploying a new theme

Creating a new theme involves creating a directory, configuring the theme using a `theme.properties` file, and adding any static resource you may require, including CSS stylesheets, JavaScript libraries, and message bundles.

For this topic, you should be able to use a pre-defined theme available from the GitHub repository at the following directory:

```
$ cd ch13/themes/mytheme/src/main/resources/theme/mytheme
```

In the `mytheme` directory, you have the following structure:

```
login/
├── messages
└── resources
        ├── css
        ├── img
        └── js
```

The `mytheme` theme was built to change only the `login` theme type. In this example, we are customizing only the login page.

When defining a theme type, you should have a standard directory structure as follows:

- The `resources` directory is the place from where Keycloak is going to look up static resources used by your theme.

- The `messages` directory is the place from where message bundles are going to be loaded.

Within the `resources` directory, it is a best practice to have specific directories for each type of resource you need in your theme, such as CSS stylesheets, JavaScript, and image files.

> **Note**
>
> In our example, the `messages` directory is empty because you will not need to define message bundles but rely on those already available from the `base` theme.

As mentioned earlier, theme types must have a `theme.properties` file to define its configuration. In our example, this file contains only the basic settings to change the login page using custom CSS styles. Let's understand how this file is defined by opening the file that is located in the GitHub repository at `ch13/themes/mytheme/src/main/resources/theme/mytheme/login/theme.properties`:

```
# Inherit resources and messages from the keycloak theme
parent=keycloak
# Define the CSS styles
styles=css/login.css css/bootstrap.min.css css/signin.css
# Mapping CSS classes from Keycloak to custom CSS classes
kcHtmlClass=login-page
kcLoginClass=form-signin
```

From the preceding snippet, you will see that `mytheme` is extending the `keycloak` theme and defining some additional CSS stylesheets. In this file, there is also a mapping between the Keycloak CSS classes to those defined in a custom CSS stylesheet at `ch13/themes/mytheme/src/main/resources/theme/mytheme/login/css/signin.css`.

Now, let's use this theme when authenticating to the account console. For that, you need to deploy the theme to the server by building the example project and deploying the JAR:

```
$ cd ch13/themes/mytheme
$ ./mvnw clean package
$ cp target/mytheme.jar $KC_HOME/standalone/deployments
```

After performing these steps, log in to the administration console as the administrator user. Once you are in the console, select the **account-console** client from the list of clients and then, at the client details page, select the **mytheme** theme from the list of options for the **Login Theme** setting. At the end, the **account-console** client settings should look as follows:

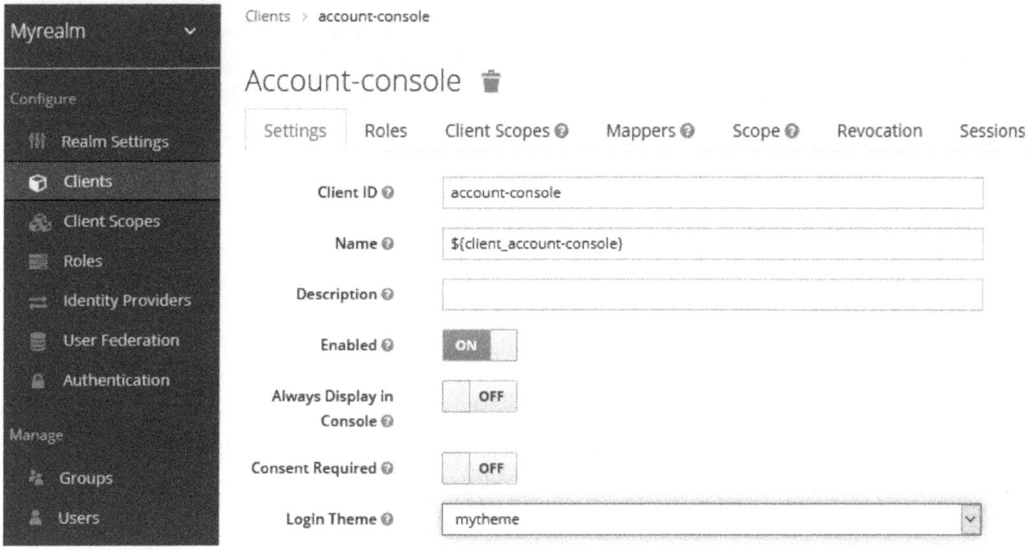

Figure 13.9 – Defining the mytheme theme as the login theme for the account console

Now, log out from the administration console and try to log in to the account console by opening http://localhost:8080/auth/realms/myrealm/account. If everything is properly configured, the login page should have a different layout, as follows:

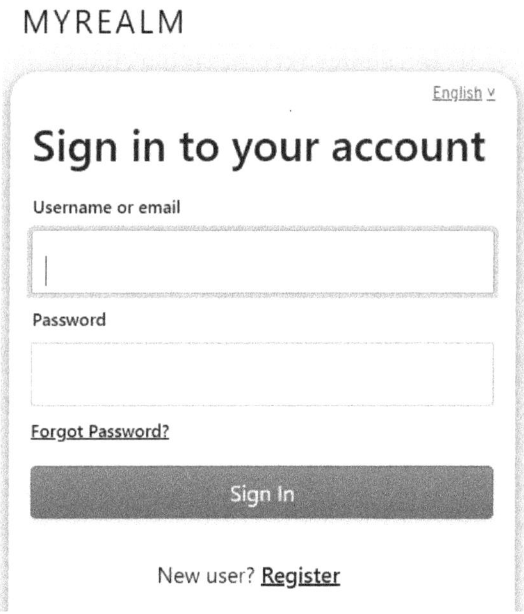

Figure 13.10 – The new layout for the login page when logging in to the account console

One important tip for when creating themes is to disable caching so that changes you are making to your theme are automatically reflected at runtime. By default, Keycloak caches templates and theme configuration for performance reasons. To disable caching, change the following settings in the $KC_HOME/standalone/configuration/ standalone.xml file:

```xml
<theme>
    <staticMaxAge>-1</staticMaxAge>
    <cacheThemes>false</cacheThemes>
    <cacheTemplates>false</cacheTemplates>
</theme>
```

In this topic, you learned about how to create and deploy a theme to Keycloak. For that, you were provided with an example from the GitHub repository that changes the layout of the login page. You also learned that when creating a new theme, you usually want to disable caching so that any change you make to a theme is reflected when reloading the server pages.

In the next topic, you are going to understand how to go even further with your customizations by changing the built-in page templates.

Extending templates

Sometimes, extending a theme using only CSS styles is not enough and you want to change the disposal of components in the page templates from the base theme.

Keycloak relies on **Apache Freemarker**, a well-known and widely used template engine, to render pages based on templates. By leveraging the templates from the base theme, you have a powerful tool to drastically change Keycloak pages.

For that, you only need to copy a template from one of the theme types in the base theme and include it in your own theme type.

However, this flexibility has a cost where any change to the built-in templates between Keycloak releases should be manually applied to your own custom templates. This approach for customizing themes is very handy, but it would require a bit more knowledge from you about how Keycloak defines these templates.

For more details about how to extend a built-in template, look at the documentation at https://www.keycloak.org/docs/latest/server_development/#html-templates.

Extending theme-related SPIs

Included in this section are code examples for customizing how themes are selected, as well as how to add custom templates and resources using an SPI.

The code is located at the ch13/themes/mytheme directory in the GitHub repository. By looking at the following two classes:

- ch13/themes/mytheme/src/main/java/org/keycloak/book/ch13/theme/MyThemeSelectorProvider

- ch13/themes/mytheme/src/main/java/org/keycloak/book/ch13/theme/MyThemeResourceProvider

You should be able to see the realization of what you learn from the *Understanding Service Provider Interfaces* section, but applied to themes. These two providers are related to the themeSelector and themeResource SPIs, respectively.

MyThemeSelectorProvider is an example of how to dynamically select a theme at runtime where, depending on your requirements, you may need to choose a theme based on information pertaining to the request, the client, or the user authenticating to Keycloak. This provider has a quite simple logic to select a theme depending on the value of a request query parameter.

The steps to deploy the provider are the same as when you deployed the mytheme theme:

```
$ cd ch13/themes/mytheme
$ ./mvnw clean package
$ cp target/mytheme.jar $KC_HOME/standalone/deployments
```

To see it in action, remove any theme you have set for the realm or client and then try to log in to the administration console again.

At the login page, append the &theme=mytheme query parameter to the URL and reload the page. After doing that, you should be able to see the login page layout from the mytheme theme, even though no theme was set to the realm or to a client. Also, note that the theme is applied regardless of the realm.

On the other hand, MyThemeResourceProvider is an example about how to load additional templates and resources to any theme. For this provider, we do not resolve any additional templates or resources, but just give you the baseline in case you require this level of customization. This provider can be handy when you have customizations that require additional pages, such as when creating custom authenticators or required actions.

In this topic, you were provided with some code examples of how to customize theme selection and how to add additional pages by leveraging the `themeSelector` and `themeResource` SPIs, respectively.

In this section, you learned about Keycloak themes and how to use them to change the look and feel of the different server pages. For that, you learned about how themes are created and configured, how they are deployed, and how to go even further with customizations by changing the built-in page templates. Finally, you were given some code to demonstrate how to dynamically select themes at runtime as well as how to add additional pages that can be used from custom authenticators or required actions.

In the next section, you are going to look at an example of how to leverage the Authentication SPI to customize how users are authenticated using a second factor.

Customizing authentication flows

As you learned from *Chapter 11, Authenticating Users*, Keycloak allows you to easily customize user authentication by changing authentication flows through the administration console. Eventually, the built-in authentication executions might not be enough to address your authentication requirements, and, in this case, you can leverage the Authentication SPI to implement your own authentication executions.

We are not going to cover in this section all the details pertaining to the Authentication SPI, but give you a code example to help you understand the steps and the mechanics when you are creating your own authenticators. The code example for this topic is available from the GitHub repository at `ch13/simple-risk-based-authenticator`.

The example here is about a quite simple authenticator that relies on a risk score to determine whether the user should provide a second factor when authenticating. The risk score is calculated based only on the number of failed login attempts, where, if a user fails to log in three times in a row, the next time they will be forced to provide a **One-Time Password (OTP)** as a second factor. However, you could leverage this example to something more complex where the risk analysis could also consider other factors, such as the device the user is using, the location, or even the score from an external fraud detection system.

To install the custom authenticator, you need to deploy the provider's JAR file as follows:

```
$ cd ch13/simple-risk-based-authenticator
$ ./mvnw clean package
$ cp target/simple-risk-based-authenticator.jar
$KC_HOME/standalone/deployments
```

After deploying the provider, you are going to use what you learned from *Chapter 11, Authenticating Users*, to configure a new authentication flow as follows:

1. Create a copy of the **Browser** flow and name it My Risk-Based Browser Flow.

2. Delete the **OTP Form** execution from the **My Risk-Based Browser Flow Browser - Conditional OTP** sub-flow. Make sure that the sub-flow is marked as **REQUIRED**.

3. Add the **My Simple Risk-Based Authenticator** execution to the **My Risk-Based Browser Flow Browser - Conditional OTP** sub-flow.

4. Add the **Conditional OTP Form** execution to the **My Risk-Based Browser Flow Browser - Conditional OTP** sub-flow. Make sure that this execution is marked as **REQUIRED**.

5. Go to the **Bindings** tab and associate the **My Risk-Based Browser** flow with the **Browser** flow.

6. Now, click on the **Actions** link for **Conditional OTP Form** execution and then click on the **Config** option:

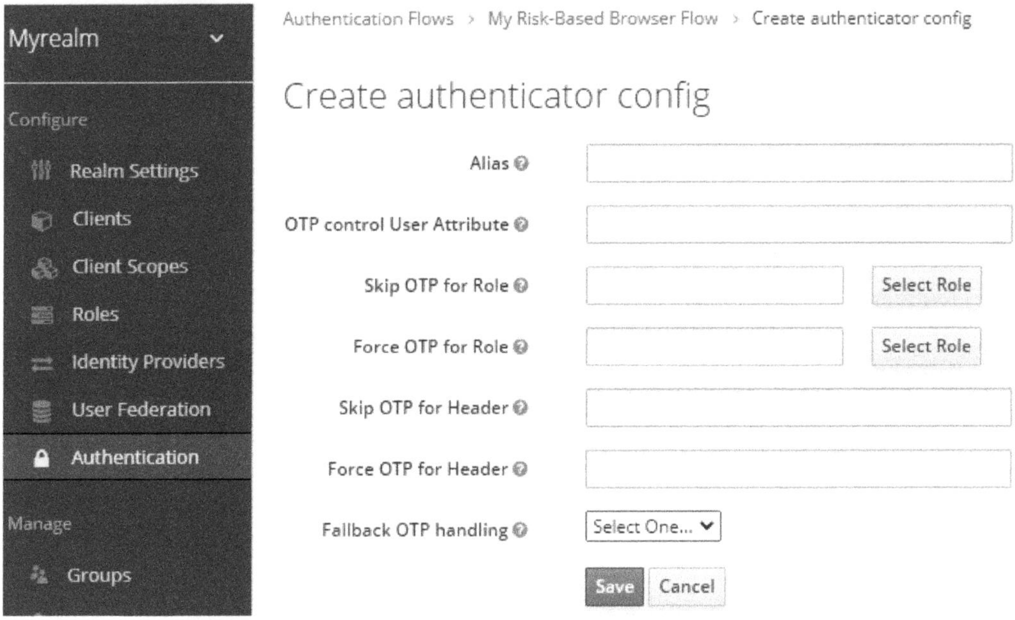

Figure 13.11 – Configuring the Conditional OTP form execution

At this page, you should provide the following configuration:

- **Alias**: `conditional-otp`
- **OTP control User Attribute**: `my.risk.based.auth.2fa.required`
- **Fallback OTP handling**: `force`

Once you are done, click on the **Save** button:

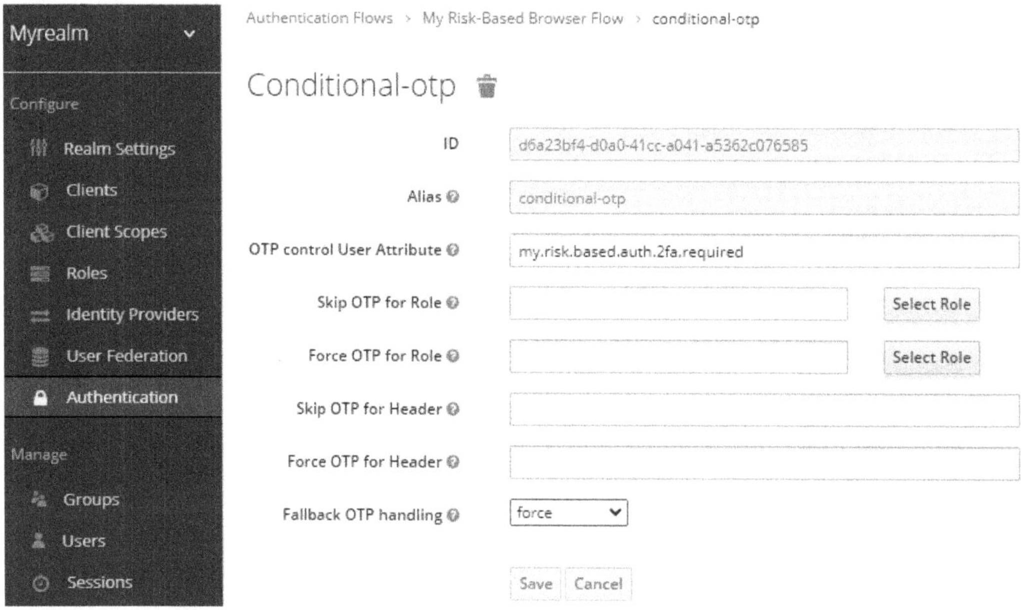

Figure 13.12 – Saving settings for the Conditional-otp form execution

At the end, the new **My Risk-Based Browser Flow** should look like this:

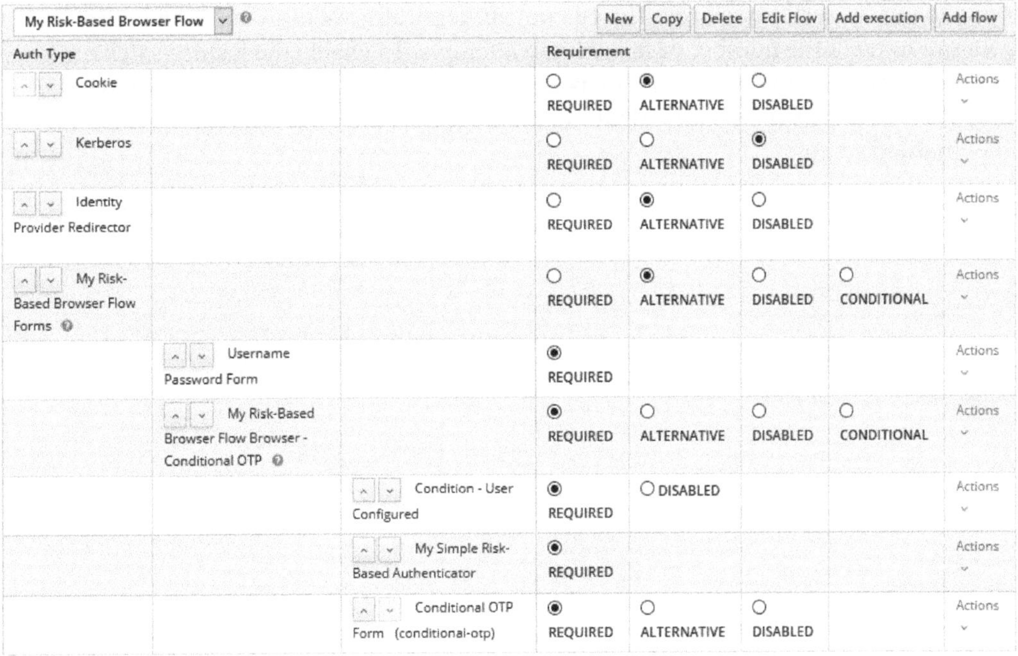

Auth Type		Requirement				Actions
∧ ∨ Cookie		○ REQUIRED	◉ ALTERNATIVE	○ DISABLED		Actions ∨
∧ ∨ Kerberos		○ REQUIRED	○ ALTERNATIVE	◉ DISABLED		Actions ∨
∧ ∨ Identity Provider Redirector		○ REQUIRED	◉ ALTERNATIVE	○ DISABLED		Actions ∨
∧ ∨ My Risk-Based Browser Flow Forms ❓		○ REQUIRED	◉ ALTERNATIVE	○ DISABLED	○ CONDITIONAL	Actions ∨
	∧ ∨ Username Password Form	◉ REQUIRED				Actions ∨
	∧ ∨ My Risk-Based Browser Flow Browser - Conditional OTP ❓	◉ REQUIRED	○ ALTERNATIVE	○ DISABLED	○ CONDITIONAL	Actions ∨
		∧ ∨ Condition - User Configured — ◉ REQUIRED	○ DISABLED			Actions ∨
		∧ ∨ My Simple Risk-Based Authenticator — ◉ REQUIRED				Actions ∨
		∧ ∨ Conditional OTP Form (conditional-otp) — ◉ REQUIRED	○ ALTERNATIVE	○ DISABLED		Actions ∨

Figure 13.13 – The final configuration for My Risk-Based Browser Flow

Finally, let's enable the **Brute Force Detection** feature to the realm. This feature is responsible to track failed login attempts and avoid brute force attacks when an attacker is trying to guess users' passwords. The custom authenticator we just configured relies on this feature to track the number of failed login attempts. To enable the feature, click on the **Realm Settings** item on the left-side panel. Once at this page, click on the **Security Defenses** tab and then click on the **Brute Force Detection** sub-tab. Once at this tab, turn on the **Enabled** setting:

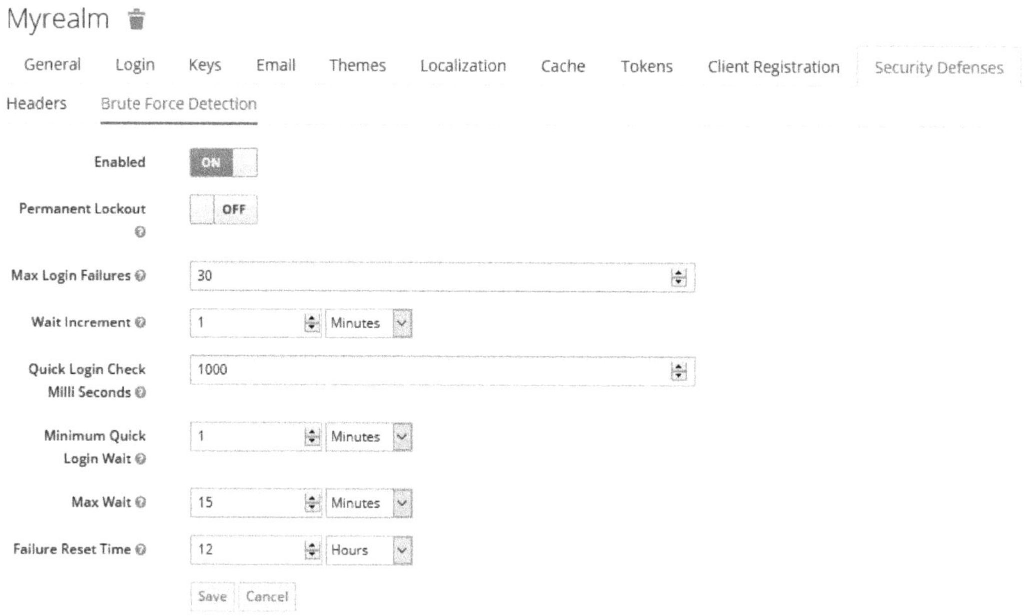

Myrealm 🗑

| General | Login | Keys | Email | Themes | Localization | Cache | Tokens | Client Registration | Security Defenses |

| Headers | Brute Force Detection |

Enabled	ON
Permanent Lockout ❷	OFF
Max Login Failures ❷	30
Wait Increment ❷	1	Minutes
Quick Login Check Milli Seconds ❷	1000
Minimum Quick Login Wait ❷	1	Minutes
Max Wait ❷	15	Minutes
Failure Reset Time ❷	12	Hours

Save   Cancel

Figure 13.14 – Enabling brute force detection to the realm

> **Tip**
> For more details about the brute force detection feature, take a look at the documentation at `https://www.keycloak.org/docs/latest/server_admin/#password-guess-brute-force-attacks`.

Let's now log in to the account console using the `alice` user. For that, open your browser at `http://localhost:8080/auth/realms/myrealm/account` and log in using the user's credentials.

At this moment, you should be able to authenticate to the account console by providing only a password.

Now, log out from the account console and, when at the login page, try to log in again but using an invalid password. Repeat this step three times.

On the fourth occasion, provide the correct password of the user. If everything is correct, you should now be asked to configure an OTP to then authenticate and access the account console. Next time you try to authenticate after failing to log in three times, you should only be asked for the OTP.

The Authentication SPI gives you the main customization hooks for adapting Keycloak to better fit into your authentication requirements. Based on what you learned from *Chapter 11, Authenticating Users*, you should be able to add your own authentication executions, required actions, add additional steps during user authentication, and so on. For more details, consider looking through the documentation available at `https://www.keycloak.org/docs/latest/server_development/#_auth_spi`.

In this section, you were provided with an example of how to leverage the Authentication SPI to create your own authenticator providers.

In the next section, you are going to be provided with additional references to other customization points provided by Keycloak.

Looking at other customization points

In the previous sections, you learned about just a subset of the customization points that you have available in Keycloak. As mentioned earlier, Keycloak is built around the concept of SPIs and there are many other customization points that you might find useful.

The best source for querying the available SPIs is the documentation available at `https://www.keycloak.org/docs/latest/server_development`. Some key SPIs are also covered by examples in the Keycloak Quickstart repository available at `https://github.com/keycloak/keycloak-quickstarts/`.

From the documentation, you may be interested in looking at the following SPIs:

- User Storage
- Event Listener

The User Storage SPI allows you to integrate Keycloak with any external identity store. A common use case for it is to fetch identity data from an existing database.

- Documentation: `https://www.keycloak.org/docs/latest/server_development/#_user-storage-spi`

- Quickstart:

  `https://github.com/keycloak/keycloak-quickstarts/tree/latest/user-storage-jpa`

  `https://github.com/keycloak/keycloak-quickstarts/tree/latest/user-storage-simple`

The Event Listener SPI allows you to customize how to handle events fired by Keycloak so that you can integrate it with your audit or fraud detection systems:

- Documentation: `https://www.keycloak.org/docs/latest/server_development/#_events`

- Quickstart:

  `https://github.com/keycloak/keycloak-quickstarts/tree/latest/event-listener-sysout`

  `https://github.com/keycloak/keycloak-quickstarts/tree/latest/event-store-mem`

As you learned at the beginning of the chapter, a list of all the available SPIs can be queried from the administration console on the **Server Info** page. You should be able to implement customizations for any SPI listed there.

However, most of them are still considered internal SPIs and they lack documentation. For these SPIs, the best you can do is look at Keycloak's code base to understand how they are implemented.

In this section, you were provided with some final references and considerations regarding other customization points not covered by this chapter.

Summary

In this chapter, you were presented with one of the main aspects of Keycloak: extensibility. You learned that Keycloak not only helps you to deploy IAM to your ecosystem, but also to adapt IAM to your needs.

For that, you were provided with the basics of how to change the look and feel of the server using themes and how to implement custom providers using some of the available SPIs. Although you were presented with only a few examples about how to extend Keycloak, you should be able to leverage what you learned from this chapter to extend Keycloak using any SPI.

In the next chapter, you will be looking at some security best practices and considerations when using Keyloak.

Questions

1. What is a public and private SPI?

2. Are any more references available regarding how to use the `KeycloakSessionFactory` and `KeycloakSession` APIs?

3. Do I need to be a Java developer in order to extend Keycloak?

Further reading

For more information on the topics covered in this chapter, you can visit the following links:

*   Keycloak Server Developer Guide: `https://www.keycloak.org/docs/latest/server_development`

*   Apache Freemarker: `https://freemarker.apache.org/`

*   Java Service Provider Interface: `https://docs.oracle.com/javase/tutorial/ext/basics/spi.html`

*   Keycloak GitHub repository: `https://github.com/keycloak/keycloak`

Section 4: Security Considerations

For any business, it is important to make life as difficult as possible for hackers. This section covers some best practices and checklists to get you on your journey toward a sufficient level of security for your business.

This section comprises the following chapter:

- *Chapter 14, Securing Keycloak and Applications*

14
Securing Keycloak and Applications

In this chapter, we will look at how to secure Keycloak for production environments. Then, we will look at how to secure the database, as well as secure cluster communication between Keycloak nodes. Finally, we will touch on some topics regarding how you can protect your own applications against threats.

After reading this chapter, you will have a good understanding of how to securely deploy Keycloak, including what is required to secure the database. Since this is a book about Keycloak and not about application security, you won't become an expert on application security, but if this is a topic that's new to you, you will have a basic understanding and an idea of how to learn more.

In this chapter, we're going to cover the following main topics:

- Securing Keycloak
- Securing the database
- Securing cluster communication
- Securing applications

Securing Keycloak

In this section, we will look at some important aspects of securing the Keycloak server itself. We will start by looking at an example of a secure Keycloak deployment, as shown in the following diagram:

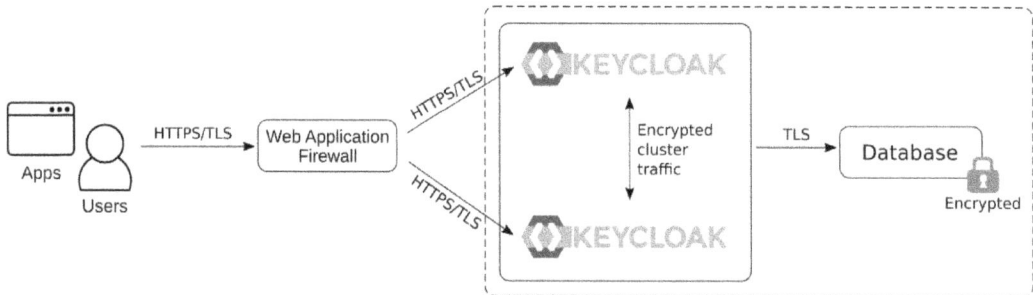

Figure 14.1 – An example of a secure deployment

In this example, Keycloak and its database are isolated from users and applications with a **Web Application Firewall** (**WAF**), all network requests are encrypted, and the database is also encrypted.

Let's look at this in a bit more detail, starting with why **Transport Layer Security** (**TLS**) is a requirement for any ingoing and outgoing traffic to Keycloak.

Encrypting communication to Keycloak

It is recommended to use end-to-end encryption for all communication to and from Keycloak. This means always using HTTPS, and never using HTTP. At the time of writing this book, the most recent security layer in HTTPS is TLS 1.3, so this is what you should use whenever possible. Most HTTP libraries will support at least TLS 1.2. If they do not support this, you should consider not using the library since TLS 1.2 has been around since 2008.

If you're leveraging a load balancer or reverse proxy in front of Keycloak, the most secure approach is to leverage TLS passthrough, which provides end-to-end encryption between the client and Keycloak.

In some cases, this may be infeasible, in which case you can use re-encrypt, where the communication between the proxy and Keycloak is encrypted again with an internal certificate.

Using unencrypted communication between the proxy and Keycloak should be avoided and only considered if the network between the proxy and Keycloak can be fully isolated, such as in cases where the proxy and Keycloak reside on the same machine.

In the next section, we'll look at why Keycloak needs to know the URL it will be exposed on.

Configuring the Keycloak hostname

Keycloak is required to know its hostname for several reasons, such as when you're sending an email to a user. Out of the box, for convenience, Keycloak infers the hostname from the request by looking at the `Host` HTTP header sent by the client. This configuration should never be used in production deployments as it could allow an attacker to send requests to Keycloak with a different value for the header.

An example of such an attack is where an attacker uses the recover password capability in Keycloak and modifies the host header, resulting in the email that's being sent to the user containing a link to a site controlled by the attacker. Unless the users realize the URL is not correct, the attacker can intercept the request to update the password. By intercepting the request, the attacker can either obtain the updated password or set a different password. In either case, the attacker gains access to the user account.

To prevent this type of attack, you can either configure a fixed hostname for Keycloak, or if Keycloak has been exposed through a reverse proxy, you can verify the host header at the reverse proxy. Configuring a fixed hostname for Keycloak is the simplest and most secure approach. To learn how to do that, read *Chapter 9, Configuring Keycloak for Production*.

In the next section, we will look at the importance of regular key rotation.

Rotating the signing keys used by Keycloak

Regularly rotating all your signing and encryption keys is highly recommended. You may want to consider doing so as frequently as once a month.

Luckily, Keycloak allows you to rotate keys in a way that is seamless and non-interrupting. This is because new keys can be made active, while the old keys are still permitted to verify tokens for a while.

Rotating keys have several benefits, such as the following:

- Reduces the amount of content that's signed or encrypted with a specific key.
- Reduces the time available to anyone who wants to try and crack your keys.

- Cleans up unused refresh tokens or long expiration access tokens, regardless of user session timeout settings.

- If an attacker were able to gain access to the keys or – even worse – such a leak was not discovered, the impact would be reduced.

To rotate the signing keys in Keycloak, open the administration console of Keycloak in your browser. Select the realm you want to rotate keys for, go to **Realm Settings**, and click on **Keys**.

First, you will see all the active signing keys in the realm, as shown in the following screenshot:

Master 🗑

| General | Login | Keys | Email | Themes | Localization | Cache | Tokens | Client Registration | Security Defenses |

Active   Passive   Disabled   Providers

Algorithm	Type	Kid	Priority	Provider	Public keys	
RS256	RSA	sed1ch3fY3a3c_EqSmKYwaKrQOQv2u5gdL_15SS2CQw	-100	fallback-RS256	Public key	Certificate
HS256	OCT	b223adad-1868-47c1-8ea4-c33fd80f7db4	-100	fallback-HS256		

Figure 14.2 – Active signing keys

The screenshot shows that the realm currently has two signing keys – one for the RS256 algorithm and another for the HS256 algorithm. Keys in Keycloak can have three different states:

- **Active**: Active keys are used to sign new tokens, where the highest priority key is used for a specific algorithm.

- **Passive**: Passive keys are not used to sign new tokens but are used to verify previously signed tokens.

- **Disabled**: Disabled keys are keys that are not currently in use.

To rotate the keys, the first step is to create a new active key. If, after creating a new active key, the previous key is disabled, all active user sessions and tokens will be invalidated. This approach should only be taken if you suspect the keys may have been compromised. Otherwise, it is better to passivate the previous key for a period to allow all user sessions and tokens to be updated with the new signing keys, before deleting the old key.

Creating additional keys is done by configuring additional key providers. Click on the **Providers** tab; then, under **Add keystore**, select **rsa-generated**. Fill in the form with the values shown in the following screenshot:

Master 🗑

General	Login	Keys	Email	Themes	Localization	Cache	Tokens

Active	Passive	Disabled	Providers

Keystores > Add Keystore

Console Display Name ❔	rsa-generated
Priority ❔	100
Enabled ❔	ON
Active ❔	ON
Algorithm ❔	RS256
Key size ❔	2048

Save Cancel

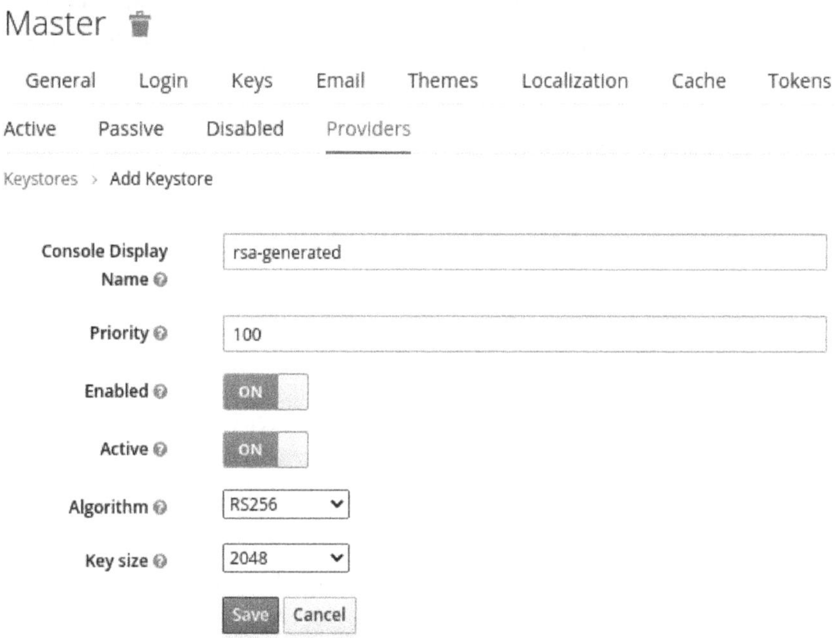

Figure 14.3 – Creating a new signing key

After creating the key, go back to the **Active** tab. You will notice that there are now two signing keys for RS256, as shown in the following screenshot:

Master 🗑

General	Login	Keys	Email	Themes	Localization	Cache	Tokens	Client Registration	Security Defenses

Active	Passive	Disabled	Providers

Search... 🔍

Algorithm	Type	Kid	Priority	Provider	Public keys	
RS256	RSA	G5sEdw-W6VKzhZbsQrfCHAu2J_ETqHkf6Nouk92PJ2c	100	rsa-generated	Public key	Certificate
RS256	RSA	sed1ch3fY3a3c_EqSmKYwaKrQOQv2u5gdL_15SS2CQw	-100	fallback-RS256	Public key	Certificate
HS256	OCT	b223adad-1868-47c1-8ea4-c33fd80f7db4	-100	fallback-HS256		

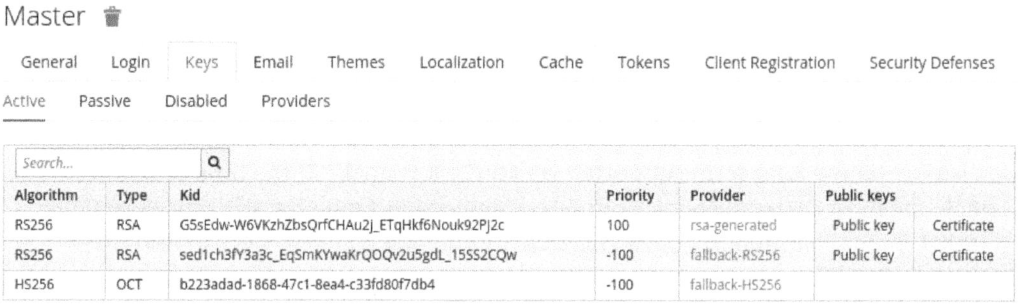

Figure 14.4 – Multiple signing keys for the same algorithm

Since the new key you created has the highest priority, it will be used to sign new tokens. Keycloak will automatically re-sign cookies and tokens with the new keys, which will be transparent to users and applications.

By default, Keycloak stores private keys in the database. Combined with good database security and regular key rotation, this is usually acceptable.

For additional security, Keycloak supports storing keys in an external store. At the time of writing this book, Keycloak can load keys from a Java keystore. There is also an extension mechanism that allows you to implement a custom source for keys. Understanding how to develop custom providers for Keycloak was covered in *Chapter 13, Extending Keycloak*.

For the highest level of security, you could also consider using an external service such as a **Hardware Security Module (HSM)** for signing tokens. Out of the box, Keycloak does not currently support any such integrations but does have extension points that allow you to develop custom providers yourself.

Next, we will look at the importance of regular updates.

Regularly updating Keycloak

Potentially one of the best sources of inspiration for an attacker comes from known vulnerabilities in unpatched software. If you do not regularly update Keycloak or the operating system, the list of unpatched known vulnerabilities the attacker can try out becomes longer and longer.

It is especially important that you have a process in place to be able to discover new releases and quickly upgrade.

One thing to note here is that Keycloak does not have long-term supported versions. Instead, it uses a continuous delivery model, or a rolling release. If there are any issues, then continuously upgrading Keycloak means that there are significantly fewer changes you need to make, so you are dealing with bite-sized chunks at a time.

Dealing with continuous releases does, in most cases, require automating the upgrade process, as well as being able to quickly test if an upgrade has any impact on your production systems.

If you prefer a long-term supported version, Red Hat offers Red Hat Single Sign-On, which is essentially a long-term supported version of Keycloak. At the time of writing this book, the most current version of Red Hat Single Sign-On is 7.4, which is essentially Keycloak 9, and is continuously receiving security and bug patches. You can find more information about Red Hat Single Sign-On at `https://access.redhat.com/products/red-hat-single-sign-on`.

In the next section, we will look at using an external vault to store secrets.

Loading secrets into Keycloak from an external vault

There are some use cases where you need to provide Keycloak with credentials to access external systems, such as connecting to an email server or federating users from a directory server. By default, Keycloak stores these credentials in the database, but it can also retrieve these from an external vault.

At the time of writing this book, Keycloak has out of the box support for an Elytron credential store, which is essentially an encrypted file, and support for leveraging secrets from Kubernetes.

As we mentioned previously, Keycloak has an extension mechanism that allows you to integrate it with any external vault. To learn more about extending Keycloak, please refer to *Chapter 13*, *Extending Keycloak*.

For more information on configuring a vault, please refer to the Keycloak server administration guide, which is available at `https://www.keycloak.org/docs/latest/server_admin/index.html#_vault-administration`.

Protecting Keycloak with a firewall and an intrusion prevention system

At a minimum, it is a good idea to leverage a firewall to control incoming and outgoing traffic to Keycloak. If possible, you should also consider completely separating Keycloak and its database from even internal applications.

With regards to incoming traffic, this can include limiting incoming traffic to only accepting HTTPS. You may also want to consider only allowing access to the Keycloak admin console and admin REST APIs from an internal network.

For outgoing traffic, it may be a little bit more difficult, depending on your use case. Some outgoing traffic you may need to permit includes the following:

- Backchannel requests over HTTPS to applications, such as logout requests.
- Connections to user federation providers, such as LDAP.
- Backchannel requests to external identity providers, such as an OpenID token request.

If you are only securing internal applications with Keycloak, it is most likely simpler to secure outgoing traffic, but this may be harder if you are also securing third-party applications that have been deployed outside your network.

It may also be a wise decision to utilize an intrusion prevention (or detection-only) system. An intrusion prevention system can be a great tool in detecting and preventing bad traffic, including helping you survive a denial-of-service attack.

For additional security, it can also be a good idea to leverage a **web application firewall (WAF)**. It is relatively complex to set up a WAF properly and it may need to be updated regularly, but if this is done correctly, a WAF can provide an extra layer of protection against attacks.

Next, we will look at arguably one of the most important aspect of securing Keycloak, which is protecting the database.

Securing the database

Keycloak stores a lot of sensitive data in its database, which makes it especially important to secure it, thus preventing attackers from accessing or modifying the databases.

Some examples of the data Keycloak stores includes the following:

- Realm configuration
- Users
- Clients

If your database became compromised, we must consider some examples of what could happen if an attacker were able to read your data:

- An attacker would get access to details about your employees or customers. The impact of this would depend on how much personal information you store about your users, but even a list of email addresses is valuable to an attacker.
- An attacker would get access to user credentials. Even though passwords are stored as one-way salted hashes in the database, the attacker may be able to crack some of the less secure passwords.
- If you are not using a vault or keystore, an attacker would have access to any secrets stored in the database, such as LDAP bind credentials, SMPT passwords, and even the private signing keys used by Keycloak.

These are only a few examples, but attackers are usually highly creative and can come up with all sorts of ways to exploit your data.

An important point to stress here is that an attacker does not care if they get the data directly from the database, or if they get it from a backup of the database, which makes it just as important to secure backups of the database as securing the database itself.

It would be potentially even worse if an attacker managed to gain access to write to the database, as this could give an attacker the ability to access any application secured by Keycloak – they would be able to alter realm configuration or user credentials to impersonate users.

It is beyond the scope of this book to cover database security in detail, but we will briefly look at some best practices, starting with using a firewall.

Protecting the database with a firewall

The first and most obvious thing to do when you're securing your database is protect it with a firewall. All traffic should be denied by default, and only required access such as from the Keycloak servers should be permitted.

In addition, you should prevent outbound connections unless there is a strong reason to permit it.

The next thing you will want to do is enable authentication and access control.

Enabling authentication and access control for the database

Only the minimum amount of people possible should have access to the database, and they should have the minimum amount of access needed to do their job. As Keycloak manages the schema as well as the data in the database, ask yourself if anyone really needs permanent access to the database at all.

Keycloak, as well as any users accessing the database, should use strong passwords, and accounts should be locked after failed login attempts. Consider using stronger authentication mechanisms, such as client certificates.

After limiting access to the database, you will want to secure the data in transit as well as at rest by enabling encryption.

Encrypting the database

To protect data in transit, all connections to the database should be encrypted by leveraging TLS.

In the event someone gains access to the server where the database is running, it is also important to encrypt data at rest. This includes making sure you encrypt any backups of the database.

There are a lot more steps involved in properly securing a database, and just like you will want to regularly update Keycloak, you should also regularly update your database. If your company has its own data center, chances are you already have people that can help you with this task. If not, you could consider leveraging a relational database service in the cloud.

In the next section, we will look at how to secure communication between nodes in a cluster.

Securing cluster communication

Keycloak embeds Infinispan, which is leveraged when you create a cluster of Keycloak nodes. Unlike the database, Keycloak does not send any very critical information through the cluster, where most of the sensitive data is kept in a local cache, thus leveraging cluster communication only for invalidations. It does store information about user sessions in the cluster, which are distributed across the cluster. Sessions themselves contain some information such as the session ID, the expiration date, and associated client sessions. Even if an attacker gains access to this information, they are limited in terms of what they can do with it, since accessing any session through Keycloak requires a token or cookie to be signed by Keycloak.

It would still be a good idea to secure cluster communication, at the very least with a firewall. For additional protection, you can enable authentication and/or encryption for cluster communication.

Tip

At the time of writing this book, the Keycloak documentation does not provide instructions on how to secure cluster communication. Neither does the documentation for the underlying WildFly application server. On the other hand, the Red Hat Jboss Enterprise Application Platform documentation, which is the Red Hat supported version of WildFly, provides great documentation for securing the cluster. You can find this documentation at `https://access.redhat.com/documentation/en-us/red_hat_jboss_enterprise_application_platform/7.3/html/configuration_guide/configuring_high_availability#securing_cluster`.

Enabling cluster authentication

Enabling authentication prevents unauthorized nodes from joining the cluster, but it does not prevent non-members from communicating with cluster members. For this reason, there is little value in adding authentication on its own, and this should be combined with asymmetric encryption.

Encrypting cluster communication

Cluster communication can be encrypted either with symmetric encryption with a shared key or asymmetric encryption combined with authentication. The simplest approach is enabling symmetric encryption, so we will look at how you can enable that.

The first step is to create a Java keystore that holds the shared secret. To create the keystore, run the following command in a Terminal:

```
$ cd $KC_HOME
$ java -c modules/system/layers/base/org/jgroups/main/
jgroups-*.jar org.jgroups.demos.KeyStoreGenerator --alg AES
--size 256 --storeName defaultStore.keystore --storepass
PASSWORD --alias mykey
```

This command will create a keystore in the root of your Keycloak home directory, with a key that can be used for symmetric encryption. You should copy this file to all Keycloak nodes.

The next step is to open the `standalone/configuration/standalone-ha.xml` file in a text editor. Search for `pbcast.NAKACK2` to find the correct location to enable encryption. This text will be repeated twice in the file – once for the UDP transport and once for the TCP transport. You should configure encryption for both transports or remove the transport that you are not using. Update the file to add the `SYM_ENCRYPT` protocol immediately before the `pbcast.NAKACK2` protocol, as shown in the following example:

```
<protocol type="VERIFY_SUSPECT"/>
<protocol type="SYM_ENCRYPT">
    <property name="provider">SunJCE</property>
    <property name="sym_algorithm">AES</property>
    <property name="encrypt_entire_message">true</property>
    <property name="keystore_name">defaultStore.keystore</
property>
    <property name="store_password">PASSWORD</property>
```

```
        <property name="alias">mykey</property>
    </protocol>
    <protocol type="pbcast.NAKACK2"/>
```

You should also make sure the changes you made to the `standalone-ha.xml` file are made to all Keycloak nodes.

If you want to make sure encryption is enabled, you can try to start one Keycloak node with encryption enabled and one without, or you can try creating a different keystore on one node. The following example shows the output from Keycloak when one node is trying to join the cluster with a different keystore:

```
21:37:54,763 ERROR [org.jgroups.protocols.SYM_ENCRYPT] (thread-
8,ejb,fedora) fedora: rejected decryption of unicast message
from non-member node2
```

This message shows that the node was not permitted to join the cluster and will also not be able to read or send any messages to the cluster.

With that, you have learned how to secure cluster communication. In the next section, we will look at securing user accounts.

Securing user accounts

With regard to securing user accounts, you will want to protect against an attacker gaining access to the user account and also protect information about the user, including their password.

Preventing an attacker from accessing a user account is mostly about enabling strong authentication, and not just accepting a password as the means of authentication. If your users are relying on passwords, even in combination with a second factor, it is important that passwords are protected. Passwords are protected by leveraging a strong password hashing algorithm, having a good password policy, and enabling brute-force protection for passwords. It is also important to educate users in terms of what is a strong password and that they should not reuse passwords with other services.

To configure a password policy, open the Keycloak administration console and select the realm you want to configure. Then, click on **Realm Settings**, then **Authentication**, and select the **Password Policy** tab. You can create your password policy by clicking on **Add policy** and selecting the policies you want to use. The following screenshot shows an example policy that requires passwords to have a minimum length of 8 and contain at least one lowercase letter, one uppercase letter, one special character, and one digit:

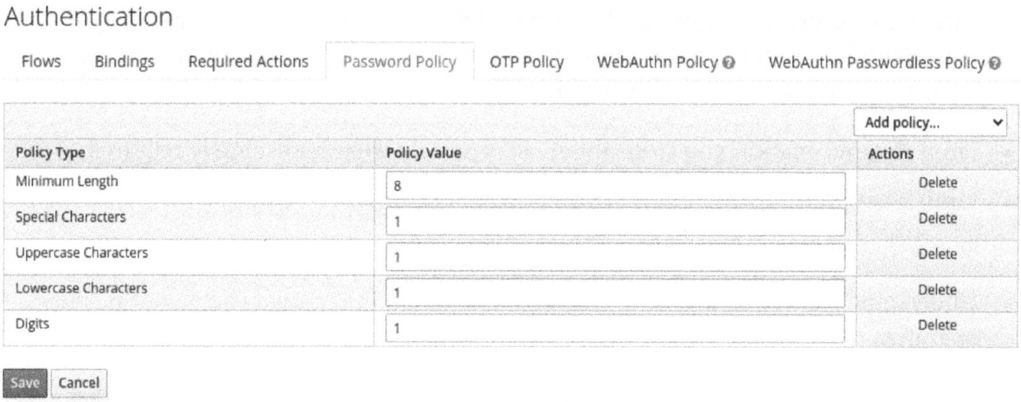

Authentication

Flows   Bindings   Required Actions   Password Policy   OTP Policy   WebAuthn Policy @   WebAuthn Passwordless Policy @

		Add policy... ⌄
Policy Type	**Policy Value**	**Actions**
Minimum Length	8	Delete
Special Characters	1	Delete
Uppercase Characters	1	Delete
Lowercase Characters	1	Delete
Digits	1	Delete

Save   Cancel

Figure 14.5 – An example password policy

It is also a good idea to enable password brute-force detection. Do this by clicking on **Realm Settings**, then **Security Defenses**, and selecting the **Brute Force Detection** tab, as shown in the following screenshot:

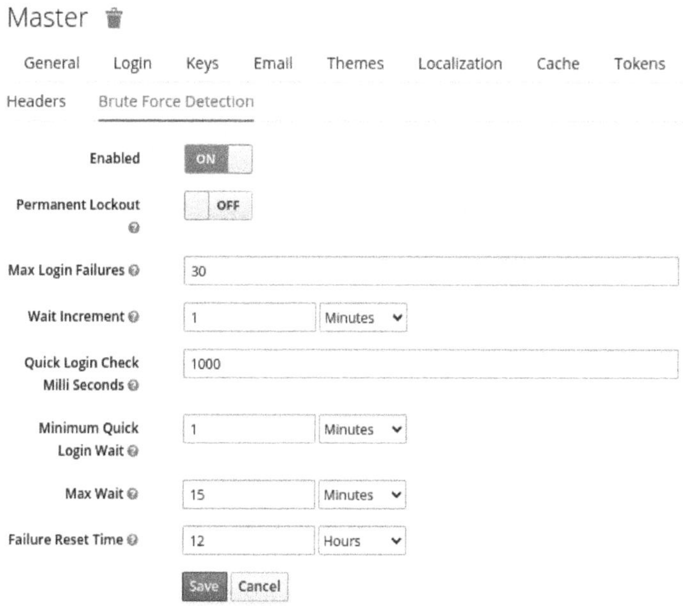

Master 🗑

General   Login   Keys   Email   Themes   Localization   Cache   Tokens   Client Registration   Security Defenses

Headers   Brute Force Detection

Enabled	ON
Permanent Lockout @	OFF
Max Login Failures @	30
Wait Increment @	1 Minutes ⌄
Quick Login Check Milli Seconds @	1000
Minimum Quick Login Wait @	1 Minutes ⌄
Max Wait @	15 Minutes ⌄
Failure Reset Time @	12 Hours ⌄

Save   Cancel

Figure 14.6 – Enabling password brute-force detection

Depending on your use case, you may be storing different levels of personal data, or personally identifiable information, about your users. There are a few steps you can take to limit your exposure to issues in this regard:

- Limit the information you store about users to only what is absolutely required.
- Limit what user information is exposed to applications.
- Secure the database.
- Understand legislation around personal information in regions where your business operates.

This topic should not be taken lightly. Personal information is invaluable to an attacker and is a commodity on its own that can be sold. Leaking such information can result in large fines and, in worst cases, cause irreparable damage to your business.

In the last section of this chapter, we will look at the steps you should take to increase the security of applications.

Securing applications

Since more applications are being exposed on the internet, the number of attacks and data breaches are growing by the day. This means it is important to secure applications properly.

Up until recently, a common practice was to leverage firewalls and VPNs as the main layer of defense against attacks. Often, this was combined with questionable security within the boundaries of the enterprise environment. This is becoming less viable with more employees working from home or using their personal laptop or phone. More and more services are also being exposed to partners or the public. This is blurring the line of the enterprise network. The whole idea of trusting what is on the inside, but not what is on the outside, was also somewhat questionable as there are often ways for attackers to get inside the enterprise network, and it also provides less protection against an internal attack.

Essentially, something better is needed than just a firewall. Keycloak is a great tool that can help increase the security of your applications, but your applications are not secure simply by using Keycloak.

It is beyond the scope of this book to provide you with all the information you need to secure your applications. Reading this section will give you some idea of this. We will start by looking at web application security.

Web application security

There are plenty of books and good resources on the internet that can help you learn how to secure web applications. Some of the steps involved in securing web applications include the following:

- **Authentication**: Since you are reading a book about Keycloak, chances are you are planning to use Keycloak to authenticate users to your applications. Once a user has been authenticated and a session has been established, it is important that the session is also secure.

- **Authorization**: Least privilege access is a great principle to follow. If you limit the access that's granted to users for them to perform their job, you are reducing the impact of a compromised account or a rogue employee.

- **Understand and protect against common attacks**: Make sure your applications are protected against common vulnerabilities such as injection and **cross-site scripting (XSS)**.

- **Regular updates**: Web application security is a continuous effort, and you should continuously strive to improve the security of your application. You should also regularly update frameworks, libraries, and any tools you are leveraging.

- **Data security**: Sensitive data should be encrypted at rest, and all data should be encrypted in transit. This should also apply to any backup data. Just like the web application itself, it is important to have good authentication and authorization in place.

- **Logging and monitoring**: Without sufficient logging and monitoring, you will not be able to identify if you have been compromised. Logging and monitoring can also be a valuable tool to prevent larger impacts due to an ongoing attack.

- **Firewall**: Firewalls and WAFs add an extra layer of defense to your web applications. Relying on only a web application firewall for protection is far from ideal, though – you should build security into the application itself.

One of the best places to start learning more about web application security is the **Open Web Application Security Project (OWASP)** Top 10. The OWASP Top 10 is a list of some of the most critical security risks to web applications. For each risk, it provides easy to understand details of the vulnerabilities, as well as tips on how to protect your application.

Another great resource is the OWASP Cheat Sheet Series, which provides several cheat sheets with very concise information on specific areas of application security.

Next, we will look at how to securely leverage OAuth 2.0 and OpenID Connect in your application.

OAuth 2.0 and OpenID Connect best practice

There are a lot of mistakes that can be made when you're using OAuth 2.0 and OpenID Connect in your applications. The specifications themselves have a lot of flexibility in how they are used, and a lot of the mechanisms to protect against common vulnerabilities are optional.

Consider the following authorization request, for example:

```
/auth?response_type=code&client_id=public-client&redirect_
uri=https://acme.corp/myclient
```

In this request, the state parameter is not included. A **Proof Key for Code Exchange (PKCE)** is also not being used. Unless the authorization server explicitly requires these parameters, this is a perfectly valid authorization request, but at the same time, it is open to several known vulnerabilities.

The same problem applies to the **JSON Web Token (JWT)** specification. It is relatively easy to make mistakes here. One example is the *none* algorithm, which is included in the specification. A valid token, according to the specification, can simply specify that it uses no signing algorithm, which obviously makes it easy for an attacker to create their own tokens.

Chapter 6, *Securing Different Application Types*, covered a fair portion of what you need to know to use OAuth 2.0 securely, but it is recommended that you learn more about this topic through other resources. The OAuth 2.0 website (`https://oauth.net/2/`) contains links to several invaluable resources that are all worth reading, including the following:

- OAuth 2.0 for mobile and native apps
- OAuth 2.0 for browser-based apps
- OAuth 2.0 threat model and security considerations
- OAuth 2.0 security best current practice

With all the options in OAuth 2.0 and the potential for not following the best practices, this may be a bit confusing. Luckily, some improvements in this regard are on their way with the introduction of OAuth 2.1. OAuth 2.1 incorporates several best practices into the specification itself, making it easier to follow best practices by simply being compliant with the specification.

Other important work regarding security is happening in the **Financial-Grade API (FAPI)** working group. This working group derives from establishing highly secure profiles of OIDC in order to leverage OIDC for open banking. However, you should not get too hung up on the name as the work they have produced applies to any use case for OIDC where additional security is required. The most important work that is coming out of this is two profiles for OIDC that are providing it with best practices:

- **FAPI 1.0 – Part 1**: Baseline API Security Profile
- **FAPI 1.0 – Part 2**: Advanced Security Profile

These profiles allow you to balance the complexity of applying the best practice with the level of security required so that it fits the use cases you have.

The Keycloak team is also making great progress in making it easier for you to enforce secure usage of OAuth 2.0 and OpenID Connect in your applications, since a feature called client policies is being created. Through client policies, it will be easy for you to enforce the use of best practices for applications, including allowing you to select different profiles for different applications, depending on the level of security needed.

We will conclude this chapter by looking at various configuration options available in Keycloak that affect the security of your applications.

Keycloak client configurations

In this section, we will look at some configuration options for an OIDC client in Keycloak that affect security.

The following screenshot show the basic settings for an OIDC client:

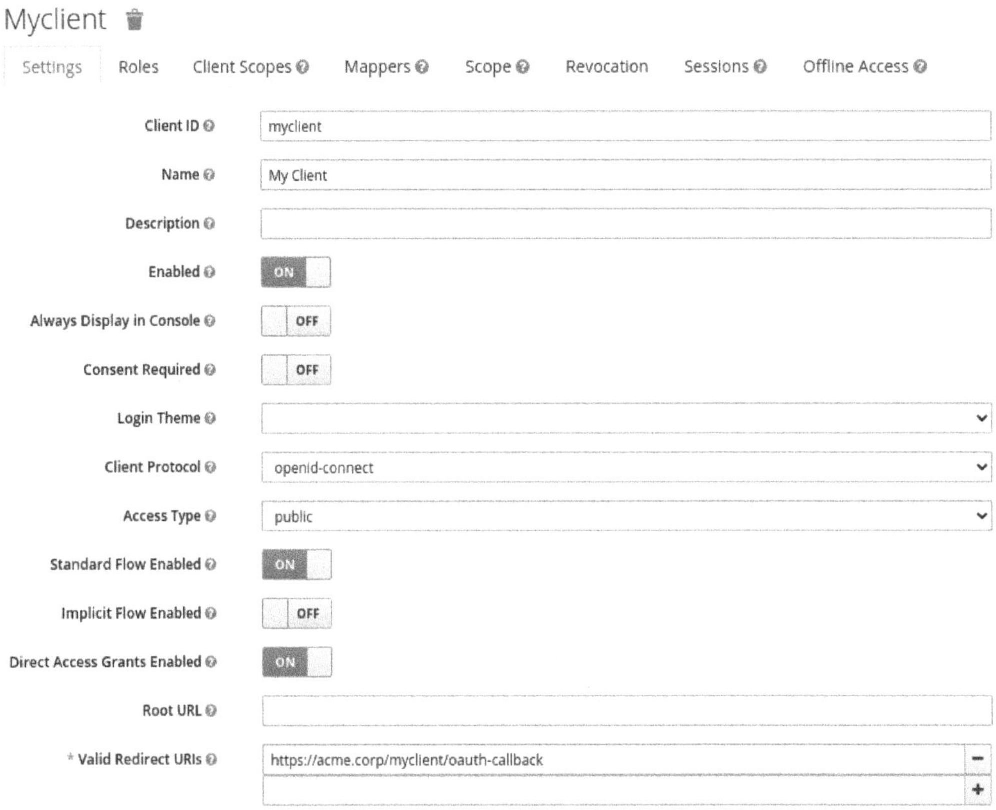

Figure 14.7 – Client settings

Let's review these and consider which are more related to security:

- **Consent Required**: If this is not enabled, the user will not see what level of access the application receives. You should enable this option for any third-party application. You should also enable this option for a native application such as a CLI.

- **Access Type**: Setting this to confidential is more secure when the client credentials can be kept securely on the server side.

- **Standard Flow Enabled**: Enables the authorization code flow for the client.

- **Implicit Flow Enabled**: Enables the now deprecated implicit flow. You should only enable this when it's absolutely required, and plan to update the application so that this can be disabled.

- **Direct Access Grants Flow Enabled**: Enables the now deprecated resource owner password flow. You should only enable this when it's absolutely required, and plan to update the application so this can be disabled.

- **Valid Redirect URIs**: It is recommended to use an exact match for the redirect URI. An example of a good redirect URI would be `https://acme.corp/myclient/oauth-callback`. Keycloak does support a wildcard in the redirect URI –any redirect URI, for that matter. You should avoid using a wildcard in the redirect URIs, but if you do, limit it to only requests that are available to the application, such as `https://acme.corp/myclient/*`.

Next, we will look at different signing algorithms that Keycloak supports:

- **Rivest–Shamir–Adleman (RSA) signature**: This is the default algorithm used by Keycloak. It is not the most secure option, but it is used as the default as it is the most widely available.

- **Elliptic Curve Digital Signature Algorithm (ECDSA)**: Considered more secure than RSA and is also significantly faster.

- **Hash-based message authentication code (HMAC)**: A symmetric signing algorithm that requires access to a shared secret.

When possible, you should use ECDSA in favor of RSA, even though RSA is still considered secure. If you want to enforce applications to use the token introspection endpoint to verify the token, you can use HMAC as the required secret. This is only available to Keycloak.

You can also choose between different lengths of the signature hash, where longer hashes provide greater security. With relatively short-lived tokens such as refresh tokens and access tokens, a 256-bit length is considered more than secure enough for most use cases.

Some other important options include configuring the lifespan of tokens. Keycloak allows you to override the access token lifespan for individual clients. It also allows you to override the client session lifespan, which controls the lifespan of refresh tokens. This allows you to have a long-lived SSO session (which could be days or weeks) with shorter-lived refresh tokens (which could be less than an hour). Shorter-lived refresh tokens reduce the impact if any refresh tokens are leaked and shortens the application HTTP session's lifespan.

Summary

In this chapter, you learned about several important aspects of deploying Keycloak securely into production. You learned how important it is to secure the database that's used by Keycloak, as well as communication between nodes. You also learned how important it is to protect user accounts from being compromised, as well as how important it is to keep information about your users secure. Finally, you got some insight into what it means to secure an application by focusing on web applications, as well as how to utilize OAuth 2.0 and OpenID Connect to secure your applications.

You should now have a good understanding of how to securely run Keycloak in production, as well as an idea of where you can start learning more about securing your applications.

This is the final chapter of this book. We hope you have enjoyed this book and have gained a good understanding of Keycloak and how you can utilize it to help secure your applications. While this book has not covered everything you may need to know, you should now have the knowledge to get started on your journey with Keycloak. As a next step, you may want to learn more about OAuth 2.0 and OpenID Connect, or web application security in general.

Questions

1. Why is it important to regularly update Keycloak?

2. Why is it especially important to protect the database that's used by Keycloak?

3. Is it sufficient to use a web application firewall to protect web applications?

Further reading

Please refer to the following links for more information on the topics that were covered in this chapter:

- OWASP Top 10: `https://owasp.org/www-project-top-ten/`
- OWASP Cheat Sheet Series: `https://cheatsheetseries.owasp.org/index.html`
- OAuth 2.0 for Mobile and Native Apps: `https://tools.ietf.org/html/rfc8252`
- OAuth 2.0 for Browser-Based Apps: `https://tools.ietf.org/html/draft-ietf-oauth-browser-based-apps`

- OAuth 2.0 Threat Model and Security Considerations: `https://tools.ietf.org/html/rfc6819`

- OAuth 2.0 Security Best Current Practice: `https://tools.ietf.org/html/draft-ietf-oauth-security-topics`

- OAuth 2.1: `https://tools.ietf.org/html/draft-parecki-oauth-v2-1`

Assessments

Chapter 1

1. Yes. Keycloak distributes container images for Docker, which runs on Kubernetes. There is also a Kubernetes Operator for Keycloak that makes it easier to install and manage Keycloak on Kubernetes.

2. The Keycloak admin console provides an extensive console to allow you to configure and manage Keycloak, including managing applications and users.

3. The Keycloak account console provides a self-service console for end users of your applications to manage their own accounts, including updating their profile and changing their password.

Chapter 2

1. The application redirects the user to the login pages provided by Keycloak. Following authentication, the user is redirected back to the application and the application obtains an ID token from Keycloak that it can use to discover information about the authenticated user.

2. For an application to be permitted to authenticate users with Keycloak, it must first be registered as a client with Keycloak.

3. The application includes an access token in the request, which the backend service can verify to decide whether access should be granted.

Chapter 3

1. OAuth 2.0 enables an application to obtain an access token that grants access to a set of resources provided by a different application on behalf of the user.

2. OpenID Connect adds an authentication layer on top of OAuth 2.0.

3. OAuth 2.0 does not define a standard format for tokens. By leveraging JWT as the token format, applications are able to directly verify and understand the contents of the token.

Chapter 4

1. Through the Discovery endpoint, an application can find out a lot of useful information about an OpenID Provider, which allows it to automatically configure itself to a specific provider.

2. The application retrieves an ID token, a signed JWT, from the OpenID Provider, which contains information about the authenticated user.

3. By adding a protocol mapper, or a client scope, to a client you can control exactly what information is included in the ID token that is made available to an application.

Chapter 5

1. An application can leverage the OAuth 2.0 Authorization Code grant type to obtain an access token from the authorization server. The application then includes the access token in the request sent to the REST API.

2. An access token can be limited through the use of the audience, roles, or scopes.

3. A service can either invoke the token introspection endpoint to verify the access token, or if the token is a JWT, it can verify and read the contents of the token directly.

Chapter 6

1. As an SPA is running in the browser, it cannot use a confidential client directly, which results in a greater risk if a refresh token is leaked. For this reason, it is more secure to have a backend running in a web server that can use a confidential client and store tokens on the server side.

2. No, any type of application can use OAuth 2.0 through an external user agent to obtain an access token, and many different types of services have support for bearer tokens.

3. An application should never collect user credentials directly as this increases the chance of credentials being leaked, and provides the application with full access to the user account. For this reason, native and mobile applications should use an external user agent to authenticate with Keycloak.

Chapter 7

1. In this chapter, you were presented with different integration options for different programming languages and platforms. If the programming language you are using already supports OpenID Connect, even if this is being done through a library or framework, you should consider using it.

    Alternatively, you can also use a reverse proxy such as Apache HTTP Server.

2. No, the Keycloak adapters were created when there were not many trusted client libraries. Nowadays, programming languages, and the frameworks built on top of these languages, already provide support for OpenID Connect.

    As a rule of thumb, do the opposite: only consider using any of the Keycloak adapters if you are left with no other option.

3. If you are using Reactive Native, you might want to look at `https://github.com/FormidableLabs/react-native-app-auth/blob/main/docs/config-examples/keycloak.md`.

    There you should find examples on how to use it with Keycloak.

    Remember that Keycloak is a fully compliant OpenID Connect Provider implementation, and you should be able to use any other library too.

4. For applications running on Kubernetes or OpenShift, both integration architecture styles would fit. Depending on the service mesh you are using (for instance, Istio), you should be able to leverage its capabilities.

    But still, you can use the embedded architectural style. This makes a lot of sense if you are already familiar with the options you have from the technology stack your application is using.

Chapter 8

1. When you put data into tokens, they actually grow disproportionately in size. One option to help here is to include only the minimum information that your application needs, and for additional information, to use the token introspection endpoint. The drawback is that your application will need an additional request to Keycloak when serving requests.

   You should also consider disabling the **Full Scope Allowed** setting in your client settings, so that only information relevant to your client is included in tokens.

2. Realm roles should be used to represent the user's role within an organization. These roles have the same semantics regardless of the clients created in a realm.

3. On the other hand, the semantics for a client role are specific to the client they belong to.

4. In this chapter, we created a realm role and a client role using the same name: manager. While the realm role could represent users with the role of manager in an organization, the manager client role could represent the permissions to manage resources in the application.

   It is up to you to choose what best fits your case; just keep in mind this conceptual difference so that you do not overuse one or the other.

5. Yes; for that, you would need to customize Keycloak through the Authentication SPI.

   It should be possible to have, for instance, additional pages in your flows to gather user information, or just use a custom authenticator to push contextual information as a session note, so that later you can map information from these session notes to tokens using a protocol mapper.

6. Yes, and this is a common task when your application is expecting to obtain roles from a claim other than the `realm_access` or `resource_access` claims. You can always change the protocol mappers to better suit your application's needs.

7. No. Applications can use different strategies depending on their security requirements. It is perfectly fine to use RBAC or groups, for instance, at the same application, or even to use ABAC or Keycloak Authorization Services, if you need fine-grained access to protected resources.

Chapter 9

1. Yes. It is recommended that you have an active-passive or active-active database so that in the event of failures, you can easily switch database instances. Note, however, that Keycloak keeps as much data as possible in caches, where reads should not be impacted at all depending on how hot the caches are (how much data is cached). Writes, however, will fail until the connection is re-established.

    Keycloak also supports setting some useful configuration options to improve failover in the event of network failures. You might want to enable background validation of connections to make sure available connections are usable, validate connections prior to obtaining them from the connection pool, or even configure the pool to fail fast when a connection is terminated to avoid validating and iterating over all connections in the pool.

2. No. The default configuration by default uses IP multicast to broadcast messages across nodes and form a cluster. The proper configuration depends on where Keycloak is being deployed. If you are deploying on bare metal or in a VM, you should consider using a different JGroups stack using either `TCPPING` or `JDBC_PING` for discovery.

3. Keycloak provides an operator that takes care of setting up most of the things we discussed in this chapter. We highly recommend using it to run Keycloak on any of these platforms. In terms of clustering, when running on OpenShift and Kubernetes `DNS_PING` is recommended for discovery.

4. By default, there is no security in this communication so that any instance listening on the same multicast address can join the cluster. To prevent unexpected nodes from joining a cluster, you can configure your JGroups stack to rely on X.509 certificates to authenticate nodes. You should also be able to enable encryption to prevent data from being intercepted and transferred in cleartext. For more details, look at the recommendations from *Chapter 14, Securing Keycloak.*

5. Ideally, yes. The reason being that, even though your instances are running within a private network, Keycloak is constantly exchanging sensitive data about users (privacy) and tokens issued by the server to applications. It is recommended to use end-to-end encryption.

6. Yes. Keycloak is CPU intensive due password hashing, token issuance, and verification using signatures and encryption. Depending on your load and how many concurrent requests you should handle, you might want to allocate two or more CPUs for each node in the cluster.

High CPU usage can also be caused by frequent GC runs. Common causes might be related to a small metaspace size, small young generation size, or the JVM reaching the overall heap size. You should constantly be monitoring and adjusting GC runs until you get as few pauses and counts as possible.

Keep in mind that TLS demands CPU. Depending on your requirements you might want to configure your reverse proxy with TLS termination and save some CPU on Keycloak nodes.

7. It depends on the use case. You should start small, using the default settings, and adjust accordingly to your load and performance tests.

8. Yes. Check the Keycloak Benchmark tool at `https://github.com/keycloak/keycloak-benchmark`.

Chapter 10

1. Yes. As we will see in the following chapters, Keycloak provides a **Service Provider Interface** (**SPI**) that allows you to integrate not only with databases but with any other form of identity store.

2. No. In addition to storing information from LDAP in its own database, Keycloak also caches data for entries that have been imported from LDAP. You have complete control over how information is cached and when it expires. Here, together with the synchronization settings, information from the LDAP directory is periodically updated without it impacting the overall performance of the server.

3. Keycloak allows you to configure mappers for identity providers. Through these mappers, you can customize how users are created by setting a specific user attribute or setting a specific role when the user authenticates for the very first time.

Chapter 11

1. Keycloak allows you to customize its look and feel entirely, not just for the pages that were presented in this chapter. As we are going to see in *Chapter 13*, *Extending Keycloak*, you should be able to change the look and feel of pages by changing the different themes provided by Keycloak. You can find more details in the documentation at `https://www.keycloak.org/docs/latest/server_development/#_themes`.

2. WebAuthn requires you to use a FIDO or FIDO2 compliant security device. You should also consider accessing Keycloak using HTTPS and using a valid domain name. WebAuthn is strict about domain names and secure connections if the server is accessed from a different domain than the client. You should also make sure the browser you are using has support for the WebAuthn API. You should also consider looking at the demo on the WebAuthn site to check how your security device works there.

Chapter 12

1. It depends on the type of session. User and client sessions are kept in memory but there is a special type of session called offline sessions that are stored in the database.

2. An offline session is a special type of session that solves a specific problem when using offline tokens, as per the OpenID Connect specification. The purpose of offline tokens is to allow clients to act on behalf of users even though the user is offline, such as when performing background tasks to access or process user information. Some people, though, use offline tokens to work around the complexities – or possible constraints – when dealing with refresh tokens, as they never expire under certain circumstances. For more details, look at the documentation at `https://www.keycloak.org/docs/latest/server_admin/#_offline-access`.

3. When running in production, you are probably running multiple Keycloak instances in a cluster. As such, you should restart nodes sequentially to avoid any data loss. Session state is distributed across a well-defined number of nodes and if all these nodes are abruptly killed, then sessions might be lost. Keycloak also allows you to keep session state outside the cluster by using a separate Infinispan server. However, this capability was originally designed for enabling clustering across multiple data centers but can be extended accordingly to support a single data center.

4. Whenever the user is authenticating using a client, a session is created. The only scenario that sessions are not created is when clients are obtaining tokens on their own behalf using the client credentials grant. In this case, there is no refresh token – therefore no user and client session – but the possibility to obtain fresh tokens through re-authentication.

Chapter 13

1. In Keycloak's code base, SPIs are organized into two main modules, the `keycloak-server-spi` and `keycloak-server-spi-private` modules. Public SPIs are located at the `keycloak-server-spi` module and Keycloak does its best to keep their interfaces backward compatible between releases. These SPIs are also usually documented. On the other hand, private SPIs are not supported in terms of backward compatibility and they usually lack documentation. As a rule of thumb, consider first looking at the SPIs available from the documentation, as they are usually what Keycloak expects people to use for extending the server.

2. There is no specific documentation for these two interfaces, just their Javadoc. The Keycloak team is working to improve this area.

3. This depends on the SPI you need to extend. As you learned from this chapter, in order to extend Keycloak themes, a basic CSS, JavaScript, and HTML background is more than enough. Other SPIs allow their capabilities to be customized through JavaScript. This is especially true for authenticators and protocol mappers. For further details, review the documentation at `https://www.keycloak.org/docs/latest/server_development/#_script_providers`. However, for other forms of customization, you will require a basic background in Java.

Chapter 14

1. There is no such thing as perfectly secure software, and mistakes are frequently made. Luckily, both the Keycloak team and its community are continuously looking for vulnerabilities and are continuously fixing any issues they find. If you don't update Keycloak, you will not receive these fixes, but anyone wanting to attack your Keycloak server will.

2. Keycloak stores a lot of sensitive data in the database, which is valuable information to an attacker. If an attacker gains write access to the database, the attacker can make changes that could allow the attacker to gain access to any application secured by Keycloak.

3. No; only relying on a web application firewall is not a good idea. You will want to enable strong authentication, as well as provide a good level of security within the application itself.

Packt>

Other Books You May Enjoy

If you enjoyed this book, you may be interest ed in these other books by Packt:

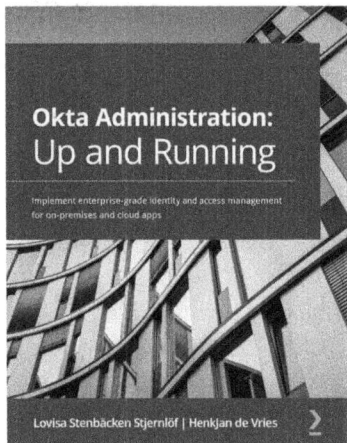

Okta Administration: Up and Running

Lovisa Stenbäcken Stjernlöf and HenkJan de Vries

ISBN: 978-1-80056-664-4

- Understand different types of users in Okta and how to place them in groups
- Set up SSO and MFA rules to secure your IT environment
- Get to grips with the basics of end-user functionality and customization
- Find out how provisioning and synchronization with applications work
- Explore API management, Access Gateway, and Advanced Server Access
- Become well-versed in the terminology used by IAM professionals

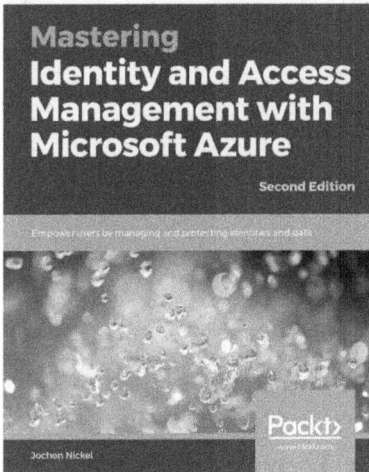

Mastering Identity and Access Management with Microsoft Azure - Second Edition

Jochen Nickel

ISBN: 978-1-78913-230-4

- Apply technical descriptions to your business needs and deployments
- Manage cloud-only, simple, and complex hybrid environments
- Apply correct and efficient monitoring and identity protection strategies
- Design and deploy custom Identity and access management solutions
- Build a complete identity and access management life cycle
- Understand authentication and application publishing mechanisms
- Use and understand the most crucial identity synchronization scenarios
- Implement a suitable information protection strategy

Packt is searching for authors like you

If you're interested in becoming an author for Packt, please visit `authors.packtpub.com` and apply today. We have worked with thousands of developers and tech professionals, just like you, to help them share their insight with the global tech community. You can make a general application, apply for a specific hot topic that we are recruiting an author for, or submit your own idea.

Leave a review - let other readers know what you think

Please share your thoughts on this book with others by leaving a review on the site that you bought it from. If you purchased the book from Amazon, please leave us an honest review on this book's Amazon page. This is vital so that other potential readers can see and use your unbiased opinion to make purchasing decisions, we can understand what our customers think about our products, and our authors can see your feedback on the title that they have worked with Packt to create. It will only take a few minutes of your time, but is valuable to other potential customers, our authors, and Packt. Thank you!

Index

P

W